Robert A. Katzmann
Editor

The Law Firm
and the
Public Good

The Brookings Institution / The Governance Institute
Washington, D.C.

Copyright © 1995
THE BROOKINGS INSTITUTION
1775 Massachusetts Avenue, N.W., Washington, D.C. 20036

Library of Congress Cataloging-in-Publication data:

The law firm and the public good / Robert A. Katzmann, ed.
     p.   cm.
  Includes bibliographical references and index.
  ISBN 0-8157-4864-7 (cl :   acid-free paper). — ISBN 0-8157-4863-9
(pa : acid-free paper)
    1. Public interest law—United States.   2. Legal assistance to the poor—United
States.   3. Law firms—United States.   I. Katzmann, Robert A.
KF336.L346   1995   95-5692
340'.115—dc20   CIP

9 8 7 6 5 4 3 2 1

The paper used in this publication meets the minimum requirements
of the American National Standard for Information Sciences—Permanence of Paper
for Printed Library Materials, ANSI Z39.48-1984.

Set in Stempel Garamond

Composition by Monotype Composition Company, Inc.
Baltimore, Maryland

Printed by R. R. Donnelley and Sons, Co.
Harrisonburg, Virginia

The Law Firm
and the
Public Good

The Brookings Institution

The Brookings Institution is an independent, nonprofit organization devoted to nonpartisan research, education, and publication in economics, government, foreign policy, and the social sciences generally. Its principal purposes are to aid in the development of sound public policies and to promote public understanding of issues of national importance. The Institution was founded on December 8, 1927, to merge the activities of the Institute for Government Research, founded in 1916, the Institute of Economics, founded in 1922, and the Robert Brookings Graduate School of Economics, founded in 1924.

The Institution maintains a position of neutrality on issues of public policy to safeguard the intellectual freedom of the staff. Interpretations or conclusions in Brookings publications should be understood to be solely those of the authors.

The Governance Institute

The Governance Institute, a nonprofit organization incorporated in 1986, is concerned with exploring, explaining, and easing problems associated with both the separation and division of powers in the American federal system. It is interested in how the levels and branches of government can best work with one another. It is attentive to problems within an orgnization or between institutions that frustrate the functioning of government. The Governance Institute is concerned as well with those professions and mediating groups that significantly affect the delivery and quality of public services. The Institute's focus is on institutional process, a nexus linking law, institutions, and policy. The Institute believes that problem solving should integrate research and discussion. This is why the Institute endeavors to work with those decisionmakers who play a role in making changes in process and policy. The Institute currently has three program areas: problems of the judiciary; problems of the administrative state; and challenges to the legal profession.

Foreword

Over the past several years, the Brookings Institution has devoted attention to a variety of problems affecting the administration of justice. Projects have concerned both civil and criminal justice, including the jury system, tort reform, crime, and relationships between the branches of government. This body of ongoing work reflects a recognition of the impact of the legal system on all Americans.

With this book, the Brookings Institution copublishes a project of the Governance Institute addressing the responsibilities of large law firms to the public good. Much time is spent attacking lawyers for the high cost of justice and for the excessive litigiousness in society generally; too little attention is devoted to the role of large law firms in addressing the legitimate, unmet needs of millions who cannot afford access to the legal system. This volume brings together the work of several distinguished lawyers eager to foster debate about what large law firms can do to contribute to the common good. It argues that self-interest, apart from moral justifications, should lead law firms to deepen their commitment to community service. The volume offers a blueprint to guide firms as they develop, implement, and monitor programs reflecting that expanded concern.

Project director Robert A. Katzmann is president of the Governance Institute, Walsh Professor of American Government and professor of law at Georgetown University, and a visiting fellow of the Brookings Governmental Studies program. At Brookings, he is grateful to Thomas E. Mann, director of the Governmental Studies program, for his critical support. Ingeborg Lockwood provided invaluable administrative work and proofreading; Laurel Imig skillfully verified the manuscript; Nancy Campbell, Deborah Styles, and Steph Selice supplied editorial expertise; Norman Turpin, Susan Woollen, and Jill Bernstein assisted with various phases of the production process; and Susan Stewart always ensured that the Governmental Studies program provided necessary administrative resources. Vicky Agee prepared the index and Eva Greene proofread the pages. Louis Holliday and Vincent Hart provided assistance in readying the manuscript. Susan McGrath and the Brookings library staff also were most helpful.

The views expressed in this book are those of the contributing authors and should not be ascribed to the persons or organizations acknowledged above, to the trustees, officers, or staff members of the Brookings Institution, or to the directors, officers, or other staff members of the Governance Institute.

Bruce K. MacLaury
President

April 1995
Washington, D.C.

Governance Institute
Acknowledgments

Special gratitude is owed to the Charles E. Culpeper Foundation and its president, Francis J. McNamara, Jr. (himself a distinguished lawyer). Without the vision and support of the Culpeper Foundation, this project could never have been attempted. The Governance Institute thankfully acknowledges a profound debt to the Culpeper Foundation for its sustained and critical involvement in this collaborative enterprise.

From the outset, the Governance Institute recognized that it could not facilitate a deepened commitment of law firms to the public good without the active involvement of leaders from the legal profession who have some responsibility for effecting change. Thus we created a small steering committee comprising members of the legal profession who are concerned about the nature of legal practice and the delivery of legal services. Our target is the large law firm.

The sustained participation of the steering committee group in every facet of the Governance Institute project on The Law Firm and the Public Good over a four-year period has been most remarkable. In addition to its general supervisory role, the committee has been responsible for developing specific topics for research and discussion. A unique aspect of the project is the contribution by virtually all of the committee members of original chapters for this study. Although each chapter reflects the individual perspective of the author, the steering committee reviewed drafts rigorously, offering advice and criticism. The group is committed to ensuring that project results are disseminated widely and implemented.

The steering committee is diverse in terms of geography and background, consisting mostly of lawyers in large firms (many with management responsibilities), but also including some lawyers from mid-sized firms and one chief operating officer (formerly a general counsel) of a large corporation. The members are: William A. Bradford, Jr., former head of the community services department, Hogan & Hartson (Washington, D.C.); Frank M. Coffin, senior circuit judge, U.S. Court of Appeals for the First Circuit (Maine); Anthony F. Earley, Jr., president and chief operating officer, Detroit Edison; Donald W. Hoagland, counsel and former chair of the managing committee, Davis, Graham & Stubbs (Denver); William C. Kelly, Jr., Latham & Watkins (an international law firm, with Kelly based in Washington, D.C.); Peter P. Mullen, partner and former executive partner, Skadden, Arps, Slate, Meagher & Flom (an international firm, with Mullen based in New York City); Edwin L. Noel, managing partner, Armstrong, Teasdale, Davis & Schlafly (Saint Louis, Missouri); Barrington D. Parker, Jr., a former New York partner in the San Francisco-based firm Morrison & Foerster and since 1994 a U.S. district court judge, Southern District of New York; and Lewis F. Powell, III, Hunton & Williams (an international firm based in Richmond, Virginia). The committee's work has also been enriched by Professors Marc Galanter and Thomas Palay of the University of Wisconsin and by Esther F. Lardent, director of the American Bar Association's Law Firm Pro Bono Challenge.

At various points, the project has benefited from the efforts of Jeffrey Adler, Daryl Capuano, Yvonne Croft, David Fagelson, Robert Granfield, Jonathan Levitsky, Jessica Pearson, Tamela Taylor, and Stephen Shannon (who assumed important responsibilities in coordinating a conference to disseminate project findings).

Apart from Governance Institute directors Frank Coffin, William Kelly Jr., and Barrington D. Parker, Jr., this project has had the counsel and support of the other Governance Institute directors, officers, and fellows, Roger H. Davidson, Jeffrey W. Kampelman, Gilbert Y. Steiner, Janet D. Steiger, Maureen Casamayou, Paul C. Light, and Robert W. Kastenmeier. The interest of Judge Robert Merhige, Judge Warren Eginton, and Judge Hugh H. Bownes is also much appreciated. Thomas E. Mann, the director of the Governmental Studies program at the Brookings Institution, played an important role in the publication of this book; more than that, his substantive advice and that of colleagues at a seminar in the Brookings

Governmental Studies program research-in-progress series was very use-ful. The Governmental Studies environment is an enriching one and was conducive to the pursuit of this work on the law firm and the public good.

Robert A. Katzmann
Project Director and President
The Governance Institute

April 1995
Washington, D.C.

Contents

1

Themes in Context

Robert A. Katzmann

A project that explores the role of the law firm in furtherance of the public good must overcome the skepticism of a society with low regard for the legal profession. Lawyers, we have been told, at least since Greek times, are rapacious, economically greedy—indeed, unscrupulous enemies of the common welfare. Aristophanes sketched the typical "lawyer" of his day as "a lawbook of legs, who can snoop like a beagle, a double-faced, lethal-tongued legal eagle" and further declared: "If you pay them [lawyers] well, they can teach you how to win your case—whether you're in the right or not."[1] Yet this very wariness of the legal profession, this "ancient grudge," provides both a spur and an opportunity for law firms to demonstrate their commitment to ensuring access to the legal system, especially to those unable to pay for services.[2]

What law firms can do to promote the common good must be understood in the context of the challenges facing the legal profession. That is, how, for good or ill, does serving the common good fit with all the other pressures? The challenges are diverse, involving equal access, the economics of law practice, adversarial legalism, and the perceived decline in professionalism. This study argues that attention to the law firm and the public good can not only help secure the paramount end of justice—equality before the law—but also help meet some of the challenges to the profession.

Challenges to the Legal Profession

Equal access, a dominant theme in the 1960s and 1970s, was typified by the rise of the public interest movement and the creation of the Legal Services Corporation. Proponents of equal access focus on the responsibilities of the legal profession to ensure that all Americans have their legal needs met.[3] The emphasis is on providing legal services; the concern is that too often justice is rationed, with undue advantage conferred on the "haves" at the expense of the "have-nots." By one account, some 80 percent of the civil needs of the poor are alleged to be unmet.[4] In 1978, exhorting the legal profession to support equal access to justice, then-President Carter chastised lawyers for not meeting their "heavy obligation to serve the ends of true justice."[5]

In an address in 1991 to the American Bar Association, Associate Justice Sandra Day O'Connor remarked:

> While lawyers have much we can be proud of, we also have a great deal to be ashamed of in terms of how we are responding to the needs of people who can't afford to pay our services. On the one hand, there is probably more innovative pro bono work being done right now than at any time in our history; on the other hand, there has probably never been a wider gulf between the need for legal services and the availability of legal services.[6]

Similarly, in the spring of 1993, Attorney General Janet Reno, noting the inadequacies of the justice system to provide legal representation to the poor, called on the legal profession to deepen its commitment to those unable to pay for such services. Reinforcing the importance of equal access is the American Bar Association's Law Firm Pro Bono Challenge, which calls on the nation's five hundred largest law firms to devote some of their resources to meeting the unsatisfied needs of the poor. James W. Jones, current chair of the Advisory Committee of the Pro Bono Challenge, observed in 1990 that "it is no exaggeration to say that, unless strong and comprehensive measures are implemented, the American system of justice will soon become essentially dysfunctional to the majority of our people."[7] Lamenting that this "state of affairs has become so familiar that it evokes little concern from most of those who spend their lives in the profession," Derek Bok commented: "the blunt, inexcusable fact is that this nation, which prides itself on efficiency and justice, has developed a legal system that is the most expensive in the world, yet cannot manage to protect the rights of most of its citizens."[8]

The *economics of firm practice* has been a dominant concern since the 1980s, encompassing a number of dimensions and a variety of alleged sins. For some, the problem is not that there are too few lawyers, but too many.[9] The malady, according to this view, is "economic deadweight."[10] Lawyers are seen as "an albatross around productivity."[11] In their zeal for increased profits, they have, from this perspective, spawned a litigation explosion. In 1992, then Vice President Quayle led the assault in a widely reported speech:

> The American people sense that something is wrong with our legal system. They believe there are too many lawsuits . . . too many excessive damage awards. They believe there is too much litigation and this is hurting the American economy. They believe too much litigation is costing American jobs. They believe that too much litigation is driving up the cost of financing federal and state and local government, that it's driving up the cost of liability insurance and the key factor, is driving up health care.[12]

Others, who would contest this negative view of the legal profession, are nevertheless concerned with the rise in costs and fees; their focus is not on blaming lawyers for a host of the nation's problems, but on exploring how changes in society alter the dynamics of practice. For them, the economics of firm practice involves examination of the extraordinary growth in size of large law firms, the push toward specialization, the increasing pressure to log more billable hours, and the rise in administrative costs.[13]

Adversarial legalism has also been faulted for constraining the efficiency and competitiveness of American business. As Robert Kagan has written, it is a style of policymaking and dispute resolution characterized by more formal legal contestation; litigant activism; more expensive and adversarial forms of legal contestation; more punitive legal sanctions; more frequent judicial review, revision, and delay of governmental decisions; more rapid legal change; and greater legal uncertainty.[14] Lawyers, according to this view, tend not to seek accommodation with competing interests, but to "invoke legal rights, duties, and procedural requirements, backed by the threat of recourse to judicial review or enforcement."[15] This manifests itself, so the argument proceeds, in "litigant activism," in which parties engage in protracted and expensive suits.[16] In the words of Mary Ann

Glendon, "Several nice issues of balance, then, confront the profession and the citizenry it serves: balance between liberty and order; balance among the branches of government; balance among the conflicting loyalties that tug at every individual lawyer; balance between traditionalism and iconoclasm in the law; balance between the artisans of order and connoisseurs of conflict in the profession as a whole."[17]

The perceived erosion of *professionalism* is still another critique leveled at lawyers.[18] Law as a public calling, so the claim goes, has been turned into a crass commercial business. Lawyers, according to this view, are guided by the bottom line, by the inexorable drive to increase profits. Norms of independent judgment, ethical behavior, and concern with the larger society have been sacrificed. In this "betrayed profession," in the words of Sol Linowitz, "Money is, of course, at the heart of the problem. Law as a profession can carry many burdens, but it cannot carry a code of values that ranks money very high among the virtues."[19] "The current ethos among lawyers," writes Lincoln Caplan, "has led to a race to the bottom."[20] Chief Judge Harry T. Edwards of the U.S. Court of Appeals for the D.C. Circuit declared in 1990 that the "structure of the work in large law firms places large firms on an institutional collision course with many humanistic values, such as truthfulness and altruism."[21] The decline in professionalism also has debilitating effects on the quality of life among lawyers. In *The Lost Lawyer*, Yale Law School Dean Anthony Kronman describes a "spiritual crisis that strikes at the heart" of professional pride, that "threatens the collective soul of American lawyers."[22] Pushed by the monetary yardstick, many attorneys find their work unsatisfying, feel increasingly isolated and less engaged in communal efforts with larger public purposes, and have less time for contemplation and independent thought. Indeed, in 1991 a "national conference on the emerging crisis in the quality of lawyers' health and lives—its impact on law firms and client services," labeled its report "At the Breaking Point."[23]

Taken together, these various concerns reveal a profession under siege. Firms may differ, as Michael J. Kelly observed, depending on the culture of house norms.[24] But the strains, especially within large firms, appear especially acute: the exponential growth in the size of firms, particularly in urban areas; the rise in costs, accompanied by the relentless pressure to log billable hours; the consequent escalation in costs; the unstable and transient loyalties of lawyers and clients to firms; the erosion of collegiality; the commercialization of law as a business; the compartmentalization of lawyers in specialized fields; and the preoccupation with law as a business all threaten to unhinge the legal profession from its professional and ethical foundations.

Nostrums abound. Proponents of access to justice have put forth a range of solutions, including increased government support of legal aid;[25] stepped-up pro bono activity by law firms (with some advocating mandatory pro bono);[26] and deregulation, in which some kinds of legal services would be performed by lay persons, presumably at a lower cost than what lawyers charge.[27] Those concerned with the economics of law practice call for an overhaul of the civil justice system, everything from malpractice to product liability reform, changing the way fees are set, and redesigning the incentives and procedures that supposedly encourage frivolous lawsuits.[28] To counter adversarial legalism, some have called for the development of alternatives to courtlike litigation; informal negotiation among contending interests; the creation of mechanisms designed to foster a "dialogic community" between administrators and beneficiaries; and a deemphasis on judicial review and simultaneous strengthening of administrative competence.[29] Critics of the decline of professionalism advocate such measures as tightening ethical standards and codes of practice; heightening concern for the values of independence; providing service to the less fortunate; and encouraging such institutions as the American Inns of Court, modeled after the British experience in which law students, lawyers, and judges examine problems of ethics in the practice of law.[30]

Arguments

The challenges facing the legal profession—inadequate access, escalating costs, adversarial legalism, and a decline in professionalism—defy easy or quick solutions (although scholars, including some at Brookings, are at work on various aspects of them).[31] This study addresses one key facet by arguing that the legal profession cannot fulfill its societal mission without honoring its responsibility to the wider community to secure justice. And that responsibility involves providing access to the legal system to those without means or with only limited resources.

The Ethical Argument

The fundamental basis of the lawyer's responsibility to ensure justice and to address the needs of those in society unable to pay can be understood by appreciating a simple proposition: access to minimal legal services is necessary for access to the legal system, and without access to the legal system, there is no equality before the law. The lawyer becomes the critical medium by which access to that legal system and the concomitant opportunity to secure justice is achieved.

But why should those services be rendered for free, if necessary, to those who cannot afford them? After all, society does not require grocers to feed the hungry free of charge, or taxi drivers to provide transit without compensation. It cannot simply be, as some courts have said, that because the state grants a license to practice law it can therefore condition that license on the performance of pro bono work: grocers and taxi drivers also have licenses from the state, yet no one would suggest that the state can make those licenses contingent upon offering services for free.

The difference between lawyers and grocers and taxi drivers is explained well by David Luban:

> The lawyer's lucrative monopoly would not exist without the community and its state; the monopoly and indeed the product it monopolizes is an artifact of the community. The community has shaped the lawyer's retail product with her in mind; it has made the law to make the lawyer indispensable. The community, as a consequence, has the right to condition its handiwork on the recipients of the monopoly fulfilling the monopoly's legitimate purpose.[32]

Unlike grocers and taxi drivers, whose essential functions—selling food or transportation—could exist without state involvement, lawyers are involved in work created by the state. And they exercise monopoly power in a variety of ways—through prohibitions against unauthorized practice and regulations and laws fashioned, in large measure, to protect lawyers.

In an adversarial system, governed by complex rules and procedures, fundamental notions of fairness and equality before the law are violated if all parties do not have access to competent legal advice. The need to minimize undue advantage in that adversarial system maintained for their near exclusive use, suggests that lawyers have a responsibility to provide legal services to those unable to pay.

The lawyer's function is grounded in role morality, the idea that special obligations attach to certain roles—in this case, to render justice.[33] Lawyers claim autonomy to perform their functions as a consequence of specialized knowledge and skill.[34] The state grants such autonomy, an effective monopoly, in exchange for lawyers, as officers of the court, discharging their duty to further equality before the law. After all, the very reason the state conferred such a monopoly was so that justice could best be served—a notion that surely means that even those unable to pay or those pursuing an unpopular cause can expect legal representation. A lawyer's duty to serve those unable to pay is thus not an act of charity or benevolence, but rather one of professional responsibility, reinforced by the terms under which the state has granted to the profession effective control of the legal system.

The Appeal to Enlightened Self-Interest

The steering committee of the Legal Profession Project believes that considerations of ethical responsibility are sufficient to support an intensified commitment to pro bono work. Nevertheless, it recognizes, given the pressures of everyday practice, that appeals to moral principle may not be enough to motivate firms to take more vigorous action. The spur of self-interest could also be a motivating force.[35] From the perspective of the law firm, a heightened concern with the public good can improve the quality of a lawyer's life, and have positive effects on lawyering and professionalism. A law firm that concerns itself with justice for all, and is motivated in part by a sense of moral purpose, recognizes values more important than the bottom line. A law firm that devotes more time to pro bono work of interest to its lawyers is likely to find morale improved and the opportunities for the refinement of legal skills enhanced. Benefits will flow not only to the law firms and the individuals and groups served; the effect of more acute attention to the public good will inevitably generate a fuller discussion about how most effectively to deliver legal services. Such is the argument of this study.

Focus and Preview

Consideration of the law firm and community service is particularly apt at a time when government support for legal aid is limited and under fire;[36] when recent U.S. presidents have sought to kindle the fires of voluntarism;[37] when the ABA Law Firm Pro Bono Challenge is under way; and when some within the legal profession have called for mandatory pro bono.[38] (Indeed, at a time when some have discussed the imposition of mandatory pro bono requirements, law firms may be especially attentive to examining their own initiatives.) Our focus is on large law firms with one hundred or more lawyers, because those typically are more likely to have resources at hand to allocate to pro bono activities. They also, if we are right in our assessment of the contribution of a realistic program for the common good to the well-being of the firm, are likely to be major beneficiaries. Whatever the package of remedies designed to address the problems of the legal system, an important element will necessarily be large law firms, as leaders of the profession. In time, our hope is that the kind of work we support will be extended to middle- and smaller-sized firms.

What is unique about this enterprise is that it is the work of major participants in the large firms that are the objects of this study. It is not advice from above or from the outside. It is the product of lengthy and probing deliberation by those who must live with all the challenges as they endeavor to give new impetus to law firms' work for the public good.

In the pages that follow, we explore the context of life in large law firms; gather information about the experiences of firms with community service; develop a rationale for expanded commitment to community service; and identify mechanisms to evaluate and monitor firm activities with regard to community service. This then is how the case unfolds.

Public Service Implications of Firm Size and Structure

We begin with an analysis of the context of law firm practice, critical to any discussion of law firms and community service. Over time, practice in large law firms has changed dramatically. To be sure, some trends have had a positive impact on the ability of different groups to enter the profession. Other, more questionable effects have included an unyielding pressure to log more billable hours, a preoccupation with compensation and profits as measures of a lawyer's worth, the evolution of increasingly large firms, diminishing morale, and the reduced sense of loyalty between and among lawyers and clients. In chapter 2, Professors Marc Galanter and Thomas Palay examine the changing nature of large firms, beginning with a historical analysis. They trace the exponential increases in the size of law firms and the concomitant rationalization, increased specialization, hierarchy, meritocracy, diversity, and market orientation of firms. Their analysis of the pro bono activities of a set of large law firms suggests—hopefully—that large firms are in a position to increase such efforts; that, in fact, it is possible to do well financially *and* fulfill responsibilities to the wider community.

Drawing upon the *American Lawyer*'s annual surveys of pro bono contributions of large firms, available from 1990 to 1993, Galanter and Palay assess the relationship between a firm's pro bono activity and several measures of its overall economic and organizational performance: total number of attorneys, total number of partners, total number of associates, gross revenue, revenue per lawyer, profits per partner, the ratio of associates to partners, and the firm's estimated profit margin. Recognizing the limits of their data, they nevertheless find that, in general, total pro bono activity was positively related to firm performance. The data indicate that the larger the firm and the greater its gross revenues, the more willing it will be to encourage or permit pro bono activity (although less than 40 percent of the lawyers in these firms provided twenty or more hours of pro bono activity). In sum, Galanter and Palay conclude that a commitment to pro bono is "not incompatible with the flourishing of the large law firm."

Structuring Pro Bono Programs

Understanding the context of law firm practice is obviously important. But as we seek to find ways to promote community service in the legal profession, we need to identify what firms have already done and evaluate the effectiveness of those efforts. To that end, Esther Lardent, director of the ABA's Law Firm Pro Bono Challenge, has gathered information about different programs undertaken by law firms, local bar associations, and corporate legal departments throughout the country. "Such programs," Lardent writes in chapter 3, "offer a blend of idealism and pragmatism that may be uniquely suited to today's larger law firms."

She begins with a discussion of various ways in which large law firms structure their pro bono programs. A few firms have community service departments—the most formal of structures, equal in stature with the firm's other practice groups—with a full-time equity partner and senior associates who rotate through the department. Most firms interested in pro bono work have committees that approve specific projects. Some have pro bono budgets, with specific annual allocations of firm resources. Increasingly, firms employ program administrators charged with monitoring pro bono activities. A few have even hired laterals with pro bono experience for the purpose of strengthening community service elements of the firm's practice.

Lardent also describes a variety of innovative programs. A few firms offer fellowships in which they underwrite the salaries of one or more persons who become staff attorneys at a public interest or legal services program. Some have developed rotation programs in which associates spend a finite period of time, usually three to six months, working for a public interest/legal services program or government department. Other firms "adopt" a program in which their services are matched with local legal services offices to supply support and assistance. Increasingly, firms have created specialized pro bono projects that target particular areas of the law, clinics, neighborhoods, or clients.

The variety of programs notwithstanding, Lardent argues that firms must guard against an erosion of commitment to pro bono. Especially in uncertain economic times, firms must be ever vigilant to ensure that financial pressures, which may work against community service, are counterbalanced by rewards and incentives that promote pro bono. With strong leadership from firm leaders, Lardent contends that firms can respond to reservations about pro bono, lessen the impact of increased billable hour targets, and combat the anxiety of young associates concerned with advancement. For instance, some firms provide "credit" or billable hour equivalency for time spent on pro bono matters.

Finally, Lardent describes the impact of external forces—the organized bar, law schools, the legal media, and major clients—on law firm pro bono. In that regard, she includes organized bar efforts, the American Bar Association Law Firm Pro Bono Challenge, mandatory pro bono, quasi-mandatory pro bono, and mandatory law firm pro bono. Although no "large law firm has established a truly mandatory pro bono program," Lardent believes such an approach is both logical and necessary.

Lawyer Morale and Public Service

Reflecting on lawyer morale in chapter 4, William C. Kelly, Jr., examines why lawyers join large law firms and what motivates them to stay. Apart from compensation, job tenure, and the thrill of combat, he believes that what is still powerfully attractive to many lawyers is the opportunity to make constructive contributions to clients, to the law firm as an enterprise, and to society. All of these goals are under siege, however, for many reasons: the erosion of the economic base, tenure, collegiality, and client loyalty; the acute concern with billable hours; and administrative burdens reflected in daily time sheets, reports, detailed monthly bills, accountant's reports, expense reports, conflict checks, marketing materials, collections, and recruitments.

Public service—whether direct, as a principal or policy adviser, or pro bono, as a lawyer on behalf of a client—can provide a safety valve against these pressures and, more important, provide the "constructive engagement that lawyers often miss in their law practices." Kelly writes that for lawyers eager to be connected to the world around them, community service raises morale and increases personal satisfaction by infusing professional life with more immediacy and larger public purposes, as well as a sense of renewal. Writing a brief related to an important public policy issue or ensuring that a poor client will be well served can energize a lawyer drained by the mundane aspects of everyday practice. With community service "often comes a shift from the anonymity of most private practice to the visibility of the public arena. The navigator becomes the captain, and the promotion can be exhilarating."

Community Service Makes Better Lawyers

From another perspective, community service can improve lawyering skills. Donald Hoagland, the former chair of the management committee of a major Denver law firm, undertakes in chapter 5 to illuminate this proposition by interviewing three categories of resource people: lawyers of all ages who have done pro bono work; lawyers who have supervised or evaluated lawyers who have (and have not) done pro bono work; and executives of substantial private and public entities who have hired or supervised lawyers from time to time for assignments that were not of a limited and technical character.

In a number of different respects, community service improves lawyering, Hoagland writes. For example, by dealing with a broader cross-section of the community, the lawyer becomes more attentive to the attitudes and values of the entire community. Such experience can better prepare a lawyer to "perceive and analyze the widest potential consequences of a possible course of action." More specifically, such work can sharpen the lawyer's ability to manage a team effort, select a jury, interrogate a witness, negotiate a transaction, or interview a prospective client or colleague. Young lawyers, Hoagland states, will mature more rapidly through having more responsibility in performing community legal services than they would in the structured setting of most law firms. They are more likely, for example, to gain litigation experience in such a circumstance than they would in a large law firm. In the end, Hoagland contends, law firms are more likely to accept community service if they believe it will have positive effects on lawyering and, as a consequence, on a firm's capacity to attract and maintain clients and business.

Fee-Shifting Statutes

The existence of fee-shifting statutes, which provide that a prevailing party may be awarded attorney's fees, reinforces the idea that law firms should encourage community service. As William A. Bradford, Jr., contends in chapter 6, public interest fee-shifting statutes reflect the view of the U.S. Congress that the rights advanced by the statute are in the public interest, and that the bar needs the inducement of fee shifting to take the cases. Thus, adding public interest fee-shifting cases to a firm's pro bono docket would satisfy a public need defined by the political process.

Moreover, such statutes, in view of their congressional sanction, could help mute ideological criticism that firms should have a restrictive view of pro bono lawyering. These fee-shifting cases "would provide lawyers to classes of persons who would otherwise have difficulty attracting and paying lawyers, and would generate money for the use of nonprofit public interest groups or otherwise to further pro bono lawyering." Bradford argues that law firms, consistent with the spirit of pro bono, should donate all or part of the fee award to the public interest group that referred that case, or to a public interest organization linked to the issue (if there was no such referral); or it should be redistributed within the law firm to fund the disbursements associated with pro bono cases.

Defining Community Service for Law Firm Practitioners

Even if law firms accept the value of community service, questions inevitably will arise as to what constitutes community service. Is it simply work for the poor? Can it include work as an unpaid director of a nonprofit charity? The American Bar Association's Model Rule and Law Firm Pro Bono Challenge seek to address these definitional concerns. Model Rule 6.1 sets forth a goal of fifty hours per lawyer per year and indicates that a "substantial majority" of this commitment should be spent on behalf of people of limited means or for organizations that are primarily concerned with the needs of persons of limited means. The historic Law Firm Pro Bono Project suggests that between fifty and eighty-five hours per lawyer—assuming an average of 1,700 billable hours per year per lawyer—be set aside for pro bono work and that a "majority" of this commitment be met by the delivery of legal services to persons of limited means or organizations that are to satisfy the needs of such people.

In chapter 7, Edwin L. Noel, Anthony F. Earley, Jr., and Lewis F. Powell, III applaud the ABA's effort to set criteria for community service and offer suggestions designed to clarify problems of definition. For them, devising appropriate standards and criteria is a delicate issue. They argue that the task is not one that lends itself to hard-and-fast definitions, but one that requires a sensitive weighing of a diversity of factors.

At least three restrictions, contend Noel, Earley, and Powell, ought to apply in determining which activities meet the definition of pro bono service: 1) the services should be for a public service organization that has a financial need for free or significantly reduced fee services; 2) the activity should call upon the lawyer's skills and training, even if legal services in the strict sense are not being performed; and 3) the services should be provided for little or no compensation. They state that a 50 percent rule, requiring that at least a majority of any lawyer's pro bono time be focused on providing legal services to persons of limited means or organizations supporting such groups, is appropriate. But they also think that both the ABA's Model Rule and Law Firm Pro Bono Challenge "appear to be somewhat restrictive of the remaining 50 percent of a lawyer's pro bono undertaking."

While recognizing the advantage of, and need for, a tight definition as the ABA launched the pathbreaking Pro Bono Challenge, they believe that once the ABA minima have been satisfied "the definitions should be made more flexible." "These services," Noel, Earley, and Powell write, "should not be restricted solely to 'legal services' or 'legal assistance' in the traditional sense, but rather should allow for greater flexibility in public service, recognizing that many of the talents lawyers bring to community organizations are other than their ability to practice law." To elaborate on this point, the authors offer a variety of hypotheticals to illustrate the kinds of activities they think merit pro bono credit.

Monitoring Compliance with the Pro Bono Challenge

Having examined the context of law firm practice, reviewed various kinds of community service, presented a variety of rationales for such service, and assessed matters of definition, the question still remains how best to monitor compliance. Judge Barrington D. Parker, Jr., a former partner in a major firm, addresses this subject, with special concern for how to encourage adherence to the ABA Pro Bono Challenge. He writes in chapter 8 that a successful monitoring program can, and should, serve not only as a mechanism to facilitate to compliance, but also as a feedback mechanism that underscores the intrinsic benefits of pro bono to lawyers and to the firm. The Challenge should include a mechanism to solicit information from lawyers working on pro bono projects about the value of their experience, including why and how a project was chosen; what skills were engaged; what was learned; how the project differed from regular client work; and mistakes made in the selection process. Evaluations should also be secured from those with managerial and supervisory authority, as to their views about the value of pro bono work, as well as from clients. The experience of firm leaders who benefited from pro bono work would be the subject of case studies that would be disseminated to lawyers at all levels of practice.

Another function of a compliance mechanism, Judge Parker states, is to assist firms to conduct far more careful analyses than most have done in the past of the real costs of pro bono work. "The conventional wisdom," he observes, "is that pro bono work involves a financial 'sacrifice' to the firm since it is work given away. This conclusion is sufficiently widely held so that it generally goes unchallenged, even among the strong proponents of pro bono work. A closer look at law firm economics causes this conclusion to unravel." Because law firms rarely operate at full capacity, "there is almost always time available for some lawyers in practically every firm to use excess capacity for pro bono work." A sound monitoring program can demonstrate that "pro bono work results in a competitive advantage in paying work that has generally been missed or seriously underestimated."

To facilitate compliance, Judge Parker proposes a number of mechanisms: for example, publicly and specifically recognizing the most successful participants; requiring frequent and detailed reports to the Pro Bono Challenge, including reasons for noncompliance or difficulties in meeting targets; vesting administrators with responsibilities to provide critiques of policies; ensuring that all pro bono coordinators and supervisors meet minimum standards of proficiency; actively encouraging the legal media to publicize the identity of firms that do not undertake community service or do little of it; supporting law schools that, with regard to on-campus interviews, seek and disseminate data about the firms that have declined to join the ABA Challenge; and encouraging corporate counsel to include inquiries about community service activities as part of the firm retention process.

Conclusion

Reflecting upon the project whose fruits are contained in this volume, Judge Frank M. Coffin writes in the afterword: "Although as an appellate judge I have been on the receiving end of lawyers' advocacy for nearly thirty years, this has been a rare opportunity to observe, over a period of four years, a group of responsible partners of large law firms come to terms with the question: How, if at all, should a large law firm respond to the call to contribute its time and talent to the public good?" He concludes that they:

> have done so by pointing out the fit between pro bono commitment and public service on the one hand and the individual's interest in the quality of firm life, the firm's interest in lawyerly development, and the profession's inherent ethical obligation on the other. . . . If efforts like this catch on, first with large firms, then with others, one can hope that the legal profession as a whole will make a seminal contribution to realizing the goal of equal access to the law. In the course of so doing, it will have ensured its own revitalization, refreshment, and reputation.

It is our hope that this work might serve as a practical primer for large law firms whose lawyers recognize that professional responsibility and self-interest support the same conclusion: that the law firm and the public good are inextricably linked and that each can draw strength from the other in ways that nourish both.

Notes

1. Lionel Casson, "Imagine, if you will, a time without any lawyers at all," *Smithsonian*, vol. 18 (October 1987), p. 122; Aristophanes, *Lysistrata/The Acharnians/The Clouds*, translated by Alan H. Sommerstein (London: Penguin Books, 1973), pp. 116,123. The "lawyers" of Athens were somewhat removed from our modern conception. They were actually rhetores, as professors of oratory were known, who instructed parties as to how they should argue their cases. Full-fledged professional lawyering, as Casson writes, did not come about until Roman times.
2. Max Radin, "The Ancient Grudge: A Study in the Public Relations of the Legal Profession," *Virginia Law Review*, vol. 32 (March 1946), pp. 734–52. If lawyer-bashing has always been in season, the reasons for the hostility have changed, as society has changed. In his perceptive analysis, Marc Galanter put it this way: "Episodes of elevated anti-lawyer feeling are never entirely new; they draw on old themes. But they are never just reruns. Such episodes are about more than lawyers: they are about people's responses to the legal system and the wider society in which it is set." Marc Galanter, "Predators and Parasites: Lawyer Bashing and Civil Justice," *University of Georgia Law Review*, vol. 28, no. 3 (Spring 1994), p. 681. See also Lawrence M. Friedman, *A History of American Law*, 2d ed. (Simon and Schuster, 1985), pp. 94–96, 303–04.
3. See, for example, Council for Public Interest Law, *Balancing the Scales of Justice: Financing Public Interest Law in America: A Report* (Washington: The Council for Public Interest Law, 1976); Mauro Cappelletti, ed., *Access to Justice* (multivolume series)

(Milan: European University Institute, 1978–81); Marvin E. Frankel, *Partisan Justice* (New York: Hill and Wang, 1980); Ted Schneyer, "Professionalism as Bar Politics: The Making of the Model Rules of Professional Conduct," *Law & Social Inquiry*, vol. 14, no. 4 (Fall 1989), pp. 677–737 (discussing the American Bar Association's Special Commission on Evaluation of Professional Standards—known as the Kutak Commission).

4. Cameron Barr, "Doers and Talkers," *American Lawyer*, vol. 12, no. 6 (July/August 1990), p. 51; Barbara A. Curran, "1989 Survey of the Public's Use of Legal Services" and the Spangenberg Group, "National Survey of The Civil Legal Needs of the Poor," both in American Bar Association Consortium on Legal Services and the Public, *Two Nationwide Surveys: 1989 Pilot Assessments of the Unmet Legal Needs of the Poor and of the Public Generally* (Chicago, 1989); Massachusetts Legal Assistance Corporation, *Massachusetts Legal Services Plan for Action* (1987); American Bar Association Consortium on Legal Services and the Public, *Legal Needs and Civil Justice: A Survey of Americans* (Chicago, 1994).

5. President Jimmy Carter, "Remarks at the 100th Anniversary Luncheon of the Los Angeles Bar Association," *Weekly Compilation of Presidential Documents*, vol. 14, no. 18 (May 4, 1978), pp. 834–41, reprinted in "President Carter's Attack on Lawyers, President Spann's Response, and the Chief Justice Burger's Remarks," *American Bar Association Journal*, vol. 64 (June 1978), p. 842.

6. Justice Sandra Day O'Connor, "Pro Bono Work—Good News and Bad News," remarks at the Pro Bono Awards Assembly Luncheon of the American Bar Association, Atlanta, Georgia, August 12, 1991 (unpublished).

7. James W. Jones, remarks at the ABA Law Firm Pro Bono Conference, October 4, 1990, Washington, D.C.

8. Derek C. Bok, "A Flawed System," *Harvard Magazine*, vol. 85, no. 5 (May–June 1983), p. 41.

9. For instance, see Ernest Gellhorn, "Too Much Law, Too Many Lawyers, Not Enough Justice," *Wall Street Journal*, June 7, 1984, p. 28; David Margolick, "Burger Says Lawyers Make Legal Help Too Costly," *New York Times*, February 13, 1984, p. A13.

10. President George Bush, remarks at the American Business Conference, Washington, D.C., *Federal News Service*, April 7, 1992; Walter K. Olson, *The Litigation Explosion: What Happened When America Unleashed the Lawsuit* (Dutton, 1991).

11. Michael Boskin, remarks at the National Economists Club, Washington, D.C., *Federal News Service*, March 31, 1992, available in LEXIS News Library.

12. Vice President J. Danforth Quayle, press conference, *Federal News Service*, February 4, 1992, available in LEXIS News Library.

13. James M. Kramon, "Lawyers Look at the Practice of Law: Some Disquieting Observations," *Maryland Bar Journal*, vol. 19, no. 11 (December 1986), pp. 6–11; Marc Galanter and Thomas Palay, *Tournament of Lawyers: The Transformation of the Large Law Firm* (University of Chicago Press, 1991).

14. Robert A. Kagan, "Adversarial Legalism and American Government," *Journal of Policy Analysis and Management*, vol. 10, no. 3 (Summer 1991), pp. 369–406.

15. Ibid., p. 372. On this point, see generally Philip K. Howard, *The Death of Common Sense: How Law Is Suffocating America* (Random House, 1994).

16. See, for example, R. Shep Melnick, *Regulation and the Courts: The Case of the Clean Air Act* (Brookings, 1983); Peter H. Schuck, "Litigation, Bargaining, and Regulation," *Regulation*, vol. 3, no. 4 (July/August 1979), pp. 26–34.

17. Mary Ann Glendon, "A Nation Under Lawyers," *American Enterprise*, vol. 5 (November/December 1994), p. 51.

18. For example, see Arlin M. Adams, "The Legal Profession: A Critical Evaluation," *Dickinson Law Review*, vol. 93, no. 4 (Summer 1989), pp. 643–44, 652–54; Robert W.

Gordon, "The Independence of Lawyers," *Boston University Law Review*, vol. 68, no. 1 (January 1988), pp. 1–83; Peter Megargee Brown, *Rascals: The Selling of the Legal Profession* (New York: Benchmark Press, 1989).

19. Sol M. Linowitz with Martin Mayer, *The Betrayed Profession: Lawyering at the End of the Twentieth Century*, (New York: Charles Scribner's Sons, 1994), p. 31.

20. Lincoln Caplan, "The Lawyers' Race to the Bottom," *New York Times*, August 6, 1993, p. A-29.

21. Harry T. Edwards, "A Lawyer's Duty to Serve the Public Good," *New York University Law Review*, vol. 65, no. 4 (October 1990), pp. 1148, 1151.

22. Anthony T. Kronman, *The Lost Lawyer: Failing Ideals of the Legal Profession* (Harvard University Press, 1993), p. 2. For another stimulating discussion, see Carrie Menkel-Meadow, "The Future of the Legal Profession: Culture Clash in the Quality of Life in the Law: Changes in the Economics, Diversification, and Organization of Lawyering," *Case Western Reserve Law Review*, vol. 44 (1994), p. 621.

23. American Bar Association, "At the Breaking Point," report of the National Conference on the Emerging Crisis in the Quality of Lawyers' Health and Lives—Its Impact on Law Firms and Client Services (Chicago, 1991).

24. Michael J. Kelly, *Lives of Lawyers: Journeys in the Organizations of Practice* (University of Michigan Press, 1994), p. 18.

25. See, for instance, American Bar Association, report of the National Conference on Access to Justice in the 1990s (Chicago, 1989), p. 43; Roger C. Cramton, "Mandatory Pro Bono," *Hofstra Law Review*, vol. 19 (Summer 1991), p. 1137; Susan E. Lawrence, *The Poor in Court: The Legal Services Program and Supreme Court Decision Making* (Princeton University Press, 1990).

26. For example, O'Connor, "Pro Bono Work—Good News and Bad News."

27. See, for example, Thomas Ehrlich and Murray Schwartz, "Reducing the Costs of Legal Services: Possible Approaches by the Federal Government," a report to the Subcommittee on Representation of Citizen Interests, U.S. Senate Committee on the Judiciary, 93d Cong., 2d sess. (1974) in Andrew L. Kaufman, ed., *Problems in Professional Responsibility* (Boston: Little, Brown and Company, 1976), pp. 582–619; American Bar Association Commission on Professionalism, "In the Spirit of Public Service: A Blueprint for the Rekindling of Lawyer Professionalism" (Chicago, 1986) pp. 243, 301; Deborah Rhode, "Policing the Professional Monopoly: A Constitutional and Empirical Analysis of Unauthorized Practice Prohibitions," *Stanford Law Review*, vol. 34, no. 1 (November 1981), pp. 1–12; Nan Aron and Samuel S. Jackson, Jr., "Non-Traditional Models for Legal Services Delivery," in Esther F. Lardent, ed., *Civil Justice: An Agenda for the 1990s*, papers of the American Bar Association National Conference on Access to Justice in the 1990s (Chicago, 1991), pp. 143–64; Alan Morrison, "Competition and Monopoly Among Lawyers," in Douglas J. Besharov, ed., *Legal Services for the Poor: Time for Reform* (AEI Press, 1990), pp. 150–55. On the subject of the circumstances in which lawyers should be subject to external regulation, see David B. Wilkins, "Who Should Regulate Lawyers?" *Harvard Law Review*, vol. 105, no. 4 (February 1992), pp. 801–87.

28. See, for instance, "A Report from the President's Council on Competitiveness," *Agenda for Civil Justice Reform in America* (August 1991); "Succeeding in the Post Gold Rush Era," *American Lawyer*, vol. 14, no. 7 (September 1992) supplement; Report of a Task Force, *Justice for All: Reducing Costs and Delay in Civil Litigation* (Brookings, 1989).

29. Robert A. Kagan, "Adversarial Legalism and American Government," p. 398.

30. Linowitz with Mayer, *The Betrayed Profession*, pp. 179–81; Sherman L. Cohn, "First We Kill All the Lawyers," *Women Lawyers Journal*, vol. 78, no. 4 (Fall 1992), pp. 6–9; Joryn Jenkins, "The Quiet Crusade: The American Inns of Court's Battle to Return Professionalism to the Practice of Law," *Federal Bar News & Journal*, vol. 39, no. 5

(June 1992), p. 320; Geoffrey C. Hazard, Jr., "The Future of Legal Ethics," *Yale Law Journal,* vol. 100, no. 5 (March 1991), pp. 1239–80.

31. For instance, see Robert E. Litan, ed., *Verdict: Assessing the Civil Jury System* (Brookings, 1993).
32. David Luban, *Lawyers and Justice: An Ethical Study* (Princeton University Press, 1988), p. 286.
33. Ibid., pp. 104–47.
34. David Fagelson discusses the autonomy concept in "Ethical Obligations of the Legal Profession," a paper prepared for the Governance Institute, September 26, 1991.
35. See Nadine Strossen, "Pro Bono Legal Work: For the Good of Not Only the Public, But Also the Lawyer and the Legal Profession," *Michigan Law Review,* vol. 91, no. 8 (August 1993), pp. 2122–23.
36. Besharov, ed., *Legal Services for the Poor.*
37. President George Bush, "Light Up the World Around You: Lawyers Can Make a Difference by Caring," *American Bar Association Journal,* vol. 76, no. 2 (February 1990), p. 9.
38. Committee to Improve the Availability of Legal Services, *Final Report to the Chief Judge of the State of New York* (Marrero Report), *Hofstra Law Review,* vol. 19, no. 4 (Summer 1991), pp. 755–883.

2

Public Service Implications of Evolving Law Firm Size and Structure

Marc Galanter and Thomas Palay

Large law firms have grown rapidly in recent years and this growth has been accompanied by increased rationalization, specialization, hierarchy, meritocracy, diversity, and market orientation. As firms have grown in size they have simply outpaced earlier methods of monitoring and coordinating personnel, recruiting associates, and generating revenues (to compensate the larger staff).[1] To survive, firms have been forced to adapt by slowing growth, generating new sources of income, remolding existing governance structures, or accepting decreased—or at least different—profit distributions.

Many observers, concerned about the commercialization of law practice, regard these developments as inimical to lawyers' commitment to public service and conclude that there has been a decline in the pro bono activities of law firms. Wary of falling into the easy assumption that things have declined since the good old days, we seek in this chapter to test the accuracy of these assertions. We shall attempt to assemble some information that illuminates the connection between firm growth and pro bono work.

We first put our inquiry into context by reviewing the growth and transformation of the large law firm in recent years. We then sketch the perceptions of decline into commercialism that have accompanied the large law firm since its founding a century ago. Finally, we present, in summary form, some data on the pro bono activities of a set of large firms.

The Emergence of the Big Firm[2]

The big firm and its distinctive style of practice emerged around the turn of the century. The break from earlier law practice can be depicted by a schematic comparison under the six headings of partners, other lawyers, relations with clients, work, support system, and new kinds of knowledge. Any of these indexes of the big firm can be found apart from the cluster, but we argue that the cluster hangs together to give the big firm a distinctive institutional character—a character that is changing as these features are rearranged.

In the big law firm, the loose affiliation of lawyers sharing offices and occasionally sharing work for clients is replaced by an environment in which clients "belong to" the firm rather than to an individual lawyer. The proceeds, after salaries and expenses are paid, are divided among the *partners* pursuant to an agreed-upon formula.

Unpaid clerks and permanent assistants in the big law firm are displaced by a select group of academically trained associates (as they came to be called), or *other lawyers,* chosen on grounds of potential qualification for partnership. These associates are salaried lawyers who are expected to devote their full efforts to the firm's clients. To provide them with the necessary incentives, the firm holds out the prospect of eventual promotion to partnership, but only after a prolonged probationary period during which the associates work under the supervision and tutelage of their seniors and are gradually assigned increased responsibility. As we have argued elsewhere, the presence of a steady supply of highly qualified but inexperienced young recruits is one of the key ingredients of the big law firm.[3] The gap between their certified promise and their untested quality of performance underlies what we refer to as the "promotion-to-partner tournament."

Large firms represent large corporate enterprises, organizations, or entrepreneurs with a need for continuous (or recurrent) and specialized legal services that could be supplied only by a team of lawyers. *Relations with clients* tend to be enduring. Such repeat clients are able to reap benefits from the continuity and economies of scale enjoyed by the firm.

The *work* of large firms involves specialization in the problems of particular kinds of clients. It involves not only representation in court, but also services in other settings and forums. The emergence of the large firm represents the ascendancy of the office lawyer and the displacement of the advocate as the paradigmatic professional figure. Litigation no longer commands the energies of the most eminent lawyers. By 1900, Robert Swaine concluded, "the great corporate lawyers of the day drew their reputations more from their abilities in the conference room and facility in drafting documents than from their persuasiveness before the courts."[4]

The emergence of the big firm was associated with the introduction of new office technologies, a new *support system.* The displacement of copying, clerks, and messengers by the typewriter, stenography, and the telephone greatly increased the productivity of lawyers.

The proliferation of printed materials—reports, digests, treatises—rendered obsolete the earlier style of legal research and required mastery of *new areas of specialized knowledge.* The acquisition of legal skills changed, too. Between 1870 and 1910 the portion of those admitted to the bar who were law school graduates rose from one-fourth to two-thirds.

The blending of these features into the big law firm as we know it is commonly credited to Paul D. Cravath. In the first decade of this century, he established the "Cravath system" of employing outstanding graduates straight out of law school on the understanding that in return for a salary, training, a "graduated increase in responsibility," and the possibility of progressing to partnership after an extended probationary period, young lawyers would work exclusively for the firm and eschew practices of their own.[5] Though most fully articulated by Cravath, many elements of the big firm had been around for several decades.[6] Cravath's innovation was to add the promise that, with the right credentials, hard work, and perseverance, the younger attorney's relationship to his or her mentors would eventually mature into an enduring and permanent partnership.

Innovative organizers elsewhere came up with similar combinations of these elements. Wayne Hobson noted that "[Louis D.] Brandeis . . . was the true pioneer of modern forms of law firm organization in Boston."[7] At Warren and Brandeis he hired Harvard graduates of high academic achievement, paid them salaries (an innovation), and "was the first Boston lawyer to organize his office on the basis of taking bright young men quickly into partnership."[8]

The core of the big firm, we submit, is the promotion to partnership. Partners and junior lawyers are not equals, but are arranged in a hierarchy with command and supervision in the former. But the latter are neither transient apprentices nor permanent employees. They are inchoate peers, fellow professionals of presently immature powers who have the potential to achieve full and equal stature.

Firms can offer this promise only when they are confident that they can attract sufficient work to keep these young lawyers busy. That is, the senior lawyers have to have either clients who produce more work than the senior lawyers can handle themselves or a reputation that will attract such clients. Reviewing early firm histories, Thomas Pinansky notes that typically it was association with a corporation or a "super-capitalist" that provided the stream of work, and "the publicity from serving such clients and the expansive contacts of these clients result[ed] in a growing network of contacts for the emergent firm."[9] For example, "when the law firm of Shearman and Sterling was established in 1873, Jay Gould promised Shearman that he would take his legal business to the new firm. . . . Gould was more than a rich client who assured the new firm a few large fees. At the time of the establishment of Shearman and Sterling, there were sixty-three cases pending involving Jay Gould. One year later, the figure had risen to ninety-seven."[10]

The frenetic pace and intense specialization of the large firm transformed the world of the younger lawyer. Conventional understandings of professionalism were violated by reducing young lawyers to anonymous employees, demanding a monopoly on their energies, and forbidding them independent relations with clients. This diminution of professional identity and status troubled many junior lawyers. William H. Dunbar, in his ninth year at Warren and Brandeis, complained that his name was acquiring "none of the value which seems to constitute the chief capital of a professional man." While he acknowledged the pecuniary benefits of his status, he remained troubled by the fact that it was the firm's, not his, reputation that benefited from "the success of all our joint labors."[11]

During these early years law firms grew in size. In every city, the number of big firms (as big was then defined) grew at an increasingly rapid rate. And over time there were ever bigger firms: first in New York, then in other large cities, then in smaller cities. This progression can be seen in Hobson's compilation of the number of firms with four or more lawyers, which grew from 15 in 1872, to 39 in 1882, to 87 in 1892, to 210 in 1903, to 445 in 1914, to "well over 1,000" in 1924.[12] The large law firm—and with it the organization of law practice around the promotion to partnership pattern—became the industry standard. Gradually, the older patterns of fluid partnerships, casual apprenticeship, and nepotism were displaced.

Circa 1960: The Golden Age of the Big Law Firm

By World War II, the big firm had become the dominant kind of law practice. It was the kind of lawyering consumed by the dominant economic actors. It commanded the highest prestige. It attracted many of the most highly talented entrants to the profession. It was regarded as the state of the art, embodying the highest technical standards. In the postwar years this position of dominance was solidified.

To get a reading on the changes over the past generation, we develop as a baseline a portrait of the big firm in its "golden age"—before the transformation that is now under way—of the late 1950s and the early 1960s, when big firms were prosperous, stable, and untroubled. The form had been tested; it was well established; it exercised an unchallenged dominance. It was a time of stable relations with clients, of steady but manageable growth, of comfortable assurance that an equally bright future lay ahead—which is not to say that its inhabitants did not look back fondly to an earlier time, when professionalism was unalloyed.

Circa 1960 New York City was home to a much larger share of big firm practice than it is now. In the early 1960s, there were twenty-one firms in New York with fifty lawyers or more, and only seventeen firms of that size in the rest of the country outside New York.[13] A few years earlier, the largest firm in New York (and the country) was Shearman & Sterling & Wright, with thirty-five partners and ninety associates, a total of 125 lawyers. Three other Wall Street firms had over one hundred lawyers. The twentieth-largest firm in New York had fifty lawyers.[14]

To examine this golden age, we compiled data from the *Martindale-Hubbell Directory of American Lawyers* on two sets of firms: Group I consists of fifty firms that were among the largest in 1986; Group II consists of fifty smaller but still large firms ranked roughly between 200th and 250th in the United States in 1988.[15]

We were able to examine the sizes of thirty-five firms from each group in 1955 and 1965.[16] In 1955 our thirty-five Group I firms ranged in size from seven to eighty-four lawyers, with an average size of forty lawyers. By 1965 their size ranged from thirteen to 112 lawyers, with an average of 62.6. The thirty-five firms in Group II ranged from six to thirty-five lawyers in 1955, with an average of 15.8; in 1965 they ranged from eight to forty-six, with an average of 25.1 lawyers. This was a period of prosperity and manageable growth for big firms. Over the decade ending in 1965, the Group I firms that twenty years later figured among the fifty largest grew at an annual rate of 5.3 percent. The Group II firms grew at an annual rate of 5.5 percent.[17]

Firms were generally located in and identified with a single city. An earlier wave of European and Washington, D.C., offices had been largely abandoned.[18] "Formation [in 1957] of a nationwide [sic] law firm with offices interlocking in Illinois, Washington, D.C. and New York" was startling, "so unusual that it had to be approved in advance by the Bar Association."[19]

Hiring

Firms in this era were built by promotion to partnership. Lateral hiring was almost unheard of, and big firms did not hire from one another. Partners might leave and firms might split up, but it did not happen very often.[20] Hiring of top law students soon after their graduation was one of the building blocks of the big firm. Most hiring was from a handful of law schools, and walk-in interviews during the Christmas break were the norm. Starting salaries at the largest New York firms were uniform— $4,000 in 1953, rising to $7,500 in 1963.[21] The going rate was fixed at a luncheon attended by managing partners of prominent firms and held annually for this purpose.[22]

Historically, the big firms had confined hiring to white, Christian males. Few blacks and women possessed the educational admission tickets to contend for these jobs, and although numerous Jews did, with a few exceptions they, too, were excluded.[23] This exclusion began to break down after World War II and accelerated after 1960. Jewish associates were hired and some moved up the ladder to partner. The lowering of barriers to Jews was part of a general lessening of social exclusiveness. In 1957, 28 percent of the partners in the eighteen New York firms studied by Smigel were listed in the Social Register; by 1968 the percentage had dropped to 20 percent. But blacks and other minorities of color were still hardly visible in the world of big law firms. In 1956 there were perhaps eighteen women working in large New York firms—less than 1 percent of their total complement of lawyers. As late as 1968, Cynthia Fuchs Epstein estimated, "only forty women were working in Wall Street firms or had some Wall Street experience."[24]

Promotion and Partnership

Only a small minority of those hired as associates achieved partnership. Of 462 beginning associates hired by the Cravath firm between 1906 and

1948, only 44 (just under 10 percent) were made partners.[25] Cravath may have been the most selective, but it was not out of line with other firms. In 1956 Martin Mayer reported that the "chance of becoming a partner . . . varies from one in seven to one in fifteen, depending on the firm and the year in which he joins it."[26] Spencer Klaw, writing two years later, provides a more optimistic assessment that partnership is achieved by "perhaps one out of every six or seven."[27]

The time that it took to become a partner varied. For New York lawyers who became partners around 1960, the average time seems to have been just under ten years.[28] Outside of New York the time was closer to seven years.[29] Throughout the decade of the 1960s, the time to partnership became shorter.[30]

One of the basic elements of the big firm is the "up-or-out" rule that prescribes that after a probationary period the young lawyer will either be admitted to the partnership or leave the firm. In this model there can be no permanent connection other than as a partner, though it is easy to overestimate the rigor with which the up-or-out rule was in fact applied.

For associates who did not make partner, firms undertook outplacement, recommending them for jobs with client corporations and smaller firms.[31] Ties might be maintained as the firm referred legal work to lawyers who left or who served as outside counsel to the corporation. And although departure from the firm was generally decreed by the up-or-out norm, some lawyers were permanent but not partners.

Partners were chosen by proficiency, hard work, and ability to relate to clients.[32] But in many cases there was some consideration of the candidate's ability to attract business.[33] And selection depended on the perceived ability of the firm to support additional partners.[34] Achieving partnership, the "strongest reward," meant not only status but security and assurance of further advancement: "they . . . know that they have tenure and feel certain that they will advance up the partnership ladder."[35] There was certainly pressure to keep up with one's peers, but competition between partners was restrained. In this environment, "Admission to the partnership of a leading firm was a virtual guarantee not only of tenured employment but of a lifetime of steadily increasing earnings unmatched by a lawyer's counterparts in the other learned professions."[36]

But this should not lead one to conclude that the classic pattern of dividing the proceeds of the big firm partnership was some approximation of giving each partner an equal share—or a share by seniority (the so-called "lockstep" system).[37] By circa 1960 the prevailing practice was to divide profits according to individualized shares, rather than a norm of equal participation.[38]

Work and Clients

The work of the big firm was primarily office work in corporate law, securities, banking, and tax, as well as some estate work for wealthy clients. Divorces, automobile accidents, and minor real estate matters would be farmed out or referred to other lawyers.[39] Litigation was not prestigious work and was not seen as a moneymaker. Mayer estimated that "litigation . . . occupies less than one-tenth the time of a large law firm" and reported that "some firms avoid it entirely."[40] He described big firm litigation in the early 1960s as involving taxes, contracts, personal injury defense, and defense of corporations and directors from shareholders suits. "But to most large law firms, the word 'litigation' connotes an antitrust suit, not because the number of such cases is large but because each of them represents so enormous a quantity of work."[41] The surge of antitrust litigation tended to elevate the standing of litigators, who had been "overshadowed by office-lawyer partners . . . who seldom, if ever, went near a courtroom."[42] Where big firms were involved in litigation, it was typically on the defendants' side. Big firms usually represented dominant actors who could structure transactions so that they got what they wanted; it was the other side that had to seek the help of courts to disturb the status quo. Disdain of litigation reflected the prevailing attitude among the corporate establishment: that it was not quite nice to sue.[43]

Relations with clients tended to be enduring. "A partner in one Wall Street firm estimate[d] its turnover in dollar volume at 5 percent a year, mostly in one-shot litigation."[44] Many big firm partners sat on the boards of their clients[45]—a practice that had been viewed as unprofessional earlier in the century, and would lose favor later.[46]

As they grew, many firms broadened their client base, becoming less dependent on a single, main client. Corporations had strong ties to "their" law firms; relations tended to be enduring and unproblematic. A 1959 Conference Board survey on the legal work of 286 manufacturing corporations found that "three-fourths of them retain outside counsel on a continuing basis. . . . Companies most frequently report that 'present outside counsel has been with us for many, many years,' or that 'we are satisfied with the performance of our outside counsel and have never given any thought to hiring another.'"[47]

We have no evidence about how many hours people actually worked or billed. Smigel reported, "Some firms believe an associate should put in 1,800 chargeable hours a year and a partner 1,500, with the hours decreasing as the partner gets older."[48] It was widely believed, perhaps with some basis, that lawyers (especially associates) were not working as hard as they had in earlier times.[49]

Outside New York

Circa 1960, New York still dominated the world of big-time law practice. Big firms elsewhere were constructed along the same promotion to partnership lines, but tended to operate a bit differently. Firms outside New York tended to be more recently founded. There was less departmentalization; lawyers were less specialized, and less supervised. Firm organization was less formal: there was less elaboration of rules about meetings, training, conflicts of interest and so on.[50] They had a smaller turnover of associates and less up-or-out pressure. Partnership was easier to attain and came earlier.[51] There was more use of such intermediate classifications as junior or limited partners and more lateral hiring.[52] Firms were also less highly leveraged. The ratio of associates to partners in Smigel's nineteen New York firms was two to one; in his non–New York firms it was one to one-and-a-half associates to one partner.[53]

For big firms, circa 1960 was a time of prosperity, stable relations with clients, steady but manageable growth, and a comfortable assumption that this kind of law practice was a permanent fixture of American life and would go on forever. Notwithstanding their comfortable situation, many inhabitants and observers regarded the big firm world as sadly declined from an earlier day when lawyers were statesmen and served as the conscience of business.[54] Echoing laments that have recurred since the last century, partners complained to Smigel that law is turning into a business.[55] No longer, Mayer reflected, do young associates regard themselves as servants of the law and holders of a public trust; "they are too busy fitting themselves for existence in the 1950s, when efficiency, accuracy, and intelligence are the only values to be sought."[56]

Big law firms enjoyed an enviable autonomy. They were relatively independent vis-à-vis their clients; exercised considerable control over how they did their work; and were infused with a sense of being in control of their destiny.

The Transformation of the Big Firm

The more numerous and more diverse lawyers of our day are arrayed in a very different structure of practice than their counterparts a generation earlier. There has been a general shift toward larger practices.[57] The number of lawyers working in sizable aggregations, capable of massive and coordinated legal undertakings, has multiplied many times over.[58] One estimate stated that in 1988 there were 35,000 lawyers at 115 firms with more than two hundred lawyers, and a total of 105,000 lawyers in 2,000 firms larger than twenty lawyers.[59]

Growth

In the late 1950s there were only thirty-eight law firms in the United States with more than fifty lawyers—and more than one-half of these were in New York City.[60] In 1985 there were 508 firms with fifty-one or more lawyers.[61]

Not only were there more big firms, but they were growing at a faster rate. The firms in our Group I (fifty of the largest firms in 1986) grew from an average size of 124 in 1975 to 252 in 1985.[62] In this period, the average size of our Group II firms (forty-four of the 200th to 250th largest in 1988) doubled, from forty-four to eighty-eight lawyers.[63] The average annual growth rate over this ten-year period was 8 percent for Group I and 7.9 percent for Group II.[64] These rates are considerably higher than the rates at which these same firms were growing twenty years earlier. From 1955 to 1965, the average annual growth rate was 5.3 percent for the Group I firms and 5.5 percent for Group II firms.[65]

In 1960 big law firms were clearly identified with a specific locality, as they had been since the origin of the big firm.[66] But by 1980, of the one hundred largest firms, eighty-seven had branches. Of all firms with fifty or more lawyers, 56.8 percent were in more than one location and 24 percent were in three or more locations in 1980.[67] Some of this branching was by "colonization," but most of it involved mergers with firms (or with groups defecting from firms) in the new locality. Washington has been the favorite site for branches. In 1980, 178 firms from outside Washington had branches there.[68] But as branching activity has increased, Washington offices have become a declining portion of all branches.

In the 1980s the home office and branch pattern was joined by the genuine multicity law firm.[69] To capture the dynamic of multicity growth, we compared twenty of the largest firms based in New York City (NY) and twenty of the largest firms based outside New York City (ONY) in 1980 and 1987.[70] The twenty NY firms had a total of seventy branch offices in 1980 and ninety-nine branches in 1987. The twenty largest ONY firms had a total of 61 branches in 1980 and 124 branches in 1987. Thus there was a 41 percent increase in branches of NY firms over this seven-year period and a 103 percent increase in branches of ONY firms.

Not only did the number of branches increase, but so did their size. The average size of each branch of a NY firm went from eight lawyers in 1980 to seventeen in 1987. The branches of the ONY firms grew from an average of fifteen lawyers in 1980 to thirty lawyers just seven years later. The growth in branches accounted for 31 percent of the total growth of the twenty NY firms and 69 percent of the total growth of the ONY firms. The percentage of lawyers outside the largest office rose from 15 percent to 21 percent for the NY firms, while doubling from 21 percent to 42 percent for the ONY firms.

We can see that branches grew much faster than main offices during this period. By 1987 there were a number of firms that had a substantial portion of their lawyers away from the largest office. Eight of the NY firms had more than 25 percent of their lawyers outside the main office (up from four in 1980); and seventeen of the ONY firms had more than 25 percent of their lawyers outside the largest office—seven had more than 50 percent outside.

Increasingly, large firms operate on an international basis. Of the one hundred largest firms in 1988, some forty-four had a total of 136 overseas offices.[71] Our comparison of the twenty largest NY and twenty largest ONY firms indicates that the largest NY firms have more overseas branches, but the gap is closing. The twenty NY firms had thirty-nine in 1980 and forty-three in 1987. Their ONY counterparts had nine in 1980 and twenty-one in 1987. Foreign offices tend to be a larger share of the offices of the NY firms (36 percent in 1987) than of the ONY firms (15 percent in 1987).

Over the past generation, there has been a marked movement away from New York City as the nation's legal center.[72] In 1957 there were twenty-one firms with over fifty lawyers in New York City and only seventeen in the rest of the country.[73] In 1980 there were 72 firms of fifty-one or more lawyers in New York State, but in the whole country there were 287.[74] In twenty years New York City's share of large firms had fallen from more than one-half to less than one-quarter. New York City has retained a somewhat larger but declining share of the very largest firms. In 1987 thirty-two of the one hundred largest firms were based in

New York (down from thirty-six in 1975).[75] The one hundred largest firms were based in twenty-four cities (up from eighteen in 1975).[76]

Work and Clients

The type of work big firms do has also been changing; there has been a surge of corporate litigation since the 1970s as well as an increase in the number, size, and responsibility of in-house legal departments.[77] Long-term retainer relations have given way to comparison shopping for lawyers on an *ad hoc* transactional basis.[78] Corporations that view legal expenses as ordinary costs of doing business rather than as singular emergencies now monitor legal costs, set litigation budgets, demand periodic reports, and require presentations from competing outside firms before awarding new business.

Law practice has also become more specialized. Within large firms, specialization has become more intense and the work of various levels more differentiated.[79] Much routine work has been retracted into corporate law departments, shifting the work of large outside firms away from office practice and toward litigation and deals.[80] With more deals, higher stakes, more regulation to take into account, and more volatile fluctuations of interest and exchange rates, there is greater demand for intensive lawyering. The large, contested, or risk-prone, one-of-a-kind, "bet your company" transaction—litigation, takeovers, bankruptcies, and such—makes up a larger portion of the work of big law firms. Since few clients provide a steady stream of such transactions, and those that have them increasingly shop for specialists to handle them, firms are under pressure to generate a steady (or increasing) supply of such matters by retaining the favors of old clients and securing new ones.

Competitiveness

The new aggressiveness of in-house counsel, the breakdown of retainer relationships, and the shift to discrete transactions has made conditions more competitive. Law practice has become more openly commercial and profit-oriented—more like a business.[81] Firms rationalize their operations; engage professional managers and consultants; and worry about billable hours, profit centers, and marketing strategies. "Eat what you kill" compensation formulas emphasize rewards for productivity and business-getting over equal shares or seniority.[82] There is more differentiation in the power and rewards of partners; increasingly, standing within the firm depends on how much business a partner brings in.[83] Rising overhead costs and associate salaries put pressure on partners. In many firms, partners work more hours with no commensurate increase in income.[84]

The need to find new business leads to aggressive marketing. Some firms take on marketing directors, a practice unheard of in 1980; but by 1985 there were forty such positions in law firms nationwide.[85] By 1989 "almost 200 law firms ha[d] hired their own marketing directors."[86] The push for new business also brings about increased emphasis on "rainmaking" by more of the firm's lawyers. Those lawyers who are responsible for bringing in business enjoy a new ascendancy over their colleagues.[87] The thrust for business-getting resonates throughout the structure of the firm. Thus a report on big firms in the southeast: "The shift from a traditional reliance upon a small number of rainmakers to the aggressive stance that everyone must make rain has resulted in a reduction in numbers of associates receiving a vote for partnership as well as—in many cases— a redivision of partners' profit pie. Many firms also go a step further by eliminating non-producing partners and restructuring or jettisoning non-productive departments."[88]

The search for new business has been directed not only toward would-be clients, but also to existing ones. In a setting where corporations are more inclined to divide their business among several law firms, firms engage in "cross-selling" to induce the purchaser of services from one department to avail itself of the other services from the firm.[89]

Lateral Hiring, Mergers

In the classic big firm, almost all hiring was at the entry level; partners were promoted from the ranks of associates. Those who left went to corporations or smaller firms, not to similar large firms, since these adhered to the same "no lateral hiring" norm. But starting in the 1970s, lateral movement became more frequent. At first firms made an occasional lateral hire to meet a need for litigators or to fill some other niche. But soon lateral hiring developed into a means of systematically upgrading or enlarging the specialties and localities they could service, and of acquiring rainmakers who might bring or attract new clients. As lateral movement increased, a whole industry of "headhunter" firms emerged, gaining respectability as it grew.[90] The number of legal search firms grew rapidly, from 83 in 1984, to 167 in 1987, to 244 in 1989.[91]

The flow of lateral movement expanded from individual lawyers to whole departments and groups within firms to whole firms. Mass defections and mergers became common, enabling firms to add new departments and expand to new locations at a stroke. A casual search of the legal press from 1985 to 1989 produced a list of seventy-one mergers involving eighty-three firms with more than fifty lawyers; in fifty-eight of these mergers, at least one of the merging firms had one hundred lawyers—a sizable portion of the whole population of firms of that size.[92] Mergers were not only a way to grow, but also a convenient device to shake out or renegotiate terms with less productive partners.

Firms hired laterally not only by mergers but also by inducing specific lawyers to change firms, "cherry picking" as it came to be called in the late 1980s. A 1988 survey of the five hundred largest law firms found that over one-quarter reported that more than one-half of their new partners were not promoted from within but rather came from other firms.[93] But lateral movement takes place not only at the partner level. The same survey found that one-quarter of the responding firms reported that more than one-half of their associates were hired laterally. Increasingly, associates move from one big firm to another. A 1989 *New York Law Journal* survey found that at twenty-three of the thirty largest firms in New York, an average of 24 percent of the associates coming up for partnership were laterals.[94]

The other side of this movement involves splits and dissolutions of firms.[95] As firms get larger the task of maintaining an adequate flow of business may become more precarious. Firms are more vulnerable to defections by valued clients or the lawyers to whom those clients are attached. Size multiplies the possibility of conflicts of interests, and the resulting tension between partners who tend old clients and those who propose new ones can be solved by a breakaway. Surrounded by other firms attempting to grow by attracting partners with special skills or desirable clients, firms are vulnerable to the loss of crucial assets. So dissolution may be catalyzed by lateral movement and merger activity, and such breakups in turn stimulate a new round of lateral movement.

Hiring

As firms have grown and required larger numbers of qualified associates, recruitment activity has intensified. Recruiting visits to law schools, extensive summer programs, brochures, and expense-paid "call-backs" of candidates have become familiar parts of the big law firm scene.[96] Starting salaries have increased dramatically, beginning with a great contraction of the supply of associates in the late 1960s. The Vietnam War draft diverted law graduates to other occupations in which they could obtain deferments, just when 1960s activism induced disdain for corporate practice among many students, who instead sought work in poverty law and public interest law. The percentage of elite law graduates entering private practice dropped precipitously.[97] Confronted by criticism that their work was unfulfilling and inimical to the public interest, many firms acceded to demands that recruits be able to spend time on *pro bono publico* activities.[98]

Firms responded to their supply problem not only by accommodating their recruits' public interest impulses, but by a sharp increase in compensation. In 1967 the starting salary for associates at elite firms in New York City was $10,000, scheduled to increase to $10,500 for 1968. In February 1968 the Cravath firm, breaking with the "going rate" cartel, raised the salaries for incoming associates to $15,000, setting in motion a new competitive system of bidding for top prospects. Firms that wanted to be considered in the top stratum had to match the Cravath rate. The change in New York starting salaries reverberated throughout the upper reaches of the profession. The salaries of more senior associates had to be raised to preserve differentials; the take of junior partners had to be adjusted accordingly; and firms outside New York, though paying less, had to give corresponding raises to maintain parity with their New York rivals. Unlike later increases in compensation, this one was not accompanied by pressure to bill more hours; in fact, it appears that hourly billings were dropping during this period.[99]

In 1986, when the highest-paid beginning associates were getting $53,000, Cravath administered a second shock by unilaterally raising salaries to $65,000.[100] At the time of the first "Cravath shock," the big firm "going rate" referred primarily to a few dozen firms, located mostly in New York; by the time the second increase occurred, the big firm world consisted of several hundred geographically dispersed firms, many of them national in scope. Long-accepted city differentials have been eroded by branching, especially by recent moves by New York firms into other legal markets, causing some firms in those localities to match the higher New York salaries.

As the number and size of large firms has increased, recruitment has become more competitive and more meritocratic, leading to changes in the social composition of the new recruits. The range of law schools from which the big firms recruit has widened and recruitment goes "deeper" into the class. Barriers against hiring Catholics, Jews, women, and blacks have been swept away. The social exclusiveness in hiring that was a feature of the world of elite law practice in 1960 has receded into insignificance.

Performance in law school and in the office counts for more, and social connections for less.[101]

By the late 1980s the population of big firm lawyers included a significant number of women and members of minority groups. A 1989 survey of the 250 largest firms found that 24 percent of their lawyers, 9.2 percent of partners, and 33 percent of associates were women.[102] A 1987 survey of these firms reported that women were "40 percent of the associates hired in the last two years, the same percentage as women in law school."[103] The percentage of women partners has been increasing at a rate of approximately 1 percent a year since 1981. These numerical gains have taken place while many women have expressed dissatisfaction with working conditions and career paths in large firms, especially as these obstruct and penalize child-rearing.[104] Women are less satisfied than their male counterparts with practice in large firms, and with law practice in general.[105] Blacks remained underrepresented in the world of large law firms: in 1987 they made up 2.1 percent of associates and 0.8 percent of partners.[106]

Leverage

Firms have become more highly leveraged over time—that is, the ratio of associates to partners has risen. Using the data from our Group I set of fifty of the largest firms in 1986, we calculated the change in associate to partner ratios at five-year intervals from 1960, the midpoint of the golden age, to 1985.[107] During that period these firms grew from an average size of 48 to 239, and the ratio of associates to partners increased 28 percent from 1:15 to 1:47. "The ratio of associates to partners rose consistently during the successive five-year intervals, with the exception of the period from 1965 to 1970 where there is a slight decrease in the ratio of associates to partners. This dip would be consistent with the initial phasing-out of permanent associates and the tightening of the labor market, both of which occurred about this time."[108]

Because of the well-known (but less well-explained)[109] difference in the leverage of large New York City firms and those located elsewhere, we again divided our firms into those whose principal office is located in New York (NY) and those whose principal office is found outside of New York (ONY). During the 1960 to 1985 period, the ONY firms grew somewhat faster, but the NY firms continued to be more highly leveraged. In New York the average ratio of associates to partners increased from 1:36 in 1960 to 1:82 in 1985. The firms in other cities, by contrast, had only an average of 1:03 associates per partner in 1960 and 1:16 in 1985.[110]

This means that the NY firms are not only more heavily leveraged than the ONY firms, but also that the differences are increasing. The average number of associates per partner in the NY firms grew by 34 percent between 1960 and 1985, while for the ONY firms it increased by only 13 percent. Moreover, in 1960, 20 percent of ONY firms had associate-to-partner ratios exceeding that of the average NY firm. By 1985 none of the ONY were more leveraged than their average NY counterpart.

Promotion and Partnership

Over the two decades preceding 1980, the period during which lawyers served as associates before becoming partners became shorter. Researcher Robert Nelson found that the average time spent as associates by those promoted to partnership in large Chicago firms during the 1950s was 7.5 years; this fell to 7.21 in the 1960s; to 6.19 for those promoted between 1970 and 1975; and to 5.64 for those promoted between 1976 and 1980.[111] But in the 1980s the time to partner began to increase again. A study of five large New England firms found that associates had to wait eight or nine years instead of seven.[112] A *National Law Journal* survey of thirty-five firms in seven localities found that some two-thirds of associates hired in the late 1970s had spent seven to eight "years to partner,"[113] and many partners anticipated a further stretchout.[114]

Generally, increases in leverage suggest that a smaller percentage of associates will be promoted to partner. A 1987 *National Law Journal* survey of promotion at the five largest firms in each of seven localities revealed both regional and interfirm disparities. The portion that made partner varied, from the lowest range of 10 to 35 percent in New York to the highest of 29 to 64 percent in Los Angeles. The portion making partner at the five largest Chicago firms ranged from 33 to 48 percent, higher than the percentage Nelson (writing in 1988) anticipated for the coming years, but lower than he reports for the period then just past.[115] Similarly, lowered estimates of the percentage that will make partner are suggested by an account of large firm practice in the southeast, which reported that "managing partners at many major firms speak openly of their expectations that no more than 10 percent of any incoming class eventually will make partner."[116]

A constriction of promotion to partnership, anticipated elsewhere, seems to have arrived already in New York's largest firms. A 1989 *New York Law Journal* survey computed the chances of achieving partnership at twenty-two of the thirty largest firms in New York City in 1980 and

1989. Some 25.1 percent of the associate classes of 1968, 1969, and 1970 (including laterals assigned to those classes) had become partners by 1980; but only 18.8 percent of the classes of 1978, 1979, and 1980 had become partners by 1989.[117] These lower figures seem more in the neighborhood of the chances of becoming a partner back in the 1950s.[118]

We noted earlier that in the 1960s firms applied the up-or-out norm with increasing stringency. In the early 1970s permanent associates were described as "a dying breed . . . being phased out by attrition at most firms."[119] But before the end of the decade the institution was reinvented.[120] Firms modified the promotion to partnership model by creating a new stratum of permanent salaried lawyers:[121] nonequity partner, special partner, senior attorney, senior associate, participating associate, and so on. As a Washington legal headhunter observed, "Everyone is studying this because everyone is running against the same economic realities. The larger classes of associates are coming up, and there is just not enough room at the top."[122]

Firms also have increased the use of personnel who are not eligible to be partners. This is most evident in the increasing delegation of work to paralegals—that is, lower salaried, nonlawyer employees performing routine legal tasks under the supervision of lawyers. Paralegals are present across the spectrum of law firms, but they have become a particularly important and growing presence at big law firms. The search for leverage without "the additional pressure created by regular associates eager to make partner" is also evident in the hiring of associates on a lower-paid, nonpartnership track.[123] The presence of these low-paid lawyers enables firms to compete for "low-end, price-sensitive business," including routine work that previously might have been done in-house by corporate law departments.[124] A 1988 survey found that twenty-three of the five hundred largest law firms had added "staff attorney" positions outside the partnership track during the preceding year.[125]

Another device for enlarging capacity without engaging new associates is the use of "temporary" lawyers. These "legal temps" are not employees of the firm, but are supplied by agencies that screen and certify them. The use of temporaries enables firms to respond to fluctuations in demand (often, but not always, in connection with litigation) without the increase in overhead necessary to accommodate additional regular employees. Such jobs attract lawyers who wish to work part-time or irregularly. Temporaries are used frequently by smaller firms to enable them to handle more business without expanding; big firms use them to enlarge capacity without adding to the partner-associate core.[126]

In these ways the classic big firm notion of promotion to partnership—that all the lawyers are potentially members of a fraternity of peers—is attenuated. But if all lawyers are no longer potential peers, some nonlawyers are being invited into the core of the firm's operations. Firms feel pressure to provide more services; we have already noted the drive to cover more specialties and more locations. Since legal services are often consumed in conjunction with other services, "Firms have brought in engineers, teachers, lobbyists, regulatory economists, banking regulators, nurses, doctors, and business managers (MBAs) and other nonlawyers to help provide client services."[127] Other firms have established coordinate "nonlegal" businesses (investment advice, economic consulting, real estate development, consulting on personnel management, marketing newsletters, and so forth). A lawyer whose firm branched out into office support services said that acquisition of this business was "like a company that makes peanut butter buying a company that makes peanut butter jars."[128] Others project a grander vision—that of the evolution of law firms into diversified knowledge conglomerates: "If the railroads had asked themselves what business they were in and had answered 'Transportation,' they might be in the airline business [today]. . . . We realized we were in the business of selling knowledge, whether we were advising legal clients, giving seminars, doing investment banking, making video tapes, or publishing newsletters."[129]

As the firm copes with the exigencies of its new competitive environment, the situation of the junior lawyers becomes more precarious and pressured (although they are more rewarded); however, the partnership core is even more affected. Partners are under mounting pressure to maintain a high level of performance—and performance that fits the business strategy of the firm. Many new features of the law firm world (mergers, lateral movement) amplify the power of dominant lawyers within a firm to sanction their errant colleagues—and the prevalent culture endorses such sanctions. So partners worry about having their prerogatives or shares reduced or even being "pushed off the iceberg" or "departnerized."[130] As with professional athletes, there are real possibilities of downward movement. "[W]ith profits being squeezed and competition on the rise," reported one consultant, "many firms can no longer afford to support these ['unproductive' or 'disaffected'] partners. Firms are trying to 'rehabilitate' these partners, decreasing some partners' incomes and asking others to leave."[131] Thus in 1982 a long-established Seattle firm of eighty-seven lawyers dismissed eight partners, along with six associates, on grounds that "the firings were necessary to increase profitability and keep talented attorneys from being hired away."[132] The unassailable security and tenured prerogative of partnership is no longer assured. "Partnership used to be for life, but it is no longer."[133]

As the world of big law firms undergoes these dramatic structural changes, many of its inhabitants experience considerable distress about commercialization, the decline of professionalism, and the loss of the distinctiveness of law practice.[134] To some extent this distress about lost virtue is a constant feature of elite law practice. But what distinguishes current worries from those of a generation ago is that the latter at least had stable expectations about the large firm as an institution. If the inhabitants of the golden age thought the large firm was already too big, they at least harbored few doubts about its durability.[135] Now this sense of stability has been shaken.

Still, the link of the big firm with aspirations to professionalism is ambivalent. Law practice—or at least that part of it that serviced large organizations—departed a century ago from the individual practice format for doing legal work, but it never arrived at the great bureaucratic corporation as a format for practice. (Perhaps the promotion-to-partnership firm should be credited with averting such developments by permitting development of sufficient scale to undertake the most large-scale and complex work.[136]) Law practice never suffered the separation of ownership from control; control of work by others was, in aspiration at least, only temporary. Compared to other business services, law remained relatively unconcentrated, decentralized, and unbureaucratic.

The Perceived Decline of Civic Virtue

Before the turn of the century, there was already a sense that the legal profession had compromised its integrity and, by too closely embracing business, its identity. In 1895 the *American Lawyer* complained that:

> The typical law office ... is located in the maelstrom of business life ... in its appointments and methods of work it resembles a great business concern ... the most successful and most eminent of the bar are the trained advisors of business men.
> ... [The bar] has allowed itself to lose, in large measure, the lofty independence, the genuine learning, the fine sense of professional dignity and honor. ... For the past thirty years it has become increasingly

contaminated with the spirit of commerce, which looks primarily to the financial value and recompense of every undertaking.[137]

After the turn of the century, John Dos Passos complained: "From 'Attorneys and Counselors at Law' they became agents, solicitors, practical promoters, and commercial operators. . . . Entering the offices of some of the law firms in a metropolitan city, one imagines that he is in a commercial counting-room or banking department."[138] It was not only a distinctive ambiance that was lost, but also the connection with the pursuit of justice:

> It may . . . be safely said that the prevailing popular idea of the lawyer, too often justified by facts, is that his profession consists in thwarting the law instead of enforcing it. . . . The public no longer calls them "great" but "successful" lawyers. . . . It is the common belief, inside and outside of the profession, that the most brilliant and learned of the lawyers are employed to defeat or strangle justice.[139]

The frenetic pace and intense specialization of the large firm repelled many established lawyers.[140] By the 1930s the scale and stability of the large law firms was recognized in the pejorative phrase "law factory."[141] Describing the bar in 1933, Karl Llewellyn observed that corporate practice had become "itself a business . . . [with] a large staff, a highly organized office, a high overhead, more intense specialization." These firms attracted the "ablest of legal technicians" and fostered a "lopsided" business perspective that ignored the wider public functions of the bar.[142] Specifically, critics deplored the distributive implications of the development of the large firm. A. A. Berle ascribed to it the abandonment of the notion that the lawyer "was an officer of the court and therefore an integral part of the scheme of justice" and its replacement by a notion of the lawyer as "paid servant of his client. . . . [T]he complete commercialization of the American bar has stripped it of any social functions it might have performed for individuals without wealth."[143]

This grim assessment was shared by Chief Justice Harlan Fiske Stone, who described "[t]he successful lawyer of our day . . . [as] the proprietor or general manager of a new type of factory, whose legal product is increasingly the result of mass production methods."[144] Stone deplored the commercialization and deprofessionalization of the large firm lawyer:

> More and more the amount of his income is the measure of success.
> More and more he must look for his rewards to the material satisfactions

derived from profits as from a successfully conducted business, rather than to the intangible and indubitably more durable satisfactions which are to be found in a professional service more consciously directed toward the advancement of the public interest. . . . [I]t has made the learned profession of an earlier day the obsequious servant of business, and tainted it with the morals and manners of the marketplace in its most anti-social manifestations.[145]

Thus the large firm was felt to be profoundly at odds with professional traditions of autonomy and public service. In its stable golden age, around 1960, inhabitants and observers regarded the large firm world as sadly declined from an earlier day when lawyers were statesmen and served as the conscience of business.[146] Echoing laments that have recurred since the last century, partners complained to sociologist Erwin Smigel that law is turning into a business.[147]

As large firms have grown and multiplied, despondency about the decline of law practice from its virtuous and collegial past has intensified. Within the legal profession itself, many share the sense that law has freshly descended from a noble profession infused with civic virtue to a commercial pursuit.[148] In the most erudite and theoretically sophisticated account of decline, the dean of the Yale Law School counsels idealistic young lawyers to stay clear of large firms, whose "harshly economizing spirit" and "increasingly commercial culture" is inimical to the commitment to public service that is the hallmark of professional identity.[149]

So we find a curious double-image in which large firm lawyers embody the professional ideal of technical proficiency and service to clients at the same time that the firm is seen as betraying other aspects of professionalism. Internal complaints about the loss of collegiality and the abandonment of public spiritedness are matched by public misgivings about the effects of large firm lawyering. For even as large firms solve the problem of providing quality legal services to large entities, they raise problems of access to justice. By efficiently assembling great concentrations of talent and resources and placing them at the service of powerful economic actors (and occasional rich individuals) who can afford their fees, large firms accentuate this disparity in the public's ability to use the legal system.[150]

In short, one of the most persistent and important critiques of the large American law firm is that it does too much for the rich and too little for the poor. This is part of a wider critique that faults the legal profession for abandoning its obligation to promote justice.[151]

Pro bono publico activity by large law firms is responsive both to the perceived decline in public service and to the sense that firms accentuate inequalities in access to justice. Unfortunately, there are no data that enable us to measure the long-term trends in public service activity by large firms, or their overall distributive effects. But we do have some data that allow us to see whether the increasing size of firms in itself marks a decline in public service.

Recent Changes in the Amount of Pro Bono Activity

The conventional view is that the growth and transformation of the large law firm portends the destruction of the public service commitment of large law firm lawyers. But one should be cautious in romanticizing the good old days as a public service utopia. Ultimately, whether the large law firm has affected the amount and type of public service provided by the legal profession is an empirical question.

We begin with the *American Lawyer*'s annual surveys of pro bono contributions of large firms available from 1990 to 1993, covering pro bono activities in the preceding years. After combining the pro bono data with the *American Lawyer* financial data, we were left with fifty-nine firms for which complete data sets exist for both 1990 and 1993. Admittedly, the data suffer from several defects. First, they are relatively recent and cover only two reporting periods. Second, the data are based largely on self-reporting by the law firms and are subject to all the potential problems associated with self-reporting. Finally, the data cover only pro bono work, not the broader category of public service.[152] However, they do provide a revealing glimpse of patterns.

The *American Lawyer* survey reports four separate measures of pro bono activity by large law firms: total hours of pro bono work done by the firm, number of attorneys with twenty or more hours of pro bono activity during the year, the amount of pro bono activity per lawyer, and the percentage of attorneys at the firm reporting twenty or more hours of pro bono activity. The results are summarized in table 2-1.

As is evident from the table, pro bono activity, according to all four measures, increased between 1990 and 1993. In this set of firms, the total hours of pro bono work increased almost 45 percent, average hours per attorney increased by almost one-third (31 percent), the number of attorneys with twenty or more hours of pro bono activity increased by almost 60 percent, and the percentage of attorneys at the firm reporting twenty or more hours of pro bono activity increased by 34 percent. To be sure,

Table 2-1. *Aggregate Pro Bono Measures for Fifty-Nine Large Firms, 1990 and 1993*

	1990		1993	
	Total	Mean	Total	Mean
Number of attorneys contributing more than 20 hours	5,731.0	97.1	9,206.0	156.0
Percentage of attorneys contributing more than 20 hours	—	29.7	—	39.9
Average number of hours contributed per attorney	—	44.9	—	59.0
Total hours pro bono (thousands)	865.5	14.7	1,262.8	21.4

Source: *American Lawyer* pro bono surveys for 1990 and 1993.

the data also show that less than 40 percent of the lawyers in these firms provided twenty or more hours of pro bono activity, so most of the increases were attributable to a minority of their lawyers.

Table 2-1 depicts the aggregate trend of pro bono activity. We also tabulated the firm-by-firm changes for the fifty-nine firms for which we had data for both 1990 and 1993. The results are summarized in table 2-2. Again, the evidence indicates a general increase in pro bono activity and most firms showed increases in all four categories.

To explore why some firms provide more pro bono activity than others, we matched the *American Lawyer* pro bono survey with the *American*

Table 2-2. *Firm-by-Firm Changes in Pro Bono Measures for Fifty-Nine Large Firms, 1990 to 1993*

	Mean	Number of firms showing increase	Number of firms showing decrease
Number of attorneys contributing more than 20 hours	58.9	50	9
Percent of attorneys contributing more than 20 hours	10.2	46	13
Average number of hours contributed per attorney	14.1	46	13
Total hours contributed	6,735.0	47	12

Source: *American Lawyer* pro bono surveys for 1990 and 1993.

Lawyer reports on firm size, revenues, and estimated profits. The data do not warrant overly sophisticated analyses. Nevertheless, we can report several interesting results.

First, we examined the relationship between a firm's pro bono activity and several measures of its economic and organizational performance: total number of lawyers, total number of partners, total number of associates, gross revenue, revenue per lawyer, profits per partner, the ratio of associates to partners, and the firm's estimated profit margin. To examine the relationship between pro bono activity and performance, we treated each of the four measures of pro bono activity as a dependent variable and regressed it against various measures of performance. In general, total pro bono activity was positively related to firm performance. As seen in table 2-3, the total number of hours of pro bono activity was most strongly associated with the size of the firm, the number of associates, and the firm's gross revenues.[153] Similarly, the number of lawyers providing twenty or more hours of pro bono service was also most strongly related to the total number of lawyers at the firm, the number of associates, and gross revenues. Hours per lawyer and the percentage of lawyers providing twenty or more hours, while positively related to the performance data, are so weakly correlated as to make these positive relationships all but meaningless. In short, within this group of large firms, bigger firms did more pro bono in absolute terms, but proportionately they did not do strikingly more such work.

Next we examined the relationships between *changes* in pro bono activity from 1990 to 1993 and *changes* in the performance data over the same period. Again, all the relationships were positive, most only very weakly so. The only relationships showing any strength were those between 1) changes in the total hours of pro bono activity and changes in the total number of attorneys, the total number of partners, and—to a substantially lesser extent—the number of associates and gross revenues; and 2) changes in the number of attorneys performing twenty or more hours of pro bono service and—to a lesser extent—the size of the firm, the size of the partnership, the number of associates, and gross revenues. The results are summarized in table 2-4.

Overall, the data suggest that the larger the firm and the greater its gross revenues, the more willing it will be to encourage or permit pro bono activity. This conclusion is supported by comparing changes in pro bono activity with changes in the performance variables. These data are summarized in table 2-5. The data show that the average percent change in each of the measures of pro bono activity (rows 8–10) greatly exceeded

Table 2-3. *Relationship between Measures of Firm Pro Bono Activity and Measures of Firm Performance for Fifty-Nine Large Firms, 1990 and 1993*

	Total number of attorneys	Number of partners	Number of associates	Gross revenue	Revenue per attorney	Profits per partner	Associate:partner ratio	Estimated profit margin
Total hours pro bono								
1990	0.1920004	0.0432492	0.21703	0.2577766	0.1361535	0.1123169	0.0453675	0.0000937
1993	0.2498967	0.2203405	0.1944513	0.2027788	0.0105995	0.0124458	0.0001715	0.0004338
Number of attorneys contributing more than 20 hours								
1990	0.4096873	0.1088324	0.4500975	0.4629425	0.1226547	0.1206781	0.0693031	0.0008326
1993	0.3337237	0.2907893	0.2610776	0.2122561	0.0018772	0.001966	0.0006655	0.0015694
Number of hours contributed per attorney								
1990	0.0112989	0.0206837	0.006182	0.0023451	0.0556011	0.0289698	0.0001282	0.0034382
1993	0.0018975	0.0010333	0.0048559	0.0006575	0.0022237	0.011365	0.0196227	0.012236
Percent of attorneys contributing more than 20 hours								
1990	0.0137742	0.0274019	0.0071113	0.0015631	0.0260577	0.0109093	0.0018525	0.0013972
1993	0.0006437	0.0049437	0.0039268	0.0041988	0.0092426	0.0208273	0.0207048	0.0125143

Source: *American Lawyer* pro bono surveys for 1990 and 1993.

Table 2-4. *Relationship between Changes in Measures of Firm Pro Bono Activity and Changes in Measures of Firm Performance for Fifty-Nine Large Firms, 1990 and 1993*

	Number of attorneys	Number of partners	Number of associates	Gross revenue	Revenue per attorney	Profits per partner	Associate:partner ratio	Estimated profit margin
Total hours pro bono	0.235814213	0.244897625	0.124012469	0.145213447	0.032149979	0.02817857	0.006677652	0.006768832
Number of attorneys contributing more than 20 hours	0.205272307	0.121932467	0.140420547	0.159238943	0.013269732	0.013340287	0.022284906	0.000216907
Number of hours contributed per attorney	0.043720723	0.087761184	0.013808943	0.022856754	0.014404592	0.008009705	0.0018238	0.000474955
Percent of attorneys contributing more than 20 hours	0.025734363	0.040173836	0.010235601	0.007015243	0.002991629	0.006037805	0.000927754	0.000130321

Source: *American Lawyer* pro bono surveys for 1990 and 1993.

Table 2-5. *Mean Percent Change in Measures of Performance and of Pro Bono Activity for Fifty-Eight Large Firms*

Measure	Mean percent change
Total lawyers	0.083469
Partners	0.132527
Gross revenue	0.168785
Revenue per attorney	0.202547
Profit per partner	−0.05486
Associate:partner ratio	−0.35207
Estimated profit margin	−0.10735
Total hours pro bono	0.97687
Number of attorneys contributing more than 20 hours	0.899028
Average number of hours contributed per attorney	0.732044
Percent of attorneys contributing more than 20 hours	0.607291

Source: *American Lawyer* pro bono surveys for 1990 and 1993.

the percent changes in any of the firm performance measures (rows 1–7). More important, when we compared the data firm-by-firm (as presented in table 2-6), pro bono activity at most firms (as measured by column variables) grew faster than performance (as measured by row variables).

Conclusion

The data presented in Part II offer confirmation of the widespread impression that large firms can readily institutionalize a commitment to systematic provision of pro bono legal services. We do not argue that such service is a necessary and inevitable feature of the large business law firm—a claim that its history surely falsifies. But current developments suggest that it is not incompatible with the flourishing of the large firm.

As the other chapters in this book suggest, large firms can adapt to pro bono commitments advantageously. They can appoint partners (or outside specialists) to manage a program and assign staff to deal with the logistical problems of finding and screening suitable cases. A high volume of pro bono work may offer an inducement for recruiting talented associates and may enable the firm to facilitate development of its lawyers' professional skills while projecting a coveted image of public service. Large firms have demonstrated their capability to provide significant amounts of pro bono work.[154]

Table 2-6. *Number of Firms (of Fifty-Eight Surveyed) where the Column Measure of Change in Pro Bono Activity is Greater than the Corresponding Row Measure of Change in Performance*

Percent change

Measure of performance	Total hours pro bono	Number of attorneys contributing more than 20 hours	Average hours per attorney	Percent of attorneys contributing more than 20 hours
Total attorneys	45	49	38	46
Partners	44	46	36	41
Gross revenue	41	47	36	37
Revenue per attorney	41	44	32	38
Profit per partner	50	50	47	50
Associate: partner ratio	56	57	55	56
Estimated profit margin	51	53	50	51

Source: *American Lawyer* pro bono surveys for 1990 and 1993.

Notes

1. Marc Galanter and Thomas M. Palay, *Tournament of Lawyers: The Transformation of the Large Law Firm* (University of Chicago Press, 1991); Marc Galanter and Thomas M. Palay, "Why the Big Get Bigger: The Promotion-to-Partner Tournament and the Growth of Large Law Firms," *Virginia Law Review*, vol. 76 (1990), pp. 747, 755.
2. This section is based on Galanter and Paley, *Tournament of Lawyers.*
3. Galanter and Palay, "Why the Big Get Bigger."
4. Robert T. Swaine, *The Cravath Firm and its Predecessors, 1819–1947,* vol. 1 (New York: Ad Press, 1946), p. 371.
5. Swaine, *The Cravath Firm and its Predecessors,* pp. 2–12. Wayne K. Hobson, *The American Legal Profession and the Organizational Society 1890–1930* (New York: Garland Publishing, 1986), pp. 195–203.
6. The term "Cravath system" was originated by Cravath's partner, Robert T. Swaine, whose history of the firm, published in 1946, is the classic of the genre.
7. Hobson, *The American Legal Profession and the Organizational Society 1890–1930,* p. 186.
8. Ibid.
9. Thomas Pinansky, "The Emergence of Law Firms in the American Legal Profession," *University of Arkansas at Little Rock Law Review,* vol. 9 (1986–87), p. 593.
10. Ibid., p. 610. On the Jay Gould litigation, see Walter K. Earle, *Mr. Shearman and Mr. Sterling and How They Grew* (Yale University Press, 1963), pp. 30–31, 69–87.
11. Letter written by William H. Dunbar to Louis D. Brandeis, Aug. 17, 1896, reprinted in Alpheus Mason, *Brandeis: A Free Man's Life* (New York: Viking Press, 1946), p. 83.
12. Hobson, *The American Legal Profession,* p. 161.

13. Erwin O. Smigel, *The Wall Street Lawyer: Professional Organization Man?* (Indiana University Press, 1969), p. 43. The roster of New York firms based upon a count conducted by Spencer Klaw in December 1957 can be found in Smigel, *The Wall Street Lawyer*, pp. 34–35.
14. Spencer Klaw, "The Wall Street Lawyers," *Fortune*, vol. 57, no. 2 (February 1958), p. 194; Smigel, *The Wall Street Lawyer*, pp. 34–35.
15. The two data sets and the shortcomings of the sources used are described in Appendixes A and B of Galanter and Palay, *Tournament of Lawyers*, pp. 143–44.
16. All calculations are based on the firms for which data were available in both years in question.
17. Our figures on growth are a little higher than those reported by Smigel. He reports that from 1957 to 1962, the number of partners in twenty large New York City firms increased by 16 percent, and that the total number of lawyers in the seventeen large firms outside New York had grown by 37 percent from 1951 to 1961. Smigel, *The Wall Street Lawyer*, p. 351. Since we were looking at firms that succeeded in becoming very large two decades later, it is not unlikely that our sample is biased toward greater growth.
18. Smigel, *The Wall Street Lawyer*, p. 207.
19. Beryl Harold Levy, *Corporation Lawyer: Saint or Sinner* (Philadelphia: Chilton Co., 1961), p. 20. The arrangement in question was the association of Adlai Stevenson and his three partners with Paul Weiss, which then had twenty-one lawyers. Richard J. H. Johnston, "Stevenson Joins a Law Firm Here," *New York Times*, April 20, 1957, p. 1, col. 3. The bar association approval (by a divided vote) is reported in "Bar Groups Back Bid by Stevenson," *New York Times*, May 7, 1957, p. 38. The arrangement lasted until 1961. John Brooks, "Advocate," *New Yorker*, vol. 59, no. 14 (May 23, 1983), pp. 46, 74.
20. The forty-two firms that responded to Roger Siddall's inquiry had been in existence an average of fifty-eight years. He asked them to detail the "number of splits in the line of succession": this was answered by forty of the offices, of which twenty-nine respondents had none; the other eleven had undergone a total of thirty splits. Roger B. Siddall, *A Survey of Large Law Firms in the United States* (New York: Vantage Press, 1956), p. 33.
21. Smigel, *The Wall Street Lawyer*, p. 58.
22. Smigel, *The Wall Street Lawyer*, p. 58; Martin Mayer, *The Lawyers* (New York: Harper and Row, 1966), p. 332.
23. Some women and Jews were hired during World War II, when the supply of so-called "desirable" candidates had evaporated. Nevertheless, a *Yale Law Journal* survey found that Jewish students from the Yale classes of 1951–62, especially those below the top one-third of their class, were less successful in obtaining work in the larger, higher-paying firms. During the 1950s and early 1960s, Jews graduating from Yale went to firms roughly one-half the size of their gentile classmates and earned the equivalent of classmates ranking an average of one-third of a class lower in law school ranking. "The Jewish Law Student and New York Jobs—Discriminatory Effects in Law Firm Hiring Practices," *Yale Law Journal*, vol. 73, no. 4 (March 1964), p. 625. This study was based on interviews with Yale students and hiring partners and on a survey of Yale graduates of 1951–62 who worked in New York. The exclusion of Jews and others from the big firms (and from the bar) is chronicled by Jerold S. Auerbach, *Unequal Justice: Lawyers and Social Change in Modern America* (New York: Oxford University Press, 1976), chapter 4 and passim.
24. Cynthia Fuchs Epstein, *Women in Law* (New York: Basic Books, 1981), p. 176. Epstein reports that "of the thirty-four women partners on Wall Street in 1979, only three achieved partnership before 1970" (p. 180).

25. Smigel, *The Wall Street Lawyer,* p. 116.
26. Martin Mayer, "The Wall Street Lawyers, Part II: Keepers of the Business Conscience," *Harper's Magazine,* vol. 212, no. 1269 (February 1956), p. 52.
27. Klaw, "The Wall Street Lawyers," p. 142.
28. In a one-hundred-lawyer firm with twenty-six partners studied in 1956, partners had taken an average of 9.1 years to partnership. Smigel, *The Wall Street Lawyer,* p. 137. In Simpson Thacher, those who became partners between 1945 and the late 1950s had spent an average of 10.6 years with the firm. Smigel, *The Wall Street Lawyer,* p. 79. In a firm that Smigel identifies as a "social" firm, the average time to partnership was 11.7 years. Smigel, *The Wall Street Lawyer,* p. 92. A respondent at Sullivan and Cromwell reported that "it now takes longer than ten years to become a partner." Smigel, *The Wall Street Lawyer,* p. 84; compare Mayer's report that most partners felt that "ten is about right." See Mayer, "The Wall Street Lawyers, Part II," p. 53.
29. Robert L. Nelson, *Partners with Power: The Social Transformation of the Large Law Firm* (University of California Press, 1988), p. 141.
30. At a 1965 Practising Law Institute forum on Managing Law Offices, a Davis Polk partner observed: "In our firm . . . [time to partnership] used to be a little more than ten years, except in the rarest cases. More recently, it has been five, six, or seven years, though in some cases it may still take ten years or more. The time varies with the individual, his department and the need of the firm for another partner from a particular department." Practising Law Institute, "Managing Law Offices," edited transcript prepared for a forum held at the Statler Hilton Hotel, New York City, May 20–21, 1965, p. 156.
31. Smigel, *The Wall Street Lawyer,* p. 64. In our circa 1960 period, corporate legal work in many cases paid better than law firms. Siddall, *A Survey of Large Law Firms,* p. 107.
32. Smigel, *The Wall Street Lawyer,* p. 97.
33. Mayer, *The Lawyers,* p. 334.
34. Nancy Lisagor and Frank Lipsius, *A Law Unto Itself: The Untold Story of the Law Firm Sullivan and Cromwell* (New York: W. W. Morrow, 1988), p. 190.
35. Smigel, *The Wall Street Lawyer,* pp. 259, 302.
36. Mark Stevens, *Power of Attorney: The Rise of the Giant Law Firms* (New York: McGraw-Hill, 1987), p. 8.
37. Compare Ronald J. Gilson and Robert H. Mnookin, "Sharing Among the Human Capitalists: An Economic Inquiry into the Corporate Law Firm and How Partners Split Profits," *Stanford Law Review,* vol. 37, no. 2 (February 1985), pp. 313, 340. They refer to "traditional methods" of apportionment. The persistent reports about the secrecy of these matters suggest that there was more to keep secret than an equal shares formula.
38. Siddall reports a great variety of compensation schemes among his forty-two firms. Siddall, *A Survey of Large Firms in the United States,* pp. 48–49. The data here do not tell us how much of the variation may be accounted for by seniority. But they cast some doubt on the notion that many or most law firms were equal shares partnerships. At least some of these firms attempted to apportion rewards according to the contribution of each partner to income.
39. Levy, *Corporation Lawyer,* p. 35.
40. Martin Mayer, "The Wall Street Lawyers, Part I: The Elite Corps of American Business," *Harper's Magazine,* vol. 212, no. 1268 (January 1956), p. 36.
41. Mayer, *The Lawyers,* p. 320.
42. Klaw, "The Wall Street Lawyers," p. 144.
43. Stewart Macaulay, "Non-Contractual Relations in Business: A Preliminary Study," *American Sociological Review,* vol. 28, no. 1 (February 1963), pp. 55–67.

44. Paul Hoffman, *Lions in the Street: The Inside Story of the Great Wall Street Firms* (New York: Saturday Review Press, 1973), p. 72.
45. Mayer noted that "lawyers want to sit on boards because . . . it sews up the client's legal business." Mayer, "The Wall Street Lawyers, Part II," p. 56.
46. Michael Gartner, in "Guest Opinion: Are Outside Directors Taking Outside Chances?" *Juris Doctor*, vol. 3, no. 3 (March 1973), pp. 4–5, 37, reported that liability and conflict-of-interest concerns were leading law firms to reappraise the desirability of directorships.
47. See "Monthly Survey of Business Opinion and Experience: Organization for Legal Work," *The Conference Board Business Record*, vol. 16, no. 10 (October 1959), pp. 463–64.
48. Smigel, *The Wall Street Lawyer*, p. 220.
49. Smigel, *The Wall Street Lawyer*, pp. 43, 104; compare Klaw, "The Wall Street Lawyers," p. 194.
50. Smigel, *The Wall Street Lawyer*, pp. 182–83, 186, 190.
51. Smigel, *The Wall Street Lawyer*, pp. 183–84. In late 1957 the twenty largest Wall Street firms (ranging in size from 46 to 125 associates and partners) had 2.28 associates for each partner. Calculated from data in Klaw, "The Wall Street Lawyers," p. 194.
52. Smigel, *The Wall Street Lawyer*, pp. 181, 183.
53. Ibid., p. 203.
54. On the "declension thesis," see Robert N. Gordon, "The Independence of Lawyers," *Boston University Law Review*, vol. 68, no. 1 (January 1988), p. 48.
55. Smigel, *The Wall Street Lawyer*, pp. 303–05.
56. Mayer, "The Wall Street Lawyers, Part II," p. 56.
57. In 1948 more than six of out of ten lawyers practiced alone; in 1980 only one-third of a much-swollen number of lawyers was in sole practice. Richard Abel, *American Lawyers* (New York: Oxford University Press, 1989), p. 179; Barbara A. Curran, *The Lawyer Statistical Report: A Statistical Profile of the U.S. Legal Profession in the 1980s* (Chicago: American Bar Foundation, 1985), pp. 8 (table 1.2.3), 10 (table 1.3.1), 14.
58. In 1980 there were almost 50,000 lawyers in firms of twenty-one or more—they made up 9.2 percent of all lawyers, 13.4 percent of lawyers in private practice, and 26.1 percent of all lawyers practicing in firms. Curran, *The Lawyer Statistical Report*, pp. 13–14.
59. Steven Brill, "The Law Business in the Year 2000," pull-out supplement to *American Lawyer*, vol. 11, no. 5 (June 1989), p. 10.
60. Smigel, *The Wall Street Lawyer*, pp. 43, 178.
61. Barbara A. Curran, *Supplement to the Lawyer Statistical Report: The U.S. Legal Profession in 1985* (Chicago: American Bar Foundation, 1986), p. 5.
62. The range was from 50 to 198 lawyers in 1975 and from 142 to 419 lawyers in 1985. These figures are somewhat lower than those in the last paragraph because they are drawn from our data set, based on *Martindale-Hubbell* rather than *National Law Journal* surveys. Our data is used here because, unlike that from the *National Law Journal*, it permits comparisons with earlier periods. See Galanter and Palay, *Tournament of Lawyers*, pp. 140–42 and cites therein.
63. The range was from 21 to 68 in 1975 and from 54 to 121 in 1985; "The NLJ 250," *National Law Journal*, supplement, September 26, 1988, pp. S1-S28.
64. These ranges are confirmed by annual surveys of the five hundred largest firms conducted by *Of Counsel* since 1986. The reported rate of growth for all of these firms was over 9 percent for each of the three years. "Of Counsel 500," *Of Counsel*, vol. 8, no. 8 (April 17, 1989), p. 1.
65. For the calculations for 1955 to 1965, see notes 16 and 17.
66. The occasional Washington or foreign branch office was anomalous. Smigel, *The Wall*

Street Lawyer, p. 207. Attempts at multicity firms were rare, suspect, and unstable, as displayed in the Adlai Stevenson/Paul Weiss arrangement (see note 19).

67. Curran, *The Lawyer Statistical Report,* p. 53.

68. Abel, *American Lawyers,* p. 188.

69. Tamar Lewin, "The New National Law Firms: Mergers Play Bigger Role," *New York Times,* October 4, 1984, p. 31. The true pioneer is Baker & McKenzie, which in the 1950s established four foreign offices, staffed largely by local lawyers, and a Washington office. Thirteen more foreign offices were added in the 1960s, and in 1988 the firm consisted of forty-one offices in twenty-five countries. "The NLJ 250," p. S-4; James Lyons, "Baker & McKenzie: The Belittled Giant," *American Lawyer,* vol. 7, no. 8 (October 1985), pp. 115–16. On their organizational strategy, see also Stevens, *Power of Attorney,* pp. 153–66. Another pioneer in the design of the multicity firm was the late Robert Kutak, whose Omaha-based Kutak, Rock and Huie, founded in 1965, was established in six regional centers by 1980. Joseph R. Tybor, "End of the Go-Go Years at Big Firms? Bad Day at Kutak Rock," *National Law Journal,* vol. 4, no. 8 (November 2, 1981), p. 1. In the late 1970s the firm planned to open an office in one new city each year, and by the end of the 1980s to have seventeen offices around the country. Walter Kiechel III, "Growing Up at Kutak, Rock and Huie," *Fortune,* vol. 98, no. 8 (October 23, 1978), pp. 112–13. The firm was unable to keep up this pace and experienced a severe contraction in late 1980.

70. This comparison is based on our *National Law Journal* "Two Twenties" data set. For convenience, we refer to "branches," but we use that term to mean an office other than the office of the firm that contains the largest number of lawyers. In 1987 only one of our forty firms (Akin, Gump) had an office larger than its home office. See Galanter and Palay, *Tournament of Lawyers,* pp. 144–45.

71. The number of overseas offices ranges from one to thirty-two; eight firms had five or more overseas offices.

72. This reflects the dispersion of corporate headquarters and financial markets. In 1960, 128 of the Fortune 500 industrial corporations had headquarters in New York City; in 1988, only 50 were headquartered there. There were comparable shifts in other categories of corporations. "The Fortune Directory: The 500 Largest U.S. Industrial Corporations," *Fortune,* vol. 62, no. 7 (July 1960), pp. 131–50; "The Fortune Directory Part II," *Fortune,* vol. 62, no. 8 (August 1960), pp. 135–44; "The Fortune 500; Largest U.S. Industrial Corporations," *Fortune,* vol. 117, no. 9 (April 25, 1988), p. D-11; "The 500 Largest Service Corporations," *Fortune,* vol. 117, no. 12 (June 6, 1988), p. D-7.

73. Smigel, *The Wall Street Lawyer,* p. 43.

74. Curran, *The Lawyer Statistical Report,* pp. 51, 166.

75. Abel, *American Lawyers,* table 47. A 1989 survey found that thirty-three of the one hundred firms with the largest gross revenues were based in New York. Steven Brill, "The Am Law 100: A Boom in Premium Deal Work," pull-out supplement to *American Lawyer,* vol. 11, no. 6 (July–August 1989), pp. 6–58.

76. The decline in the predominance of New York-based firms points to, but overstates, the decline of New York City as a locus of legal activity. A significant portion of the branching activity discussed in the preceding paragraphs consists of the establishment of New York branches by ONY firms. In 1980 only three of our ONY firms had offices in New York (average size seventeen). By 1987 ten of the twenty ONY firms had New York offices (average size thirty-nine).

77. For a preliminary report on this see Marc Galanter and others, *Corporations in Court: Recent Trends in American Business Litigation,* unpublished report prepared for the 1990 annual meeting of the Law & Society Association, Berkeley/Oakland, May 31–June 3, 1990. There is some indication that there are more large corporations that have corporate law departments. A 1959 survey of manufacturers found that 134 of the 286

companies surveyed had legal departments. A 1985 survey found that 74 of the 126 manufacturing companies replying had in-house counsel. This is an increase from 47 to 59 percent. However, the degree to which the numbers are comparable is unclear. See "Monthly Survey of Business Opinion and Experience," pp. 463–68; Arthur Andersen & Co., "The Corporate Market for Legal Services: A Marketing Study" (Arthur Andersen & Co., 1985), p. 4, exhibit 3.

78. Frances Flaharty, "Comparison Shopping Hits the Law: Companies Cut Costs," *National Law Journal*, October 31, 1983, pp. 1, 9; Rita Henley Jensen, "Banking Clients More Willing to Shop for Firms," *National Law Journal*, January 18, 1988, p. 1; Emily Couric, "New Relationships, New Rules," *National Law Journal* supplement, August 1, 1988, pp. S2–S27.

79. Nelson, *Partners with Power*, p. 171.

80. Abram Chayes and Antonia Chayes, "Corporate Counsel and the Elite Law Firm," *Stanford Law Review*, vol. 37, no. 1 (January 1985), pp. 277, 295, report that major corporations responding to a small survey reported one-half of all legal fees paid to outside lawyers were for litigation. Compare Nelson, *Partners with Power*, p. 8.

81. It should be recalled that similar observations have been echoed periodically since the early days of big law firms.

82. Bruce D. Heintz, "New Trends in Partner Profit Distribution," *Wisconsin Bar Bulletin*, vol. 55 (October 1982), pp. 24–26; Gilson and Mnookin, "Sharing Among the Human Capitalists," p. 313; but compare Nelson, *Partners with Power*, pp. 202–04.

83. Reflecting on Smigel's contention that law firms lack the hierarchy, rules, and levels of conflict characteristic of other organizations because they are organized around professional norms, Nelson concedes that if this was so in "the stable professional community of New York law firms in the late 1950s . . . [i]t is clearly not accurate today. Large firms are the regimes of client-producers, and this stratum of partners dictates the policies of the firm and projects the ideology of professionalism that justifies the structure of the firm and the client-producers' role in it." Nelson, *Partners with Power*, p. 276.

84. A survey by Altman and Weil of median earnings of partners in 700 large (75 + lawyers) firms found 1986 earnings increased by 78 percent over ten years earlier, but inflation was up 93 percent. Average hours billed were up 8 percent to 1,685 hours annually. Rita Henley Jensen, "Partners Work Harder to Stay Even," *National Law Journal*, August 10, 1987, p. 12. A Price Waterhouse survey of medium and large firms found that from 1978 to 1988 partner earnings rose only 1 percent after accounting for inflation. Brill, "The Law Business in the Year 2000," p. 6.

85. Mary Ann Galante, "Firms Finding More Value in Marketing," *National Law Journal*, November 18, 1985, pp. 1, 28. The next year it was reported that "more than 60 law firms, ranging in size from 14 lawyers to nearly 600 . . . [in] about 25 cities . . . had hired a marketing administrator." A National Association of Law Firm Marketing Administrators was established in the same year. Sally J. Schmidt, "Firm Development Mobilized By a 'New Breed' of Resource," *National Law Journal*, August 25, 1986, p. 15.

86. Merrilyn Astin Tarlton, former president of the National Association of Law Firm Marketing Administrators, quoted in "New Partner in the Firm: The Marketing Director," *New York Times*, June 2, 1989, p. B-19.

87. Phyllis Weiss Haserot, "How to Get Associates into the Act," *National Law Journal*, August 25, 1986, p. 15; Rita Henley Jensen, "The Rainmakers," *National Law Journal*, October 5, 1987, pp. 1, 28, 30.

88. Lee Ann Bellon, "Southeast Boasts an Expanding Legal Community," *National Law Journal*, January 18, 1988, pp. 19–20.

89. Diane Netter Weklar, "System is Key: Strategies for Legal Marketing," *National Law*

Journal, August 1, 1988, pp. 22, 26; Suzanne O'Neill, "Firm Marketing Responsibilities: Associates Can Attract Clients, Too," *National Law Journal*, January 16, 1989, p. 17.

90. Legal headhunter firms emerged in New York in the late 1960s in response to the constriction in the supply of lawyers. At first such activity was regarded as a discreditable departure from professional decorum. "In 1967, when Lois R. Weiner . . . decided to specialize in finding jobs for lawyers, the publishers of Martindale-Hubbell refused to sell her a copy." Tom Stevenson, "The Talent Peddlers," *Juris Doctor*, vol. 3, no. 2 (February 1975), pp. 12–13.

91. Abel, *American Lawyers*, p. 188; "Legal Search Profession Annual Survey," *National Law Journal*, June 12, 1989, p. S-3.

92. Galanter and Palay, *Tournament of Lawyers*, p. 54, n 115.

93. *Of Counsel* survey, reported in Larry Smith, "National Study: Lateral Hiring Continues Unabated," *Lawyer Hiring and Training Report*, vol. 9, no. 13 (June 1989), p. 6. Approximately four hundred firms provided information on lateral hiring. The figures in this survey were close to those in a 1986 survey.

94. Edward Adams, "Longer Partnership Odds at N.Y. Firms," *New York Law Journal*, July 17, 1989, pp. 1, 6.

95. According to Hildebrandt and Co., about one hundred law firms dissolved in 1987, including about a dozen with more than thirty lawyers. Jill Abramson, Stephen J. Adler, and Laurie P. Cohen, "The Strange Case of the Vanishing Firms," *Wall Street Journal*, July 29, 1988, p. 17; Abel, *American Lawyers*, pp. 186–87. Although there have been some spectacular breakups of large firms, such as the notable dissolution of Finley Kumble in 1987, the pressure to merge or dissolve was thought to be most severe for midsized firms. In 1988 a Hildebrant consultant reported that "in the past two years, more than 60 midsize firms—more than 10% of the total nationwide— have either dissolved or merged. . . . Though midsize firms make up 10% of all law firms they accounted for 25% of the field's mergers and closing in the past two years." Amy Dockser, "Midsize Law Firms Struggle to Survive," *Wall Street Journal*, October 19, 1988, p. B-1.

96. This has transformed the law school scene by linking law students early and tightly to the world of law practice, a development that has been described to one of the authors of this chapter by Roger Cramton, former dean of Cornell Law School, as "the new apprenticeship."

97. "From 1964 through 1968 . . . the number of Harvard Law School Graduates entering private law practice declined from 54 to 41 percent." Yale graduates entering private practice dropped from 41 percent in 1968 to 31 percent in 1969; the percentage of Virginia graduates entering private practice dropped from 63 percent to 54 percent from 1968 to 1969. Jerry J. Berman and Edgar S. Cahn, "Bargaining for Justice: The Law Students' Challenge to Law Firms," *Harvard Civil Rights-Civil Liberties Law Review*, vol. 5, no. 1 (January 1970), pp. 16, 22–23. "In 1970, none of the thirty-nine law review editors graduating from Harvard expects to enter private practice." Mark Green, "Law Graduates: The New Breed," *The Nation*, vol. 210, no. 6 (June 1, 1970), pp. 658–60. A similar drop among Michigan graduates is documented by David Chambers, who found that those entering private practice dropped from 74 percent in the classes of 1965 and 1966 to about 60 percent for the years from 1967 to 1970. Chambers shows that most of the decrease was due to diversion into teaching and graduate work to secure draft deferments. David Chambers, a presentation to the annual meeting of the Law and Society Association, Madison, Wisconsin, June 8–11, 1989.

98. Berman and Cahn, "Bargaining for Justice," pp. 16–22.

99. Smigel, *The Wall Street Lawyer*, p. 43.

100. Tamar Lewin, "At Cravath, $65,000 to Start," *New York Times*, April 18, 1986, p. B-33.

101. But even absent deliberate exclusion, selection on the basis of educational credentials and the candidates' social affiliations, personal preferences, and career expectations will maintain some degree of association between legal roles and the social origins of lawyers. Compare John P. Heinz and Edward O. Laumann, *Chicago Lawyers: The Social Structure of the Bar* (New York: Russell Sage Foundation; Chicago: American Bar Foundation, 1982), p. 332; Abel, *American Lawyers*, pp. 109–10 argues that the inclusion of women and the erection of higher educational hurdles have worked to "narrow the class background of lawyers, whose origins have grown even more privileged." See also Abel, *American Lawyers*, p. 228.

102. Rita Henley Jensen, "Minorities Didn't Share in Firm Growth," *National Law Journal*, February 19, 1990, pp. 1, 28–31, 35.

103. Doreen Weisenhaus, "Still a Long Way to Go For Women, Minorities," *National Law Journal*, February 8, 1988, pp. 1, 48.

104. Judy Klemesrud, "Women in the Law: Many Are Getting Out," *New York Times*, August 9, 1985, p. B-14; Patricia A. Mairs, "Bringing Up Baby," *National Law Journal*, March 14, 1988, p. 1; Jennifer A. Kingson, "Women in the Law Say Path is Limited by 'Mommy Track,'" *New York Times*, August 8, 1988, p. B-1. Compare Deborah Holmes, "Structural Causes of Dissatisfaction Among Large-Firm Attorneys: A Feminist Perspective," Working Paper 3:3 (Madison: Institute for Legal Studies, University of Wisconsin Law School, 1988).

105. Barbara Kate Repa, "Is There Life After Partnership?" *American Bar Association Journal*, vol. 74, no. 6 (June 1, 1988), pp. 70–75; Marilyn Tucker, Laurie A. Albright, and Patricia L. Busk, "Whatever Happened to the Class of 1983?" *Georgetown Law Journal*, vol. 78, no. 153 (1989), pp. 153–95; Ronald L. Hirsch "Are You on Target?" *Barrister Magazine*, vol. 12, no. 1 (Winter 1985), pp. 17–20, 49–50; Robert Nelson, "Analysis of Hirsch Data by Robert L. Nelson," in Geoffrey C. Hazard, Jr. and Susan P. Koniak, eds., *The Law and Ethics of Lawyering* (Westbury, NY: Foundation Press, 1990), p. 1033. The contours of dissatisfaction remain to be mapped. A study of Michigan graduates of 1976–79 five years after graduation revealed that both men and women found the balance of family and work obligations the least satisfactory aspect of their professional lives. But, surprisingly, full-time women lawyers with children reported higher overall career satisfaction and higher satisfaction with the balance of their family and professional lives than did their male counterparts. David L. Chambers, "Accommodation and Satisfaction: Women and Men Lawyers and the Balance of Work and Family," *Law and Social Inquiry*, vol. 14, no. 1 (Winter 1989), pp. 251, 273, 275.

106. Weisenhaus, "Still a Long Way to Go for Women, Minorities," p. 50. The percentage of black associates had fallen slightly since 1981, while the percentages of other minorities rose.

107. See Galanter and Palay, *Tournament of Lawyers*, table 3, pp. 60–61.

108. These calculations are reported in Galanter and Palay, *Tournament of Lawyers*, pp. 59–61. For reasons noted there we regard these as an accurate representation of trends rather than a depiction of the absolute levels of leverage in any given firm at any specific point in time.

109. At least part of the difference between New York firms and firms elsewhere probably lies in the different meaning attributed to the term "partner" by the NY and ONY firms. If firms designate as partners those lawyers who have been given that title (and a promise of permanent tenure) but not a share of the firm profits, then they would display lower associate to partner ratios than if the partner designation were reserved to lawyers who had a share of the profits. There is reason to think that in at least some cities outside New York the designation partner is used more expansively. Daniel Wise, "Psst! Wanna Make Partner?" *National Law Journal*, October 26, 1987, pp. 1, 32–33. Since this practice simultaneously reduces the number of associates and increases

the number of partners used in calculating these ratios, our comparisons overstate the difference in leverage.

110. In Galanter and Palay, *Tournament of Lawyers,* pp. 61–62, we examine several other data sets and conclude that the trends are basically consistent, though the absolute numbers differ.

111. Nelson, *Partners with Power,* p. 141.

112. Eve Spangler, *Lawyers for Hire: Salaried Professionals at Work* (Yale University Press, 1986), p. 55.

113. Wise, "Psst! Wanna Make Partner?" A survey of 150 medium-sized firms found that the median time to achieve partnership had lengthened between 1975 to 1985 from five years to six years. Telephone interview with D. Weston Darby, Jr., of Cantor and Co., August 4, 1989. The survey was reported in D. Weston Darby, Jr., "Are You Keeping Up Financially?" *American Bar Association Journal,* vol. 71, no. 12 (December 1985), pp. 66, 68.

114. Nelson, *Partners with Power,* p. 140.

115. Wise, "Psst! Wanna Make Partner?" p. 32; Nelson, *Partners with Power,* pp. 138–39.

116. Bellon, "Southeast Boasts an Expanding Legal Community," pp. 19–20.

117. Adams, "Longer Partnership Odds at N.Y. Firms." These figures should not be overinterpreted. Not only is the time interval for the more recent group one year shorter than for the older group, but the findings are equally consistent with lengthening of time to partnership.

118. As reported by Mayer, "The Wall Street Lawyers, Part II," p. 52, and Klaw, "The Wall Street Lawyers," p. 142. Compare Smigel's analysis of Cravath in *The Wall Street Lawyer,* p. 116. Contemporary associates have their own golden age myth of a time when young lawyers were trained as generalists rather than being pushed early into a specialty, received intensive mentoring, and "could expect to make partner after a certain number of years" if they "performed well and committed no egregious blunders." Holmes, "Structural Causes of Dissatisfaction Among Large-Firm Attorneys," p. 20.

119. Hoffman, *Lions in the Street,* p. 44.

120. Larry Bodine, "Law Firm Ladder Gets a New Rung," *National Law Journal,* March 12, 1979, pp. 1, 17.

121. Deborah Graham, "New 'Senior Attorney' Program Draws Attention at Davis Polk," *Legal Times,* February 28, 1983, pp. 3, 7; Kirk Hallam, "Big Firms Search for Alternatives to Traditional Form," *Los Angeles Daily Journal,* March 18, 1983, p. 1; Mary Ann Galante, "Firms Look Closer At How to Create Lawyer Categories," *Los Angeles Daily Journal,* August 22, 1983, p. 1; Mary Ann Galante, "Meet the Permanent Associate," *National Law Journal,* October 24, 1983, pp. 1, 28; Amy Singer, "Senior Attorney Programs: Half A Loaf," *American Lawyer,* vol. 9, no. 1 (January/February 1987), p. 12; Martha Freeman, "Alternatives to the Old Up or Out," *California Lawyer,* vol. 7, no. 12 (December 1987), pp. 44–45, 104–5; Bill Blum and Gina Lobaco, "When Associates Don't Make Partner," *California Lawyer,* vol. 8, no. 1 (January/February 1988), pp. 51–54. As noted above, the up-or-out norm had rarely been applied with absolute rigor. A Davis Polk partner observed that the new senior attorney program "just regularizes what's been the fact for some time in the past." Graham, "New 'Senior Attorney' Program Draws Attention at Davis Polk," p. 3.

122. Peter Griggs and Daviryne McNeill, "Upper Ranks Add Heft at Most Big D.C. Firms," *Legal Times,* December 28, 1987/January 4, 1988, p. 4.

123. Steven Susman, "Eighties Shakeout," transcript from presentation at American Lawyer symposium, June 1–2, 1987, in New York City.

124. Michael Orey, "Staff Attorneys: Basic Work at Bargain Prices," *American Lawyer,* vol. 9, no. 7 (September 1987), p. 20.

125. Steve Nelson, "Law Firms Adopt Staff Attorney Option at 'Revolutionary' Pace," *Of Counsel*, vol. 7, no. 8 (April 18, 1989), p. 14.

126. Stephen Labaton, "Lawyers Debate Temporary Work," *New York Times*, April 18, 1988, p. 26; Barbara Berkman, "Temporarily Yours: Associates for Hire," *American Lawyer*, vol. 10, no. 2 (March 1988), pp. 24, 26–27; Laura Mansnerus, "Law Firms, Too, Hire Lawyers by the Hour," *New York Times*, March 4, 1988, p. B-10. The New York City Bar Association's reproach of these agencies' percentage fees as offending the ban on fee-splitting chilled the business there, engendered heated protest, and was withdrawn. Laura Mansnerus, "Rule on Temporary Lawyers Changes Again," *New York Times*, June 2, 1989, p. 19.

127. Phyllis Haserot, "How To Get Associates Into the Act," *National Law Journal*, August 25, 1986, pp. 15, 21.

128. Alexander Stille, "When Law Firms Start Their Own Businesses," *National Law Journal*, October 21, 1985, pp. 1, 20–22.

129. Ibid., p. 20. The shift in perspective is succinctly put by one general counsel reflecting on the change in the nature of professionalism: "Most lawyers think of themselves first and foremost as lawyers, when in reality, they are a very small part of a much larger profession or industry. That industry is the industry of information management." Carl D. Liggio, "Conference Proceedings," Federal Bar Council, 1984 Bench and Bar Conference, Dorado, Puerto Rico, January 29–Feb. 5, 1984 (New York: Goldner Press, Inc., 1984), pp. 105–14.

130. Margaret Fisk, "What Does the Future Have in Store?" *National Law Journal*, September 26, 1988, pp. 49–50.

131. Bruce D. Heintz, "Elements of Law Firm Competition," *National Law Journal*, December 26, 1983, pp. 15, 17–19, 42.

132. "Mass Firing in Seattle," *National Law Journal*, July 24, 1989, p. 2. Compare the report that in the early 1980s "[d]issatisfied with the performance of some of its partners, Willkie Farr & Gallagher of New York has asked about a half dozen to leave...." Peter W. Bernstein, "Profit Pressures on the Big Law Firms," *Fortune*, vol. 105, no. 8 (April 19, 1982), pp. 84–87, 90, 94, 98, 100.

133. Bernstein, "Profit Pressures on the Big Law Firms," p. 100.

134. See, for example, American Bar Association Commission on Professionalism, *In the Spirit of Public Service: A Blueprint for the Rekindling of Lawyer Professionalism* (Chicago: Commission on Professionalism, American Bar Association, 1986).

135. Smigel reports that in the early 1960s most lawyers in firms of one hundred or more lawyers "feel they have reached or passed their optimum size." Smigel, *The Wall Street Lawyer*, p. 350.

136. Apparently the big firm enjoyed some comparative advantage over internal law departments within corporations. See Pinansky, "The Emergence of Law Firms in the American Legal Profession," p. 610.

137. "The Commercializing of the Profession," *The American Lawyer* (March 1895), pp. 84–85. (This is not the intense monthly that has since 1979 chronicled—and cheered on—rapid change in the world of large law firms, but a long-extinct legal newspaper of the same name, published in New York from 1893 to 1908.) "Bar" is used here not in the English sense, but in the American sense of the entire body of legal professionals.

138. John R. Dos Passos, *The American Lawyer: As He Was—As He Is—As He Can Be* (New York: The Banks Law Publishing Co., 1907), p. 46.

139. Dos Passos, *The American Lawyer*, pp. 130–31.

140. Hobson, *The American Legal Professional and the Organizational Society 1890–1930*, pp. 88–103.

141. This term is used by Karl Llewellyn in a 1931 book review, *Columbia Law Review*, vol. 31, no. 7 (November 1931), p. 1218. In a 1932 *New Yorker* profile of Paul Cravath,

the author notes that "the blasphemous youngsters just out of law school refer to [the Cravath firm] . . . as 'the factory,' and it does have, indeed, the efficiency and production of a first-rate industrial plant." Milton Mackaye, "Profiles: Public Man," *New Yorker*, vol. 7, no. 46 (January 2, 1932), p. 23.

142. Karl Llewellyn, "The Bar Specializes—With What Results?" *Annals of the American Academy*, 167 (1933), p. 177.

143. A. A. Berle, "Modern Legal Profession," *Encyclopedia of the Social Sciences*, vol. 9 (1933), pp. 343–44.

144. Harlan Fiske Stone, "The Public Influence of the Bar," *Harvard Law Review*, vol. 48, no. 1 (November 1934), p. 6.

145. Stone, "The Public Influence of the Bar," pp. 6–7.

146. On the golden age, see Galanter and Palay, *Tournament of Lawyers*, pp. 20–36.

147. Smigel, *The Wall Street Lawyer*, pp. 303–05.

148. The latest entry is Sol M. Linowitz with Martin Mayer, *The Betrayed Profession: Lawyering at the End of the Twentieth Century* (New York: Charles Scribner's Sons, 1994). The most scholarly is A. T. Kronman, *The Lost Lawyer: Failing Ideals of the Legal Profession* (Harvard University Press, 1993). The most dyspeptic is Peter Megargee Brown, *Rascals: The Selling of the Legal Profession* (New York: Benchmark Press, 1989). The literature is vast. See, for example, Arlin M. Adams, "The Legal Profession: A Critical Evaluation," *Dickinson Law Review*, vol. 93, no. 4 (Summer 1989), p. 652. ("The most pervasive manifestation of the change in the legal climate is the decline of professionalism and its replacement with commercialism"); Norman Bowie, "The Law: From a Profession to a Business," *Vanderbilt Law Review*, vol. 41 (1988), pp. 741–59; Lincoln Caplan, "The Lawyers' Race to the Bottom," *New York Times*, August 6, 1993, p. A-29. The bar's "official" account of the danger of commercialization is the American Bar Association Commission on Professionalism, *In the Spirit of Public Service* (1986), commonly known as the Stanley Report, for Chair Justin Stanley.

149. Kronman, *The Last Lawyer*, at 378–9.

150. Marc Galanter, "Why the 'Haves' Come Out Ahead: Speculations on the Limits of Legal Change," *Law and Society Review*, vol. 9 (1974), p. 95.

151. On this "public justice" critique and other misgivings about the legal profession, see Marc Galanter, "Predators and Parasites: Lawyer Bashing and Civil Justice," *Georgia Law Review*, vol. 28, no. 3 (Spring 1994), pp. 633–81.

152. *American Lawyer* defines pro bono activity as time spent by lawyers (not paralegals or support staff) performing legal services for free. They exclude time spent on nonlegal good works such as serving on a board or fundraising. "The Am Law 100: The Retrenchment Continues," *American Lawyer*, vol. 15, no. 6 (July/August 1993), p. 17. An interesting paper that also uses the *American Lawyer* Survey of Pro Bono Activity, but which came to our attention too late to be integrated into our work, is Debra Burke, Reagan McLaurie, and James W. Pearce, "Pro Bono Publico: Issues and Implications," *Loyola University Chicago Law Review*, vol. 26 (1994), pp. 61–97.

153. Implicitly, we are testing whether there is a simple linear relationship between the dependent and independent variables. R^2 is a summary statistic showing the proportion of the total variation in the dependent variable explained by the regression of the dependent variable on the independent variables. Thus it is a measure of how closely the estimated function approximates or resembles the actual function. The higher the R^2, the closer the relationship.

154. But smaller firms, unable to enjoy these economies of scale, find it more disruptive and burdensome to take on systematic pro bono commitments. If systematic and regular pro bono is to be generalized, it is necessary to offset this disparity of burdens. Elsewhere, with regard to smaller practices, we argue for extending the principle of

transferability to include interfirm as well as intrafirm transfers. Marc Galanter and Thomas Palay, "Let Firms Buy and Sell Credit for Pro Bono," *National Law Journal,* September 6, 1993, pp. 17–18. Other proposals for transfer of pro bono obligations and credits may be found in David Luban, *Lawyers and Justice: An Ethical Study* (Princeton University Press, 1988), pp. 277–89; Mary Coombs, "Your Money or Your Life: A Modest Proposal for Mandatory Pro Bono Services," *Boston University Public Interest Law Journal,* vol. 3, no. 2 (Fall 1993), pp. 215–38; Linowitz with Mayer, *The Betrayed Profession,* pp. 161–62.

3

Structuring Law Firm Pro Bono Programs:

A Community Service Typology

Esther F. Lardent

T he dramatic changes in the practice of law in large firms during the past fifteen years, together with an increased emphasis on businesslike management and the bottom line, pose a serious but not insurmountable threat to the pro bono publico and community service activities of major firms.

To counteract these financial pressures, many law firms in recent years have accelerated efforts to develop more formalized pro bono programs whose structure, policies, and practices are designed to accommodate the practical realities of large firm law practice. These activities are also, in part, a response to the heightened emphasis on pro bono publico service by the organized bar and other external influences. This chapter discusses in some detail the approaches taken by firms to support and encourage pro bono practice in the current legal climate. Such programs offer a blend of idealism and pragmatism that may be uniquely suited to today's larger law firms.

Structuring the Pro Bono Program

Until recently, many firms' pro bono efforts, even those of the most active firms, were typically, even consciously, unstructured and laissez-faire in character. Firms with a strong pro bono bent relied on the oral tradition of the firm to attract young lawyers with a commitment to pro bono and on the active, hands-on participation in pro bono by the firm's most visible leaders to inculcate these newcomers with the firm's enthusiasm for public service.

As firms grew in size—and as their management structures evolved—pro bono supporters within the firms realized that a more structured, less ad hoc approach to pro bono was needed, one that embodied the firm's institutional commitment to pro bono. This approach mirrors the general trend toward greater structure and formalism in other areas of firm administration, such as compensation and hiring, and signals the integral role of pro bono in the firm. The creation of a pro bono structure, if effectively implemented, enables the firm to recreate—or, in the case of those firms without a strong pro bono tradition, to create for the first time—the modern equivalent of the pro bono oral tradition among firms and firm leadership. That is, the structure signals the firm's visible and ongoing commitment to pro bono, serves as a source of pro bono opportunities, and, most notably, encourages and supports younger lawyers in their pro bono engagements. A variety of such structures characterize firm approaches: the community services department; pro bono committees; adopting a pro bono budget; pro bono staffing; and hiring experienced laterals.

The Community Services Department

First established in 1969 by Hogan & Hartson in Washington, D.C., the Community Services Department (CSD) is the most formal of the structures adopted by firms in an effort to institutionalize pro bono within the firm.[1] The department, with a full-time equity partner and several associates who rotate through it, is viewed as giving pro bono work stature within the firm equal to its commercial practice. The CSD provides stability and visibility for the firm's pro bono efforts. While many other partners and associates in the firm participate actively in pro bono work, the attorneys assigned to the department develop expertise in various areas of public interest law and work closely with Washington's diverse and broad-based public interest bar. That visibility and in-depth experience has enabled Hogan & Hartson to take on many highly desirable pro bono projects over the years.[2] It is notable that the partner in charge of the CSD has typically been selected from among the firm's commercial partners and, in most instances, has returned to that practice within the firm after spending three or four years as head of the department.

Despite the success and longevity of Hogan's Community Services Department, no other firm replicated that model until recently. Some firms have cited concern about cost, while others believe that this model may discourage firmwide participation in pro bono, although that has not been the case at Hogan. In recent years, however, three other firms have adopted the CSD model or a variant of it. In 1990 Holland & Knight, a Florida firm with a long pro bono tradition inculcated by Chesterfield Smith, the firm's chairman emeritus, created its Community Services Team with a substantial annual budget, a full-time partner, and a full-time associate position that rotates every eighteen months.[3] Arent Fox Kintner Plotkin & Kahn in Washington, D.C., has also established a Community Services Team, staffed by two partners who spend a substantial percentage of their time on pro bono projects, as well as several associates.[4] Finally, Morgan, Lewis & Bockius has a firmwide Public Interest Practice Group that has equal rank with the firm's other practice groups. It is charged by the firm's management to encourage the firm's lawyers to do pro bono work and to develop broader areas of pro bono practice to better utilize lawyers in all specialties within the firm.[5] In practice, the group's responsibilities appear to more closely resemble those of a firm pro bono committee, described in greater detail below.

The Pro Bono Committee

The most widely used firm pro bono structure is the pro bono committee, although these committees vary widely in their roles, effectiveness, and composition. In an era in which so many firms use committees to oversee the administrative work of the firm, the existence of a pro bono committee, while not as definitive a commitment as the creation of a department, certainly helps to establish the visibility and parity of the firm's pro bono work.

Committee composition is key. The most effective pro bono committees have a broad-based membership, often including lawyers from many of the firm's key departments or practice areas as well as representatives of branch offices to ensure a uniform firm pro bono culture. Cross-fertilization with other firm committees in related areas, such as evaluation and compensation, associates, training and professional development, and—perhaps most notably—the firm's executive or management committee, has proven quite useful. The participation of an attorney who is a noted rainmaker or part of the firm's formal or informal leadership is highly beneficial, as is the presence of firm members who are not the "usual suspects" with respect to pro bono. Most pro bono committees are composed of both partners and associates, and, in the case of firms whose legal assistants play a particularly active role in pro bono work, paralegals may also be asked to participate. The most successful committees have a highly visible and active chair, typically a well-respected equity partner.

The pro bono committee, by its very existence, ideally serves as the visible reminder of the support of the firm and its leadership for pro bono service. It may also undertake a variety of administrative roles, including approval of pro bono engagements; development of policies with respect to pro bono matters on subjects such as supervision of pro bono matters and firm payment of out-of-pocket costs; ongoing assessment of attorney participation and overall firm participation in pro bono, including review of the firm's pro bono docket and periodic and annual reports on pro bono hours; securing and publicizing pro bono opportunities; soliciting attorney participation in pro bono matters referred to the firm; maintaining contact with public interest and community groups that are potential sources of referrals; making pro bono work a visible part of the firm's evaluation, advancement, and compensation decisions; ensuring that pro bono attorneys have adequate training, support, and supervision; ascertaining individual lawyers' areas of interest and expertise; and publicizing the firm's pro bono achievements through a variety of means. Of course, not all pro bono committees take responsibility for all of these areas, but the most successful committees play a very active and aggressive role in promoting pro bono practice.

The Pro Bono Budget

A number of firms have structured their pro bono program through the adoption of a firm pro bono budget—that is, a specific annual allocation of firm resources to pro bono activities. Typically, pro bono budgets establish an overall firm goal in terms of total attorney pro bono hours to be expended (or the dollar value of these donated hours), but more recently this portion of the budget has been expressed as a percentage of total firm billable time. During the past year, a number of firms have adopted the goals established by the Law Firm Pro Bono Challenge—either 3 percent or 5 percent of total billable hours—as a budget "floor."[6] Indeed, some firms have a goal of spending 8 to 10 percent or more of their billable time on pro bono work. While attorney time is clearly the major component of the budget, other expenditures, such as firm resources (for example, support staff, messengers, long-distance telephone tolls, and copying and printing charges) as well as litigation-related expenses (for example, filing fees, expert witnesses, stenographers, travel, discovery costs) are often included as line items in the overall pro bono budget. Far less frequently the pro bono budget includes the expense of administering the firm's pro bono program (for example, non-client-related attorney and support staff time, training costs, pro bono meeting and event expenses).

The establishment of a budget for firm pro bono work is not new. Many firms have long required that an estimate of hours and disbursements be prepared for each new pro bono engagement accepted by the firm—essentially a per-case budgeting process. Firmwide pro bono budgets, however, adapt the approach used by a number of firms with respect to revenue-generating legal work. These budgets establish a target amount of pro bono work that the firm should generate annually, based on past performance and the firm's assessment of its current caseload and capacity to increase its activity level.

The budget is overseen by the management committee or, more typically, the pro bono committee of the firm. The committee tracks the firm's progress in meeting the budget and takes steps to promote increased pro bono work if the firm is below its targeted budget, just as the firm's management reviews revenues received and takes measures to enhance revenues if they fall below the targeted amount. Some firms, as part of their oversight, establish per-office, per-practice area, or per-attorney targets toward meeting the overall firm pro bono goal and assess the performance of individuals or offices/departments in the firm in meeting these goals.

A budget that reflects an appropriate allocation of firm resources can be very helpful in promoting a firmwide commitment to pro bono, ensuring broader and more balanced participation, and increasing the firm's overall pro bono contribution. However, a budgeting approach can also have a detrimental impact on the firm's pro bono program. In some situations the resources budgeted for pro bono work are inadequate, the budgeted amount is viewed as an absolute maximum, and review of pro bono hours and expenditures focuses solely on whether the firm has exceeded its budget rather than ensuring that the firm is not "under budget" with respect to its pro bono work. Such use of a budget can strongly discourage pro bono participation, particularly in more complex matters. For example, if a firm establishes a pro bono budget, as some firms have, based on the premise that 50 percent of the firm's attorneys will spend no more than twenty hours annually on pro bono time, the firm's pro bono work will amount to far less than one-half of 1 percent of the total billable time. (This assumes that the average attorney at the firm bills approximately 1,800 hours annually—a very conservative figure.) The adoption of such a low pro bono budget for a major law firm, particularly if the budgeted amount is viewed as a ceiling, clearly sends a strong negative message regarding pro bono.[7]

Pro Bono Staffing

Increasingly, as ad hoc efforts give way to more formal programs, firms are hiring pro bono program administrators either in lieu of a pro bono committee or as staff to that committee. The background, responsibilities, and job titles for these positions vary widely. Some pro bono staff are attorneys, often with a public interest background or strong interest in pro bono work, who serve as special counsel or pro bono counsel. Unlike the Community Services Department model, however, these attorneys are almost never equity partners or shareholders in the firm. When the pro bono staff person is an attorney, that individual often provides direct representation in firm pro bono matters as well as administration of the pro bono program. That individual may also supervise and train other attorneys in the firm with respect to pro bono work.

Although the number of lawyer pro bono staff has increased substantially in recent years, pro bono staffing is most frequently provided by nonlawyers.[8] These pro bono coordinators may be full-time administrators with backgrounds as public interest or legal services advocates, social workers, paralegals, or support staff. Others combine their work on pro bono with other responsibilities within the firm in areas such as professional development, training, recruitment, or paralegal or support work. The role of the pro bono administrator in a firm with a structured pro bono program is typically quite different from that of the "coordinator" of an ad hoc firm pro bono effort that lacks the administrative complexity of more formal programs. While many firms with relatively informal programs have traditionally appointed an individual attorney to serve as the point person for community service activities, that attorney typically carries a full commercial caseload and spends relatively little time on administration.

As the discussion of the range of possible tasks for a pro bono committee makes clear, an ambitious formal pro bono program requires substantial administrative resources. The availability of an individual whose day-to-day responsibilities include oversight of the pro bono program clearly increases the capacity and reach of that program. However, because pro bono staff are typically not highly placed in the firm hierarchy, the creation of a staff position, in the absence of strong, consistent leadership involvement in pro bono through a prominent individual or pro bono committee, often fails to accomplish the most fundamental goal of a structured program—ensuring that pro bono is an integral, valued part of the culture and daily life of the firm.

Hiring Experienced Laterals

One of the most innovative and successful approaches to the creation of an institutional pro bono capacity was developed by the South Carolina firm of Nelson, Mullins, Riley & Scarborough.[9] Despite strong support from firm leadership, the firm determined that its traditional ad hoc approach to pro bono, as the firm grew and established additional branch offices, was not producing the desired level of commitment of time and resources. At its annual planning retreat, the firm adopted four long-range goals, one of which was: "To earn an honest reputation as a leader in [the] area of public concern/public service, individually and as a law firm, giving of our time and financial resources."[10]

To accomplish this goal, the firm approached the development of a heightened pro bono capacity in much the same way as it would develop a new practice area. It conducted in-depth research, including a survey of what worked and what did not at larger law firms; an examination of different models; and the development of a detailed plan for expansion that included deadlines and quantitative goals. Most notably, recognizing the benefit of having in-house expertise in pro bono programs, it hired a lateral with substantial experience in pro bono, an attorney who had formerly served as director of the state's legal services support center and who is now an equity partner in the firm. The firm's new lateral hire brought with him the pro bono equivalent of "portables," that is, pro bono clients who presented a number of exciting and noteworthy pro bono opportunities that engaged the interest of a wider range of firm attorneys, particularly the more senior attorneys in the firm. To ensure that its new practice area was well launched and to demonstrate its keen interest in pro bono, the pro bono program was cochaired by the firm's best-known partner, a former governor of the state.

The careful planning, clear setting of goals, attention at the highest levels of the firm, and hiring of a lateral with expertise in a new area of the law is not an unfamiliar process for firms, of course. It is one that well-managed firms frequently use to plan for expansion into additional practice areas and in launching branch offices. Its use in making the transition from an ad hoc pro bono program to a structured program, however, is relatively unique. A positive development is that several firms, including Crowell & Moring and Steptoe & Johnson in Washington, D.C., and Katten Muchin & Zavis in Chicago have also recently hired attorneys with substantial experience in pro bono work to administer their firms' pro bono programs.[11]

Innovative Pro Bono Programs

In structuring their pro bono programs, firms have put in place a number of specialized and innovative programs, including fellowships, rotation programs, "adopt-a-program" projects, and firmwide projects, most notably firm-sponsored clinics. These innovative programs often complement existing effective formal pro bono programs through which attorneys maintain a high level of pro bono service.

Fellowships

Fellowship programs may be more accurately characterized as charitable giving, rather than pro bono, since the firm underwrites the salaries of one or more fellows who become staff attorneys at public interest or legal services programs, rather than donating the services of its own attorneys. The most ambitious fellowship program is that sponsored by Skadden, Arps, Slate, Meagher & Flom of New York City, which committed $10 million to place twenty-five fellows per year for five years. Skadden Arps met its original obligation and has decided to continue the program indefinitely.[12]

A number of other firms have developed more modest fellowship programs, ranging from Covington & Burling's program, which funds four fellows annually in the Washington, D.C., Neighborhood Legal Services Program, to the single fellowship programs recently implemented by Crowell & Moring and Pillsbury Madison & Sutro in San Francisco.[13] Hale and Dorr in Boston has for some time contributed $30,000 annually to defray the expense of a lawyer at Greater Boston Legal Services, while continuing its annual financial contribution through that program's lawyers' fund drive.[14] Several New York City law firms have offered to supplement the public interest salaries of associates who work for a year at a legal services or public interest program prior to joining the firm. The Philadelphia Bar Association and the Philadelphia firm of Drinker Biddle & Reath have created a program in which newly hired associates at participating firms may elect to spend their first year of practice at a legal services/public interest program before coming to the firm.[15] In this fellowship program the associate's customary first-year salary is paid over the course of two years. As a result, the individual attorney is, in effect, contributing to the program, with the firm's financial outlay relatively minimal in comparison with other fellowship programs.

Rotation Programs

A large number of law firms consistently provide associates—typically more senior associates—who spend a finite period of time, usually three to six months, working full-time for a public interest/legal services program or government agency. The longest-established rotation program is sponsored by Covington & Burling of Washington, D.C., which for more than twenty-five years has sent a new team of lawyers, paralegals, and secretaries to that city's legal services program every six months without ever missing a rotation period.[16] Indeed, the firm has far more applicants for the rotation program than it has slots. Bingham, Dana & Gould has sent one of its lawyers to Greater Boston Legal Services for more than a decade, and many other firms also have long-standing rotation programs.[17]

Although there was no appreciable growth in the number of firm-sponsored rotation programs in the 1980s, there has been a significant expansion in the early 1990s. At the urging of Volunteers of Legal Services (VOLS), a New York City program that promotes pro bono among larger law firms, a number of firms in that city have established rotation programs at legal services offices.[18] Several firms in Cleveland have made a commitment to send a firm lawyer to that city's Legal Aid Society for one month or more.[19] In Chicago, several firms have responded to a plea for assistance from that city's hard-pressed public defender program.[20] A 1994 survey conducted by the ABA's Law Firm Pro Bono Project found that many firms have sponsored intermittent rotation placements in the past and have expressed a willingness to do so in the future.[21]

Some firms do not characterize their rotation programs as pro bono in nature, but rather consider them as training and professional development opportunities. This is particularly the case for those firms that regularly send associates for three- to six-month stints with a prosecutor's office or public defender program. The intensive trial experience obtained by the associate—experience that cannot be duplicated at the firm—is viewed as a benefit to both the firm and the attorney. Most firms, however, view rotation opportunities as public service that provides ancillary benefits to the firm.

Rotation programs pose a number of unique issues for firms. Because they typically involve more senior (third- or fourth-year) associates, the firm, in cooperation with the rotation placement site, must ensure a smooth transition to and from the rotation program, make certain there is adequate supervision on site, and develop a plan and policy to deal with any conflict of interest issues that may arise. In addition to the training and professional growth provided by rotation placements, such programs provide an excellent opportunity for firms to quickly supplement their pro bono hours. For the public interest program, the benefits of adding a full-time staff attorney are many. If, however, the rotation attorney is provided for a very short period of time (for example, one to two months) and there is no provision for continuity in the completion of the rotation attorney's unfinished caseload, a rotation program may not justify the time and resources that the public interest organization must expend in training, orienting, and integrating the rotation attorney.

One of the most interesting applications of the rotation model is its usefulness in making the resources of large urban law firms available to more rural programs. Colorado's "Lend-a-Lawyer" program, which provides rural placements for Denver attorneys, is one example of such a program.[22] A highly successful version of this model is the ProBAR program developed by the State Bar of Texas and the American Bar Association.[23] Attorneys from large law firms around the nation have spent weeks or months providing representation in immigration matters to detainees in a remote area of Texas, supplementing the limited pro bono resources available from the small local bar.

"Adopt-a-Program" or "Matching" Projects

Since the early 1980s major law firms in Boston and New York City have been matched with local legal services offices to provide a wide range of support and assistance to these offices.[24] Firms participating in these matches typically offer nonsubstantive support services, including access to the firm's library, computerized research, training programs, consultation with firm administrators on topics such as computerization and telephone systems, donations of surplus or replaced furniture and equipment, and, in appropriate situations, access to the firm's word-processing or other administrative services.

In addition, the firm's attorneys may serve as mentors for program lawyers; participate in moot courts of important cases; consult on a variety of issues with which legal services attorneys have little familiarity, such as intellectual property or banking matters; and serve as counsel to the organization, representing the program in contract negotiations, lease and purchase of real estate, employment issues, and governance and tax matters. Some firms have detailed staff to the legal services program for finite periods of time.[25] For example, litigation paralegals may assist program lawyers in preparing exhibits for trial in a particularly complex matter, or the firm librarian may develop an acquisitions policy or library manual for the program or serve as its part-time librarian.[26]

As the resources of legal services and public interest programs continue to shrink, in recent years there has been a renewed interest in matching programs that can provide access to services and expertise that the legal services and public interest programs could not otherwise afford. The American Bar Association Section of Litigation, for example, has encouraged its members to make their firms' training programs available to legal services lawyers in the community and, in response to the highly positive evaluation of that initiative, is investigating the feasibility of a more expansive matching program.[27]

Firmwide Projects

Increasingly firms are developing specialized pro bono projects that focus on particular areas of the law, neighborhoods, or client groups. Some question the value of firmwide projects, believing that firm pro bono programs are most effective when they offer a broad menu of options in response to the varied interests and skills of firm attorneys.

However, most firms use these projects to supplement a more general pro bono practice, citing benefits ranging from the heightened efficiency and impact of pro bono work undertaken by a firm with specialized expertise to the benefits in firm morale when staff and attorneys from every part of the firm have the opportunity to work together on matters of common concern. In 1988 Morrison & Foerster of San Francisco, one of the nation's strongest pro bono firms, selected the area of children's rights as its primary pro bono focus while continuing to support a very broad and diverse pro bono caseload.[28] Similarly, Howrey & Simon of

Washington, D.C., while maintaining an active general pro bono program, has played a leading role in the efforts to protect the rights of homeless persons in that city.[29] In Boston, Goulston & Storrs, which has an extensive commercial real estate practice, has been a leader in the development of affordable housing, not only providing direct pro bono service to community groups, but also recruiting other firms locally and nationally to provide assistance.[30] Long, Aldridge & Norman of Atlanta has undertaken a guardian *ad litem* project, using firm teams, composed of lawyers, paralegals, and support staff, to represent the' interests of children in contested custody cases.[31]

For the past decade or more, Chicago and San Francisco law firms have regularly staffed walk-in legal services clinics established by pro bono organizations in those cities, and the D.C. bar initiated a law firm clinic program in 1993 involving eighteen of the city's largest law firms on a rotating basis.[32]

Some firms have expanded the clinic concept by establishing their own legal clinic programs, staffed and administered exclusively by the firm. In Richmond, Virginia, Hunton & Williams attorneys provide legal services at the firm's neighborhood legal services clinic.[33] Schwabe Williamson & Wyatt lawyers regularly travel twenty miles to their clinic, located in a low-income Hispanic community outside of Portland, Oregon. Jennings, Strouss & Salmon of Phoenix has established the first free legal clinic located in a supermarket, and in 1994 Leonard, Street & Deinard hired an administrator and opened its clinic at a community health center in Minneapolis.[34] These clinics offer all of the benefits of other firm-sponsored projects, including the opportunity to develop special expertise about a part of the community in which the firm is located, socialization with colleagues, and an improved sense of firm identity and pride.

Guarding Against an Erosion of Law Firm Commitment to Pro Bono: Policies and Practices

Particularly in uncertain economic times, the challenge for law firms is to maintain support for pro bono by taking steps to ensure that financial pressures are counterbalanced and neutralized by rewards and incentives that promote pro bono service. Firms, in fact, have developed mechanisms to respond to reservations about pro bono expressed by some firm attorneys ("negative signaling"), reduce the impact of increasing billable hour targets, and combat the anxiety of young associates concerned with advancement within the firm.

Responses to Negative Signaling

All firms, even those with the strongest pro bono culture, have attorneys who do not support pro bono. Even proponents of volunteer service can on occasion voice their frustration over the unavailability of a colleague who is working on a pro bono matter, the amount of firm resources expended on a particular engagement, or the firm's involvement in highly controversial matters such as abortion or death penalty appeals. Firm responses to economic downturns in recent years have heightened associate insecurities, increasing the negative impact of even an isolated comment or action. Although some measure of negative signaling is probably inevitable, firms have developed a number of institutional responses designed to minimize its effect.

Most notably, many firms ensure that their pro bono program has highly visible support from the firm's leadership—support that is reinforced and reiterated periodically. The involvement of firm leadership/management at the highest levels in the firm's pro bono program or the presence of an active and supportive pro bono committee, headed by a well-regarded partner, sends an important message. The most common demonstration of support is the development of a comprehensive, written pro bono policy that clearly sets out the firm's unconditional support for pro bono. However beneficial such a policy might be, it must be supplemented by actions that accord with the policy, so that attorneys know that the firm is not merely paying "lip service" to the concept of pro bono.

Visible participation in pro bono activities by senior partners, firm management, and rainmakers can also help neutralize negative signaling. A thoughtless remark criticizing the time an attorney is spending on a pro bono project has considerably less bite in an environment in which the firm's leading attorneys are also spending substantial time on pro bono matters.

When firms hire local attorneys to establish branch offices or bring in a large number of laterals to their home office, the laterals and branch lawyers who are not steeped in the culture of the firm's support for pro bono may be particularly prone to negative signaling. A number of firms have made conscious efforts to involve these attorneys in the pro bono program, so that they clearly understand the firm's commitment.

Because the absence of support for the firm's pro bono program may be a function of lack of knowledge or participation, a number of firms have broadened available pro bono opportunities and encouraged attorney-generated projects, so that all lawyers in the firm can find a matter of interest to them. Although litigators still undertake the majority of pro bono work in many firms, larger firms have become increasingly creative in developing pro bono matters that use the expertise of transactional and business lawyers, including real estate, tax, bankruptcy, banking, and intellectual property attorneys. In addition, many firms have consciously broadened their pro bono docket to include cases that attract attorneys from across the political/ideological spectrum.

Muting the Impact of Increased Billable Hour Targets

Regional and interfirm differences notwithstanding, most firms have substantially increased their billable hour targets or expectations during the past decade. Some firms state that they have no enunciated billable hour target; however, in an era in which the firm leadership and, in some firms, the entire partnership has access to detailed time/billing records, there is great pressure to bill at the same level as one's colleagues in all firms. At these higher levels, billable hour expectations, assuming some shrinkage from hours worked to hours billed, leave little room for other activities, including pro bono work. Associates and partners are also increasingly expected to undertake firm administrative responsibilities, such as committee work or recruitment, as well as training and business development—activities that may constitute billable time at some firms but are considered nonbillable at others. Clearly, the pressure of billable hours can consume all of a lawyer's work time, leaving no time for pro bono involvement.

Minimizing the impact of billable hour targets so that pro bono work can be an integral part of an attorney's work life is a difficult task. As a beginning, firms should view pro bono work as an asset, rather than a drain on firm resources. Pro bono opportunities provide substantial, if unquantifiable, benefits to the firm, including an increased capacity to compete for new associates, improved firm morale and *esprit de corps,* free training, enhanced good will and positive publicity, and opportunities for accelerated professional development of associates. A strong pro bono culture can also help the firm retain productive attorneys and even promote business development.

In recognition of the benefits that enure to firms from pro bono, and in support of their philosophical commitment to pro bono and community service, an increasing number of firms provide "credit" or billable hour equivalency for time spent on pro bono matters. Some firms limit the number of pro bono hours that can be counted toward the firms' billable hour target, typically permitting attorneys credit for fifty, one hundred, or two hundred hours annually without firm review. Most place no limit on the number of pro bono hours that are treated as billable-equivalent time. Despite their commitment to equal treatment of pro bono hours, most firms, in reporting hours, distinguish between pro bono time and time spent on commercial clients. One firm, for example, reports total "creditable" time per attorney on a quarterly basis, further identifying, within creditable time, client billed hours and client pro bono hours. Relatively few firms simply aggregate all client billable time, without distinction between paying and pro bono clients, in their periodic printouts.

Although many firms assert that they treat pro bono hours no differently than time spent on commercial practice, ensuring equivalency is a complex process. Firms must account for pro bono activity in a manner that credits that time in assessing the productivity of an individual attorney or department, while also "backing out" the pro bono hours so that the lawyer or department does not appear to have a substantial amount of uncollectible or unproductive time. That is, the firm must avoid an inflated revenue expectation.

In addition, ensuring equivalency for pro bono time is not simply a matter of "crediting" that time toward billable hour targets; it is also important, particularly for associates, that pro bono time be treated just as billable work is for purposes of evaluations and compensation. Each attorney's pro bono work should be reviewed and assessed as part of the firm's periodic evaluation process. This in turn makes it essential that pro bono work be supervised by a more senior attorney who has input into the evaluation process. The attorney may be the associate's supervising attorney, mentor, or department head, or a member of the pro bono committee. For those firms that do not have a lockstep compensation system, bonuses based on additional time billed should be awarded on the basis of both compensated and pro bono time.

A small number of firms, perhaps because of the complexities of establishing true parity for pro bono time, have instead instituted two separate hourly expectations—one for billable hours and a second for pro bono time. Such an approach will succeed only if the firm's billable hour target is relatively low.

Combating Associate Anxiety

The economic downturn experienced by firms in many regions of the nation during the past few years took its toll on associates' willingness to perform pro bono work. Firm downsizing, involving both associates and partners, created an atmosphere of unparalleled insecurity in which associates were reluctant to undertake any "risky" behavior, including reporting diminished billable hours because of their pro bono practice. In the cities and firms in which downsizing occurred, associates' concerns about their future have become so severe that firms have developed new approaches to reassure associates that pro bono work is valued and that they will not jeopardize their future at the firm by performing volunteer service.

Many of the policies and procedures cited above were instituted in firms as a means of dealing with associate insecurity. These include detailed pro bono policies, which often overtly address the issue of whether an attorney would be penalized for pro bono service. Such policies may contain a pro bono hourly or percentage "expectation," call for more visible support for pro bono by the firm's leadership, and include pro bono work as a specific topic to be addressed in evaluations. Firms have also initiated a number of innovative programs to communicate their support for pro bono, such as bonuses for exceptional pro bono performance, firmwide awards and pro bono recognition dinners and ceremonies, and heightened internal publicity for pro bono through newsletters, e-mail, and annual reports.

The Impact of Outside Groups on Law Firm Pro Bono

Although the pro bono performance of each major law firm is affected most directly by the firm's culture, the economic climate, and the approach to pro bono taken by peer firms, several outside institutions have had an impact on law firm pro bono. They include the organized bar, law schools, the legal media, and major clients.

Organized Bar Support for Pro Bono Publico

The tradition of pro bono publico within the legal profession is far from new. Nor is organized bar support for pro bono a recent development. In the first half of this century, bar associations sponsored pro bono programs as an integral part of the ABA's efforts to promote the growth of legal aid programs. Inspired by the populism and activism of the times, bar-sponsored pro bono reached another peak in the 1960s. With the advent of the Legal Services Corporation and the increased federal funding for full-time legal services staff in the 1970s, many of these bar programs disappeared or became relatively moribund. Since 1981, however, there has been an unparalleled resurgence of support among the organized bar for enhanced pro bono publico service by attorneys. The Reagan administration's attempt to eliminate all federal funding for legal services to the poor, at a time when the number of Americans living in poverty was at an all-time high, generated strong opposition from the organized bar. Under the leadership of the American Bar Association, state and local bars became key players in the effort to save the Legal Services Corporation. When the corporation was saved but stripped of 25 percent of its funding, the organized bar, once again at the urging of the ABA, became actively involved in the expansion of pro bono resources to supplement the federal funds available for legal services.[35]

Increased bar support was complemented by a new infusion of resources available to establish pro bono programs—the result of a controversial requirement imposed on recipients of federal legal services money mandating that they use a portion of their federal funds to involve private attorneys in the delivery of legal services. As a consequence of the bar's support and new program initiatives, the number of organized programs that offered pro bono opportunities for the private bar increased from approximately fifty in 1980 to more than nine hundred programs in 1993–94.[36] The emergence of populations with new or newly visible legal needs—the elderly, people with AIDS, the homeless, children, undocumented aliens, and others—has also contributed to the increase in programs and the continued strong support of the bar.

Organized bar support for pro bono has taken many forms. In some areas, bar associations are the primary sponsors of pro bono programs. More typical are bar initiatives to find funding for these programs and to recruit volunteers.

Bar Association Aspirational Resolutions

More than fifty state and local bar associations have adopted resolutions urging private attorneys to undertake pro bono work.[37] While these resolutions vary widely in content and level of detail, most are aspirational in nature, containing a definition of pro bono service and a quantified annual goal for pro bono service. Goals established in these resolutions range from the very modest—fifteen hours per year or less—to the more substantial—for instance, eighty hours annually. These resolutions are designed to accommodate all members of the bar and do not specifically speak to the appropriate level of pro bono service by lawyers in larger law firms. They tend to focus on the individual obligation of each lawyer without addressing the obligations of the lawyer's firm or office.

Organized Bar Efforts Targeting Law Firms

In urban areas with a substantial number of larger law firms, some bar associations have begun to specifically focus on larger law firms. The first initiative of this type was developed in New York City by Volunteers of Legal Services. In 1984 VOLS launched a highly publicized campaign by leaders of the Association of the Bar of the City of New York to enlist firms that would pledge a pro bono commitment of thirty hours per lawyer per year, based on a relatively narrow definition of pro bono service. A substantial number of New York City's largest law firms have accepted that pledge and complied with it.[38]

In Chicago the Public Interest Law Initiative (PILI) asked each of the city's largest law firms to agree to a policy that promoted a structured firm pro bono effort as well as a pledge of thirty hours per lawyer annually of pro bono service. To date, approximately forty-five firms have signed on to PILI's program.[39]

In other areas of the country, bar associations have sponsored less ambitious initiatives targeted at law firms. The Minnesota State Bar Association has developed a model law firm pro bono policy and has encouraged firms of all sizes to adopt that policy. Similarly, the Philadelphia Bar Association has also promulgated several alternative model policies for firms of all sizes. The State Bar of Wisconsin has adopted a similar approach. The State Bar of Michigan has taken its general aspirational pro bono standard and emphasized its applicability to larger law firms, as has the District of Columbia, which asks firms participating in its Pro Bono Attorney Recruitment Team (PART) program to pledge to meet the bar's forty-hour pro bono goal. In St. Louis, Missouri, large firms are asked to participate in the 25/25 program, in which firms strive to ensure that one-quarter of their attorneys spend at least twenty-five hours annually on pro bono work.

With the exception of the New York City and Chicago efforts, these bar initiatives do not appear to target larger law firms exclusively. None establish a unique standard or model for these firms, despite the differences in structure, operation, resources, and economics that characterize larger law firms.

Revised Model Rule 6.1

The efficacy of aspirational pro bono resolutions by general bar associations has been called into question. Data reported by the American Bar Association indicate that only 16.9 percent of the bar participates in organized pro bono programs, a number that has remained relatively static for several years.[40] The ABA freely admits that its statistics are incomplete and that "participation" is not defined and may include inactive volunteers who have not been dropped from program rosters. Whether the ABA figure understates or overstates attorney participation is unclear, but certainly there has been no documented growth in attorney participation in pro bono since the 1980s, despite the plethora of bar resolutions.

The American Bar Association adopted a widely used definition of pro bono publico service in 1975 and an aspirational pro bono resolution in 1988, suggesting fifty hours of service annually.[41] Prompted by the desire to more effectively promote voluntary pro bono service, in 1993 the ABA adopted a revised version of Model Rule 6.1 of the Model Rules of Professional Conduct. The revised model rule retains the voluntary nature of the original Model Rule 6.1, but supplements that very sketchy and uninformative rule by adding a suggested level of participation—fifty hours of pro bono service per lawyer per year. It also defines pro bono service by incorporating a modified version of the elements of the ABA's two aspirational resolutions. The definition includes the provision of "legal services without fee or expectation of fee to: (1) persons of limited means, or (2) charitable, religious, civic, community, governmental and educational organizations in matters which are designed primarily to address the needs of persons of limited means."[42] The definition also encompasses:

(1) delivery of legal services at no fee or substantially reduced fee to individuals, groups or organizations seeking to secure or protect civil rights, civil liberties or public rights or charitable, religious, civic, community, governmental and educational organizations in matters in furtherance of their organizational purposes, where the payment of standard legal fees would significantly deplete the organization's economic resources or would be otherwise inappropriate; (2) delivery of legal services at a substantially reduced fee to persons of limited means; or

(3) participation in activities for improving the law, the legal system or the legal profession.[43]

The most notable change effected by the revision was the priority given to legal services for individuals of limited means and the organizations that serve these individuals. The revised rule calls upon lawyers to spend a substantial majority of pro bono time on these activities.

The proponents of the revised model rule believed that a detailed discussion of an attorney's pro bono obligation in the model rules would have a greater impact than any bar association aspirational resolution, because law students, applicants for the bar, and practicing lawyers are far more likely to have access to and consult the model rules. A number of states had adopted a revised pro bono model rule with a recommended annual hourly goal prior to the ABA's adoption of Model Rule 6.1, as revised, including Arizona, Kentucky, and Georgia, with Florida and Virginia following suit after the ABA's adoption of Model Rule 6.1.[44] While only Hawaii has as yet followed the ABA's lead in adopting revised Model Rule 6.1, this change is under consideration in a number of jurisdictions.

ABA Law Firm Pro Bono Initiatives

Since 1980 the American Bar Association has provided oversight, policy analysis, and technical assistance to state and local bar associations, legal services and public interest programs, and others through its Standing Committee on Lawyers' Public Service Responsibility and the Center for Pro Bono (formerly the ABA's Private Bar Involvement Project). In 1989, with support from the Ford Foundation, the ABA, in acknowledgement of the critical role played by large law firms in pro bono and of the unique needs and issues faced by these firms in enabling their attorneys to perform pro bono service, created the Law Firm Pro Bono Project. The project provides technical assistance and training to law firm managers, produces several publications for law firms, and maintains a national clearinghouse of information and materials on the subject of law firm pro bono. The project provides, for the first time, a national forum for the exchange of information and expertise among law firms in the development and administration of successful pro bono programs and projects.

The Law Firm Pro Bono Challenge

One of the first activities of the Law Firm Pro Bono Project was its sponsorship of a series of regional and national conferences for managing partners and law firm pro bono contact persons. The discussions at these meetings focused the project's attention on the lack of any national normative standard for pro bono participation by large law firms. The conferences revealed that there were wide variations in the pro bono performance of larger firms, as a result of economic factors, the presence or absence of a strong local or firm culture supportive of pro bono, and the availability or lack of a broad range of pro bono opportunities. General bar association policies promoting pro bono, and even some of the bar initiatives tailored to firms, had had very little impact on the larger firms. This was due, in part, to the fact that larger firms often looked to peer firms, rather than the organized bar, as exemplars. It was also the result of the lack of guidance provided to firms by general bar resolutions on their role in promoting pro bono. Many firm representatives at the conferences called for a single national pro bono standard for larger firms, particularly those with multiple branch offices, which face a patchwork of inconsistent local and state bar pro bono resolutions.

The project's advisory committee, composed of managing partners and several general counsel of major corporations, reviewed the results of the project's conferences and designed a unique national set of normative principles for larger law firms engaged in pro bono publico service. These principles, a distillation of the elements common to successful law firm pro bono programs, were promulgated to the project's target audience, the nation's five hundred largest law firms, as the Law Firm Pro Bono Challenge.

The Challenge provides that:

1. Our firm recognizes its institutional obligation to encourage and support the participation by all of its attorneys in pro bono publico activities. We agree to promulgate and maintain a clearly articulated and commonly understood firm policy which unequivocally states the firm's commitment to pro bono work.

2. To underscore our institutional commitment to pro bono activities, we agree to use our best efforts to ensure that, by no later than the close of calendar year 1995, our firm will either:
   (1) annually contribute, at a minimum, an amount of time equal to 5 percent of the firm's total billable hours to pro bono work; or
   (2) annually contribute, at a minimum, an amount of time equal to 3 percent of the firm's total billable hours to pro bono work.

3. In recognition of the special needs of the poor for legal services, we

believe that our firm's pro bono activities should be particularly focused on providing access to the justice system for persons otherwise unable to afford it. Accordingly, in meeting the voluntary goals described above, we agree that a majority of the minimum pro bono time contributed by our firm should consist of the delivery of legal services on a pro bono basis to persons of limited means or to charitable, religious, civic, community, governmental, and educational organizations in matters which are designed primarily to address the needs of persons of limited means.

4. Recognizing that broad-based participation in pro bono activities is desirable, our firm agrees that, in meeting the minimum goals described above, we will use our best efforts to ensure that a majority of both partners and associates in the firm participate annually in pro bono activities.

5. In furtherance of these principles, our firm also agrees:

    a. To provide a broad range of pro bono opportunities, training, and supervision to attorneys in the firm, to ensure that all of our attorneys can avail themselves of the opportunity to do pro bono work;

    b. To ensure that the firm's policies with respect to evaluation, advancement, productivity, and compensation of its attorneys are compatible with the firm's strong commitment to encourage and support substantial pro bono participation by all attorneys; and

    c. To monitor the firm's progress toward the goals established in this statement and to report its progress annually to the members of the firm and to the American Bar Association's Law Firm Pro Bono Project.

6. This firm also recognizes the obligation of major law firms to contribute financial support to organizations that provide legal services free of charge to persons of limited means.

7. As used in this statement, the term pro bono refers to activities of the firm undertaken normally without expectation of fee and not in the course of ordinary commercial practice and consisting of (i) the delivery of legal services to persons of limited means or to charitable, religious, civic, community, governmental and educational organizations in matters which are designed primarily to address the needs of persons of limited means; (ii) the provision of legal assistance to individuals, groups, or organizations seeking to secure or protect civil rights, civil liberties or public rights; and

(iii) the provision of legal assistance to charitable, religious, civic, community, governmental or educational organizations in matters in furtherance of their organizational purposes, where the payment of standard legal fees would significantly deplete the organization's economic resources or would be otherwise inappropriate.[45]

To date, 171 of the nation's largest law firms have become Challenge signatories. For a number of firms, particularly many of those that have adopted the 5-percent level of pro bono service, the Challenge is simply an extension of their existing programs. Indeed, a number of firms not only meet the 5-percent level but greatly exceed it. For other firms, the 3-percent level of pro bono service represents a major increase in their current level of participation, requiring these firms to double or triple their pro bono time.

The Challenge contains a number of unique provisions, some of which have proven quite controversial among law firms. The Challenge is a departure from virtually all of the voluntary, aspirational goals promulgated by bar associations in two respects. First, it seeks a commitment from the firm, rather than the individual attorney, in recognition of the critical role that firm support, policies, and procedures play in promoting or discouraging individual lawyer pro bono participation. Second, its aspirational goal is stated as a percentage of the total firm output of billable hours, rather than as a per-lawyer hourly expectation. In so doing, the Challenge seeks to underscore that the commitment is an institutional, aggregate one, and to ensure that it is progressive in nature, increasing as the firm's revenue-generating work increases.

The Challenge definition, while developed to be as consistent with revised Model Rule 6.1 as possible, is also consciously more rigorous than that general definition, in recognition of the special responsibilities of this most prosperous segment of the bar. Unlike the rule, for example, partially compensated work is not included in the definition. Most notably, the Challenge pro bono definition does not include activities for improving the law, the legal system, or the profession. The project's advisory committee felt that this aspect of the model rule definition, if applied to law firms whose members are often very active on boards of directors and in bar association leadership, would not advance the Challenge's goal of increasing large firm involvement in the direct delivery of legal services to those unable to otherwise obtain assistance. The Challenge focuses, accordingly, on representational activities provided at no cost to the client.

In concentrating not only on the level of pro bono participation but also on the breadth of that participation within the firm, the Challenge is also unique. The principle that a majority of both associates and partners participate in pro bono service is quite foreign to many firms. However, the drafters of the Challenge determined that broad-based participation and visible partner involvement were key elements of successful pro bono programs. The Challenge's emphasis on structural issues reflects the project's belief that without certain policies and structures larger law firms will be unable to substantially increase their pro bono commitment. Finally, the Challenge, unlike most other aspirational goals, has a reporting requirement to ensure oversight within the firm and to help the project assess the impact of the Challenge.

Because firms need not implement the Challenge until the beginning of calendar year 1995 and will not report on their progress in meeting the Challenge until the close of that year, it is not possible to make any definitive judgment about the feasibility and impact of its approach. However, many firms have already made substantial changes in response to the Challenge. These firms are developing new or revised pro bono policies and projects, implementing or revising an administrative structure for pro bono and promoting greater awareness of pro bono within the firm.

In many firms pro bono activities have increased visibility, support, and energy. The project's 1996 report on the status of the Challenge will answer the question of whether that heightened activity has resulted in substantial new services to the communities in which the firms practice.

Mandatory Pro Bono

The vast gap between the need for free legal services, particularly for the poor, and the limited resources available to address that need, coupled with the disappointing response of lawyers to appeals for voluntary service, have led some leaders of the bench and bar to call for mandatory pro bono publico service as a condition of licensure. Mandatory pro bono first surfaced in the late 1970s, when proposals were submitted to the State Bar of California and the Association of the Bar of the City of New York. Both proposals established an annual expectation of approximately forty hours of service and a moderately broad definition of pro bono. Each encountered intense opposition and was defeated.[46] A similar fate befell the quasi-mandatory language initially proposed in 1980 for the Model Rules of Professional Conduct, despite the fact that the proposed language contained no specific hourly requirement, provided no enforcement mechanism, and included only a general reporting requirement.[47] The response to that proposal was so hostile that the model rule on pro bono that was adopted was particularly weak, consisting of hortatory language, a highly ambiguous definition of pro bono, and no quantifiable measure of activity. As noted above, it was only thirteen years later that the ABA put some definitional flesh on this skeletal rule.

In recent years bar associations—either on their own initiative, at the urging of the state's highest courts, or in response to legislative proposals or litigation challenges—have addressed the mandatory pro bono issue in states as diverse as Maryland, New York, North Dakota, Texas, Washington, Hawaii, Nevada, and Florida. While action on a number of these initiatives is still pending, most have failed to win approval. There has been one striking new development that may signal a fruitful new approach. The Florida Supreme Court has approved an amendment of that state's model rules that includes a voluntary pro bono commitment of twenty hours per year, but also contains a mandatory reporting requirement.[48] A number of commentators believe that the impact of mandatory reporting, particularly when the information is readily available on an individual attorney basis to the public and the media, is the equivalent of a mandatory program. The program is still in its formative stages and its ultimate impact is still unknown.

"Quasi-Mandatory" Pro Bono

Although no jurisdiction has yet enacted a true mandatory pro bono provision, several "quasi-mandatory" programs exist. For instance, court-ordered programs mandating pro bono service are in effect in El Paso, Texas, and Westchester County, New York.[49] While both programs have been operating for some time without any major challenges, there has been no comprehensive, objective evaluation of these efforts or the several other court-ordered programs in existence.

Despite some opposition when these programs were created, they appear relatively noncontroversial today. However, it is not clear that non-participating attorneys are, in fact, sanctioned in any way. In addition, these programs typically handle a limited range of legal problems and require participants to make a very modest annual commitment of time. The lack of an assessment makes it difficult to generalize about the feasibility of court-ordered mandatory programs.

In other jurisdictions, local voluntary bar associations have made participation in the bar's pro bono program a condition of membership, creating another quasi-mandatory model. In Orange County, Florida, the site of the oldest "voluntary mandatory" program, the bar reports that a very high percentage of bar members either perform pro bono service or "buy out" their obligation by making a $350 financial contribution to the Legal Aid Society.[50] While it does appear that this and other similar programs have established a bar culture that strongly promotes participation in pro bono activity, the absence, once again, of an objective analysis and clear data make any definitive assessment of this model premature.

Mandatory Law Firm Pro Bono

The reluctance of state bars to adopt mandatory pro bono requirements is understandable. The heterogeneity of the bar's membership—which includes sole practitioners barely eking out a living, government attorneys who are often statutorily barred from the outside practice of law, and major law firms—makes the development and imposition of a single pro bono requirement a complex and politically charged task. In addition, the paperwork and administrative expense required to make such a require-ment truly enforceable would impose a substantial new burden on the states. A mandatory pro bono requirement imposed by a law firm upon its own attorneys, however, is, in theory, far more manageable. The firm already requires its attorneys to follow its directives, policies, and proce-dures in many other contexts. It obtains detailed time and client data from them and would need no additional administrative structure to oversee compliance with a pro bono requirement.

Despite the apparent logic of a mandatory approach within a law firm, there is no indication that any large law firm has established a truly mandatory pro bono program. Although some law firms assign individual pro bono matters to attorneys, particularly associates, rather than soliciting volunteers, the vast majority of firms depend on willing recruits. A number of firms have clearly articulated pro bono requirements. Holland & Hart in Denver, for example, expects "between 5 and 20 percent of the total hours expectancy for three years over a rolling 3-year period" on pro bono/public service projects.[51] Several other firms have policies that re-quire associates to be involved in at least one pro bono matter. At least one firm, Heiskell, Donelson, Bearman, Adams, Williams & Caldwell, which conditions associate eligibility for bonuses on the lawyer's comple-tion of one hundred hours of pro bono service annually, indicates that it takes this requirement very seriously.[52] But most firms are unlikely to penalize rainmakers or other highly productive lawyers who have not satisfied the firm's pro bono expectations.

Law Schools

Law schools are placing increasing emphasis on law firm pro bono, with many highlighting the issue in their requests for information from firms interviewing at the school. In addition, law student interest in public interest law is also on the upswing. With a very limited number of full-time public interest jobs available to new graduates, many students are evaluating potential employers, in part, on the basis of their pro bono commitment. One indication of the growing student interest in firms with a strong pro bono culture is the inclusion of information about pro bono programs in publications designed to help students learn more about law firms.[53]

The Legal Media

The legal press, which has contributed to the current focus on firm profitability and attorney compensation, has begun to provide more coverage of other aspects of firm practice, including pro bono publico service. In 1994 two legal newspapers with wide circulation, the *National Law Journal* and the Washington, D.C.-based *Legal Times*, which is an affiliate of the *American Lawyer*, have initiated regular columns that focus on pro bono in larger firms. The *American Lawyer* itself has adopted the Law Firm Pro Bono Challenge definition of pro bono for purposes of its survey of the nation's one hundred highest-earning law firms and has also indicated a willingness to produce more regular feature stories that focus on public service. Firms are keenly aware of this coverage, particularly the *American Lawyer* survey report, which assigns each firm a pro bono grade. Pro bono work is being integrated into legal press coverage in more subtle ways as well. For example, the *American Lawyer*'s annual midlevel associate survey uses law firm support for pro bono as one factor, among many, to evaluate the desirability of firms as employers.[54] *Legal Times* includes major pro bono cases and projects in its reports of major deals and cases. Despite an increase in coverage, however, the legal media's reports on law firms are still dominated by bottom-line issues.

Corporate Clients

The perceived attitudes of major clients toward pro bono work can have a substantial impact on larger law firms. Some firms are fearful that corporate clients will shy away from firms with expansive pro bono programs, particularly those that focus on controversial clients or causes. In fact, many corporate CEOs and general counsel are supportive of firm pro bono efforts, seeing them as analogous to the tradition of charitable giving and community service among many major corporations. Several law firms have reported that clients specifically asked about the firm pro bono programs during the course of "beauty contests," in which several firms competing for a corporation's business make presentations on the firm's assets and expertise, and responded favorably to the firm's strong emphasis on pro bono work.

Under the aegis of the American Bar Association's Section of Business Law, John Martin, vice president and general counsel of the Ford Motor Company, launched a corporate law department challenge in 1993 that has been endorsed by a number of in-house law departments.[55] One recent innovation that may help to allay law firm concerns is the development of pro bono projects jointly sponsored and staffed by a law firm and a corporate law department. LeBoeuf, Lamb, Greene & MacRae and the legal department of ITT in New York City, for instance, provide pro bono corporate advice and representation to nonprofit childcare providers.[56] Several firms are experimenting with legal clinics that are jointly staffed by firm and in-house lawyers. Typically, the partners in a jointly sponsored pro bono project have an ongoing commercial relationship as well. Corporate clients and their legal departments have had a substantial impact in encouraging firms to increase the diversity of their attorney work force. Although corporate endorsement of pro bono has not received a similar level of attention, clear indications by corporate clients that pro bono enhances a firm's stature and marketability with the client could greatly increase support for pro bono within the firm.

Conclusion

A series of thoughtful initiatives developed by pro bono supporters both in major law firms and in other institutions that interact with those firms has, thus far, preserved a strong pro bono culture within many firms. At present, firm pro bono resources are, for the most part, increasing or remaining level. But absent the implementation of strong internal pro bono programs that are reinforced by the organized bar, clients, the legal media, and other opinion shapers in the legal profession, economic pressures could erode pro bono. Such an erosion would be troubling because of the pivotal role played by the firms particularly in more complex, controversial, and time-consuming pro bono matters. In addition, any retreat from pro bono on the part of larger firms may well lead to a diminution in pro bono service throughout the legal community, since these firms are typically the trendsetters for that community.

Notes

1. Hogan & Hartson Community Services Department, *1992 Annual Report,* Washington, D.C. (January 8, 1993), p. 1.
2. Hogan & Hartson, *1992 Annual Report.*
3. Holland & Knight, *The Community Services Team: Continuing a Holland & Knight Tradition* (Tampa Bay, Florida, 1993), p. 1.
4. Arent Fox Kintner Plotkin & Kahn, *Non-Billable Matters—Policies and Procedures,* Washington, D.C. (November 8, 1990), p. A-15.
5. Morgan, Lewis & Bockius, Public Interest Practice Group, "Short Summary of Morgan, Lewis & Brockius's Public Interest Practice Group and the Recent Activities of its Attorneys in the Public Interest Area," Philadelphia (May 2, 1990), p. 1.
6. American Bar Association, press release, "ABA Launches Major Law Day Initiative to Dramatically Increase Availability of Free Legal Services," April 30, 1993.
7. Pro Bono Survey, *American Lawyer,* pull-out supplement, vol. 16, no. 5 (July/August 1994).
8. Material gathered from firm reports on file with the ABA Law Firm Pro Bono Project.
9. Discussion drawn from pro bono plan of Nelson, Mullins, Riley & Scarborough, "A National Model for Developing and Nurturing a Dynamic Pro Bono Program," 1988.
10. Nelson, Mullins, Riley & Scarborough, "1988 Firm Goals, Objectives and Strategic Plans," October 28, 1988.
11. Steve France, "Innovation Jump-Starts Firm's Pro Bono Effort," *Legal Times,* Week of May 20, 1991, pp. 2, 16; Steptoe & Johnson, Public Service Program description, attachment to 1993 letter, Washington, D.C.; Donna Gill, "Katten Hires Full-time Pro Bono Lawyer to Beef Up Services," *Chicago Lawyer* (October 1993), p. 6.
12. *Skadden Fellowship Foundation Report,* 1989–93 (New York: Skadden Fellowship Foundation, 1994).
13. The Crowell & Moring Public Interest Law Fellowship, announcement by the National Association for Public Interest Law, Washington, D.C., 1993; HomeBase and Pillsbury Madison & Sutro, "Public Service Attorney to Combat Low-Income Housing Discrimination," press release, San Francisco, April 1994.
14. Hale and Dorr, "Summary of Pro Bono Activities," Boston, 1993.
15. Drinker Biddle & Reath, "In The Public Interest" (newsletter), Philadelphia, December 1993.
16. Covington & Burling, Neighborhood Legal Services Program, in *Public Service Activities Annual Report,* 1992.
17. Boston Bar Association, "Description of the Law Firm Resources Project," Boston, June 30, 1987.
18. William J. Dean, "Law Firms Matched with Legal Services Offices," *New York Law Journal* (February 20, 1991).
19. Hahn Loeser & Parks, "Policy Statement Regarding Pro Bono Work," memorandum

to all attorneys (September 16, 1992); Jones, Day, Reavis and Pogue, "Statement of Public Service Policy, Organization and Procedures," 1994.

20. Katten Muchin & Zavis, *Law News* (pro bono newsletter), vol. 1, no. 1 (June 1994).

21. ABA Law Firm Pro Bono Project, Law Firm Pro Bono Directory survey of five hundred largest law firms in the nation, March 1995.

22. Diane Goldie, "Free Work Makes Job Worthwhile: State Bar Starts Lend-a-Lawyer Program," *Rocky Mountain News* (February 11, 1990).

23. Allan Van Fleet and Laurie Van Fleet, "ProBAR: Two Weeks That Made a Difference," *Texas Bar Journal,* vol. 54, no. 4 (April 1990), pp. 380–83.

24. Legal Services Corporation, *Quality Improvement Project: Evaluation Report, Executive Summary* (September 1981), pp. 1–18.

25. Ibid., pp. 25, 86.

26. Ibid., pp. 2–3.

27. Personal communication with Lawrence J. Fox, incoming chair, ABA Section of Litigation, October 5, 1994.

28. Morrison & Foerster, "Office Summaries of Pro Bono Work and Community Activities" (San Francisco), 1993.

29. See "Note of Thanks," in *Homefront,* newsletter of the Washington Legal Clinic for the Homeless (January 1995), p. 1.

30. Goulston & Storrs, *Pro Bono Publico Projects,* Boston, 1994.

31. Long, Aldridge & Norman, description of Guardian Ad Litem Project, September 1994.

32. Chicago Volunteer Legal Services Foundation Letter to Robert E. Hirshon, chair, ABA Standing Committee on Lawyers' Public Service Responsibility, February 16, 1992; Cynthia A. Coe, *The San Francisco Legal Services Project,* memorandum describing the pro bono clinic that the San Francisco Lawyers' Committee for Urban Affairs sponsors in San Francisco (March 25, 1993); D.C. Bar Public Services Activities Corporation, "Law Firm Pro Bono Clinic: Clinic Description" (May 1993).

33. George H. Hettrick, "Doing Good: How One Law Firm Started a Low-Fee Branch Office to Help Those in Need," *ABA Journal,* vol. 78, no. 12 (December 1992), pp. 77–81.

34. Gail Dana, "Equal Justice: Volunteer Lawyers Make the System Work for Those with Limited Resources," *Portland Downtowner* (March 23, 1992), p. 54; "Jennings, Strouss Opens Private Clinic at Food City," *Maricopa Lawyer* (October 1991); Donna Halvorsen, "The Law for All: Legal Services Center Opens in Phillips Community Clinic," *Minneapolis Star Tribune,* March 15, 1994, p. 1B.

35. Esther F. Lardent, "Mandatory Pro Bono in Civil Cases: The Wrong Answer to the Right Question," *Maryland Law Review,* vol. 49, no. 1 (1990), p. 87.

36. American Bar Association Consortium on Legal Services and the Public through the Center for Pro Bono, *1993/94 Directory of Private Bar Involvement Programs* (Chicago: American Bar Association, 1993), p. iii.

37. Memorandum to author from Stephen Dressel, American Bar Association Center for Pro Bono, Chicago, September 26, 1994.

38. Volunteers of Legal Services, Inc., "Program of Volunteers of Legal Services," New York, Summer 1991.

39. Donna Gill, "Pro Bono Effort Tallies Commitment From 45 Illinois Firms," *Chicago Lawyer,* December 1992, pp. 18, 19.

40. Lardent, "Mandatory Pro Bono," pp. 78–102.

41. American Bar Association, Special Committee on Public Interest Practice, "Montreal Resolution," 1975; "Toronto Resolution," 1988.

42. Model Rules of Professional Conduct, Revised Model Rule 6.1, Voluntary Pro Bono Publico Service, Adopted by the American Bar Association House of Delegates, February 8, 1993.

43. Ibid.
44. Ibid.
45. Copyright © American Bar Association 1993.
46. Lardent, "Mandatory Pro Bono," p. 94.
47. Ibid., p. 98.
48. Amendments to Rules Regulating the Florida Bar—1–3.1(a) and Rules of Judicial Administration—2.065 (Legal Aid), Supreme Court of Florida, No. 74,538 (June 23, 1993), pp. 1–4.
49. Lardent, "Mandatory Pro Bono," p. 96.
50. In Re: Petition for Provision of Legal Aid to the Poor (Amendment to the Rules Regulating the Florida Bar and the Rules of Judicial Administration); Petition for Rule Establishing Local Procedure to Meet Legal Needs, Supreme Court of Florida, No. 74,538, August 8, 1989, p. 18.
51. Holland & Hart, "Public Service/Pro Bono Publico Policy and Procedure," December 1987.
52. Heiskell, Donelson, Bearman, Adams, Williams & Caldwell, Law Firm Pro Bono Policy, 1994.
53. *The 1993–94 Insider's Guide to Law Firms,* compiled and written by Harvard University Law School students.
54. Annual Midlevel Associates Survey, *American Lawyer,* vol. 16, no. 8 (October 1994), p. 9.
55. Resolution Adopting a Corporate Law Department Pro Bono Challenge for the Members of the Committee on Corporate Law Departments of the Business Law Section of the American Bar Association (April 16, 1993).
56. Files of American Bar Association Law Firm Pro Bono Project.

4

Reflections on Lawyer Morale and Public Service in an Age of Diminishing Expectations

William C. Kelly, Jr.

This chapter is an impressionistic survey of life in large law firms— firms with more than 150 lawyers—gathered over the course of a year of discussions with lawyers from around the country. Insiders believe that each firm has its own personality; outsiders see little difference among them.[1] My unscientific belief is that much of what follows applies in substantial degree to all large firms, whatever their differences. My thesis is that public service, including pro bono legal work, can help reestablish ties between lawyer and community, the fraying of which in recent years has contributed materially to the lowered state of morale in large firms.

The Satisfactions of Large Firm Practice

To understand the developments of recent years, we need first to under- stand the background. What, to begin, has brought lawyers to the typical large law firm, and what motivates them to stay?

For some, employment in a large law firm has been a high-pay, low- risk business proposition. Partner draws have for years exceeded the incomes of most senior executives of corporate clients and, by a wider margin, those of nonprofit executives and individual clients. Associate salaries in the range of $60,000 to $80,000 per year for first-year lawyers put them on this fast track.

Job tenure has been another magnet. By agreement and tradition over the years, partners have been protected in their partnerships through good and bad times. The partnership format has also protected the partner from arbitrary executive decision, in contrast to the exposed position of even the senior manager in a traditional business hierarchy.

The thrill of combat ranks high among the incentives to join the profession and remains a source of satisfaction for many lawyers, especially trial lawyers but also negotiators and others.

More elusive but still powerfully attractive to many lawyers has been the opportunity to make constructive contributions to clients, to the law firm as an enterprise, and to society. These lawyers take satisfaction from guiding an enterprise toward progress, or as a proxy for progress, toward growth; they take pride in being, and in being seen as, contributors to a better future. A better future, in the eye of the beholder, may be as mundane as higher incomes for lawyers in an expanded firm, or as typical as developing a joint venture for a client or a better solution to a public policy dilemma. The ingrained sense is that to be productive one must be building something.

As a new partner, I had the extraordinary experience of being principal counsel to two joint ventures seeking to use new technology to make fuller use of America's coal supply. The psychic rewards of trading ideas with senior policymakers and bringing the legal perspective to board deliberations were extraordinary. Another such experience in my own career is a decade of working with nonprofits to develop and preserve low-income housing. To the extent that a lawyer has client relationships of this kind, the lawyer feels that his or her ideas and judgments can make a difference.

Large Law Firms Under Siege

The last twenty-five years, save the last four or five, were a period in which incomes rose and job security remained high, at least among partners and associates on track to partnership. Indeed, incomes in the major firms rose faster than the incomes of any reference group, and expansion in scale brought an ever higher share of top talent to these firms.[2]

Several years ago, however, the economics of most large law firms turned sharply for the worse.[3] Mirroring the regional features of national economics, the firms anchored on the East and West coasts, which grew and profited the most over the last quarter century, generally fell farther and from higher peaks.[4]

Erosion of the Basics

What happened? First, the demand for certain types of legal services, such as real estate lawyering, fell with the industries that formed the client base. Second, an oversupply of lawyers and firms competing for the work of institutional clients depressed prices and forced firms to assume risks formerly borne by clients. Morale was hit hard by declining incomes and expectations. At a time of falling revenues, a large share of firms faced rising costs for rents, computer equipment, and nonpartner salaries.[5] In the best of times, most firms distribute no more than 30 to 40 percent of revenues to partners. A modest reduction in revenue and a modest increase in expense can therefore be amplified into a sharp decline in partner incomes. The threat of unstable incomes is the backdrop against which morale issues are played out.

As the economic base—predictable high incomes—slipped away, so, too, did tenure and collegiality. Several major firms collapsed altogether, leaving the former partners with bank debt and liability for long-term leases.[6] Dozens fired or forced out partners;[7] nearly all laid off associates who a decade before would have retained a shot at partnership. Many who remained grieved the loss of their valued colleagues and became more nervous about their own futures.

Partners now find that they have trouble building practices because the associates upon whom they rely are often forced out. One lateral "in play" had developed a seven-figure practice in an emerging area, but found that his firm, controlled by a main office in New York, simply would not promote to partner the associates he trained or, indeed, any associates in the Washington office. Associates are unsure whether their firms are investing in them for the long term, or simply providing a job; in turn, they are unsure of how deeply to invest themselves in their firms.

The internal scramble for money can be divisive and debilitating. In the 1980s an increasing number of lawyers took on the trappings of inherited or entrepreneurial wealth, assuming living expenses that now must be fed by escalating incomes. As compensation has fallen, internecine warfare about compensation has risen. "Business producers" have become the free agents of the legal world. For better or worse, law firm management has come to seem largely the recruiting of such free agents and the defensive restructuring of compensation to keep valued "home team" players from defecting. The "nonproducers" are expected to grin and bear it; when some, instead, leave, that too is often seen as potentially aiding the firm's economics. Others accept their diminished income and status as their due, or as the best they can do in today's market. Still others hustle for new business and become part of the close fighting for business production credit. At its extreme, the law firm has come to seem less a team and more a series of franchises licensed to use the law firm's name. Loyalty and, with it, morale have suffered as lawyers no longer identify their fortunes so closely with those of their law firms.

Recent signs that the demand for large firm services has rebounded with the economy has temporarily improved morale in many firms, but the recent traumatic experiences and the persistence of the fundamental trends counsel that the underlying morale problems will persist.

Client Turmoil

Changing relationships with clients have also contributed to the decline of law firm morale. What some clients expect of their firms has changed dramatically, and these changes go far beyond the sensible and much-publicized trend toward greater accountability of outside counsel for their bills and their litigation strategies.

Client relationships are as diverse as the nature of legal problems and the clients themselves. One dimension of the relationship is its profitability as a business matter for the firm. What is the volume of work? What are the rates? Does the work keep flowing even in recessions? A second dimension records a quite different aspect of the relationship—the level of involvement of the law firm in the client's development of business or other programmatic strategies. Does the day-to-day client have a policy role in the client organization? Does the client view the firm's legal work as a commodity to be purchased from a quality firm on the best competitive terms, or does it view the firm or some of its lawyers as key members of the client's team?

Many firms, with respect to most of their services, and most firms, with respect to some of them, are selling commodities. A firm may be handling all disputes with franchisees in a four-state area for a Fortune 500 company, for example, or all loan closings for a bank in a metropolitan area. This can be profitable business, even when the client conducts a periodic price competition, and firms value it highly. That a service is a commodity does not mean that a particular trial will not be exciting or a particular deal unchallenging. What it does mean, though, is that the lawyers are not engaged with the client's senior management in coping with crises or formulating a strategy to position the client for a better future. In this mode, the lawyer is not a long-term counselor.[8]

An increasing proportion of the work done by large firms falls into the category of commodity work. The greater sophistication of in-house lawyers, who now often fill the counselor role once filled by outside counsel, has been partly responsible for this trend. The recognition that legal services such as high-volume litigation can be bundled and put out for competitive bidding has accelerated the trend. Law firms become extensions of in-house staff, available to handle overflow work. Again, there is nothing inherently wrong with this approach, which has derived from the perception in the client community that outside counsel fees have run amok.

One associate's reasons for leaving a major firm illustrate a client-related aspect of the morale problem: the isolation that can characterize specialized practices. The lawyer was working with a sophisticated, personable group of lawyers that was building a major practice. She was a strong performer, highly regarded by her supervisors. Her concerns? The clients were always large institutions with whom she had little sustained contact, and her long hours were consistently devoted to defenses of the status quo. In discussions with friends, she found that her complex work projects usually came across as being esoteric, of little general interest.[9] Her work lacked immediacy.

Other lawyers see themselves as trapped in multiyear lawsuits, with clients rightly feeling that they have made an investment in the lawyer's knowledge and should not be expected to educate a replacement.

Clients are no longer stable navigation points. Policy and personnel changes, mergers, restructurings, and layoffs are endemic among clients— even more so than among law firms. Few are the partners in law firms that have not lost clients to mergers; rare is the lawyer whose client collaborator has not been fired or demoted. One partner worked for five years with the president of a hospitality company in the development and negotiation of a worldwide joint venture only to see the entire structure collapse when the president was forced out in a corporate power struggle. Dozens of consultations and months of negotiations produced nothing of broader value than a fee.

The Press of Time

Another tributary to the stream of discontent is the accumulation of day-to-day pressures reflected in the increasing hours junior and senior lawyers spend on the job.[10] The insistence that lawyers meet firms' standards for billable hours is only the most notorious of the sources of time pressure. Increasingly, the overhead time spent on nonclient matters is an equal source of frustration.

Every law firm has an administrative maw that must be fed with reports: daily time sheets; monthly bills reflecting minute details in an array of formats prescribed by clients; conflict checks; accountants' letters; entries for internal newsletters and external marketing materials, each shaped for a different audience; year-end reports; recruiting evaluations; expense reports; and dozens more items too tedious to list. Pervasive evaluation of business production, client hours, collections, supervisory skills, and administrative contribution, necessary as that evaluation has become, is a voracious consumer of time.

Meetings are no less prolific. Meetings of partners, associates, and both together are organized by office, department, cross-cutting practice group, and administrative committee. To this mix are added interviews of prospective lateral partners, associates, and paralegals and job search assistance for those who have been laid off. Firms fail to gather the reports and hold meetings at their peril, because without them schisms develop and practice opportunities are lost. But, however well or poorly thought through in a particular firm, these internal reports and meetings crowd out time for reflection and planning.

Business development has become more demanding and sophisticated. In addition to more traditional presentations, dinners, and the like, lawyers and firms now regularly prepare extensive written proposals, which often include substantive analysis. Responding to international "terms of reference" can involve dozens or hundreds of pages of new drafting, explaining in detail the firm's experience, knowledge of the field and country in question, and proposed work plan. Many domestic competitive bids require nearly comparable proposals. Selection often involves a two-step process of being selected from a list of five or ten firms for a short list, and then submitting a more detailed proposal.

Nor is it merely a matter of sitting through meetings and grinding out reports. The navigation and coordination required to ensure, for example, that partner candidates have enough of the right kind of challenging work without upsetting others can be stressful. Equally so is dealing with a client frustrated by a colleague's delay or poor performance, or coping with an overbearing client whose complaints about service or bills are ill-founded. The evaluation process also produces tensions on all sides. And all of this—meetings, reports, business proposal writing, and the rest—is overhead time, putting further pressure on basic economics.

These time demands have had a much-lamented effect on the lawyer's time for family and friends, general reading, and relaxation. They have also endangered "quality time" within the firm—time for becoming immersed in an issue, for savoring its nuances, for debating the merits of the latest Supreme Court decision, and for telling and listening to war stories.

Many of the causes of low morale are beyond the capacities of law firms and certainly of individual lawyers to remedy easily. Larger economic trends have changed the lawyer/client relationship, the growth in the lawyer population has increased competitive pressure, and coping with these market trends requires nonclient time. These trends challenge the firms to produce creative responses.

Public Service in the Mix

Against this background, what does public service offer to enhance personal satisfaction and morale within law firms? To put this question in context, it bears repeating that public service is an ethical obligation, not merely a tool to improve morale. Equally important is the recognition that an approach to increased job satisfaction relying exclusively on pro bono work or other public service will, for most lawyers, fall short of the mark.

We all know lawyers, and indeed have colleagues, who are fully satisfied with their practices because they produce the income to support school tuition, vacation travel, or a retirement plan. We know others who are sustained by adrenalin surges from jury trials, and still others who relish the role of substantive expert. For these, the comfortable, public service has little to offer as a morale booster.

Others are simply ill-equipped by personality and skills to practice in large law firms. Some see law practice as a continuation of law school, the passive taking and completion of research and writing assignments. Many lack the basic analytical capacity required of a first-rate lawyer.

For such lawyers, participation in pro bono and public service activities will not mean redemption.

For the rest of us, public service has the potential, if not to reduce time pressure or improve economics, at least to offer the constructive engagement that lawyers often miss in their law practices. What constitutes public service, what should "count" toward meeting bar association guidelines, and who should be eligible as pro bono clients are exhaustively discussed elsewhere; public service, very broadly conceived, can boost morale however these issues are resolved. For present purposes, one threshold distinction may still usefully be made: between what might be called direct public service—service as a principal or a policy adviser— and pro bono service—service as a lawyer on behalf of a client that, in the firm's view, warrants free or low-fee representation.

Direct public service can provide engagement in the major issues of our time that is not provided by specialized law practices. For a lawyer in a large firm practice, full-time service in a government policy position can be a productive interlude in a long career of private practice, stimulating in its own right and enriching the lawyer's practice in later years. For the partner weary of the time pressures of private practice, the competition for clients and dollars, and the provision of commodity services removed from client strategy, the different opportunities, pressures, and frustrations of public office can impart a sense of renewal and provide an occasion for reorientation.

With this form of public service often comes a shift from the anonymity of most private practice to the visibility of the public arena. The navigator becomes the captain, and the promotion can be exhilarating. Most firms can tell stories of talented associates or partners, worn down by their firms and in trouble under the firm's prevailing standards, who left to become government officials or assistant U.S. attorneys and blossomed with the greater freedom they found. Many of these have returned in triumph to their former firms or built thriving practices in comparable firms.

Selection for an appointive position means, for the lawyer, disengagement from client work, a sharp drop in income, a demanding learning process, and unpredictable timing. For the lawyer's firm it often means the temporary or permanent loss of a productive colleague and, potentially, younger lawyers who may follow the appointee; disruption in established client relationships; and a distraction from day-to-day business. Law firms have an important role to play, however, in accommodating and encouraging this service. The firm is often uniquely positioned to continue the lawyer's income until final departure and to help the lawyer divest prohibited investments. Of equal importance, colleagues in the firm can be encouraged to help the lawyer prepare for his or her new responsibilities by, for example, briefing the lawyer on issues that will be raised during confirmation hearings. All of these forms of support are readily provided by most firms for lawyers who receive prominent appointments, and firms should be, and many are, equally supportive of their junior lawyers moving to government.

Part-time service on a government commission or board, or with a private institution that has a public issue focus, can offer many of the same rewards. The variations are as endless as our society is complex, from service on a blue-ribbon commission or as head of a foundation for the homeless to participation in a campaign to incorporate a new town.

This form of service has been one of the building blocks of the careers and reputations of prominent practitioners in most major cities. For retired Supreme Court Justice Lewis F. Powell, Jr., service on bodies such as the Richmond School Board, the Virginia State Board of Education, and the Virginia Commission on Constitutional Revision were key to his preeminence in the Richmond legal community.[11]

The hundreds of lawyers who participated in various ways in President Clinton's transition, and others before it, grappled for a time with the main issues that face the nation: health care reform, global warming, infrastructure finance, and antitrust policy. They worked around the clock to address hard questions about conflicting agendas amid resource scarcity.[12] For a time, they put aside their usual concerns about particular litigations, rulemakings, or transactions and forced themselves to try to bring the big picture into focus. Their client was the public interest.

Local and state settings offer similar opportunities. Dozens of lawyers, most from large firms, donated thousands of hours to the Christopher Commission's 1992 inquiry into police practices in Los Angeles, bringing them face-to-face with some of the city's toughest problems.[13] Others work with community groups, spend time in the neighborhoods of South Central Los Angeles, and bring their skills to its reconstruction.

More conventional pro bono work can offer some or all of the same satisfaction: visibility to the client and in the broader community, personal contact with the client, direct involvement in the community on the pressing issues of the day, a broad scope for advice, and a grateful client.

Representation of poor individuals contrasts with handling mega-projects in two important ways. Mega-projects tend to be staffed with multiple tiers of lawyers, reducing the opportunity of the junior lawyers to work personally with clients. And the consequence of success or failure for the client is likely to be a marginal increase or decrease in client profitability rather than triumph or catastrophe.

Pro bono representation can bring lawyers face-to-face with their clients, often presenting sharp contrasts. One lawyer who frequently handles pro bono projects such as social security appeals and wills for indigent elderly individuals often must visit them in their apartments. This humanizes his practice, which otherwise involves representing construction companies in litigation around the country. Working one-on-one with an indigent client facing a pressing legal problem, the lawyer becomes personally involved with the client and understands the immediate consequences of his professional efforts: deportation or not, receipt of disability benefits or not, and, often, jail or not. At the extreme, hundreds of lawyers from large firms have provided pro bono representation to inmates on death row. The constitutional issues posed by these cases are intellectually stimulating, some rising to the level of the Supreme Court, and recall the issues that lawyers debated in law school. Time and efficiency pressures are less than for most commercial work, allowing greater opportunity for reflection. The clients are enormously grateful for the representation, and judges regularly go out of their way to commend pro bono counsel for undertaking the work.

Pro bono representation of nonprofits often entails working directly with the board and chief executive to define and carry out a charitable mission. The chief executive may be a priest or a social worker or a school teacher. The poor themselves may serve on the board. The social needs the client serves are readily accessible to the imagination, and the lawyer directly addresses those needs, often seeing parts of the community that are foreign to large firms and institutional clients. Such a project can be an antidote to a series of similar projects for a large client that keeps the lawyer in his or her office, library, or conference room and is connected only indirectly to the public welfare.

Immediacy has other benefits. When a struggling pro bono client needs legal services, those services are not commodity services and the client does not see them as fungible. The terms of a nonprofit's lease can make a big difference to the nonprofit's future. Is the lease renewable? How will the rent escalate? Does the nonprofit have a right to sublease? The client is likely to have little experience with these issues and to value highly the lawyer's advice, which can have a material effect on the ability of a financially precarious client to serve the poor.

The pro bono client usually needs and wants all the strategic thinking even an experienced lawyer can muster. This scope can afford a contrast to the narrow, specialized roles many lawyers are asked to fill by corporate clients. Lawyers engaged in forming community banks, for example, are using their transactional skills to participate in a major initiative to infuse capital into the inner city.[14] The lawyer may propose a creative financing technique to rehabilitate the nonprofit's office building or a strategic alliance with another nonprofit to reduce costs or enhance program effectiveness. A good idea can quickly become the basis for action, upon which the individual or nonprofit client may rise or fall.

Nonprofits face day-to-day issues as well, upon which junior lawyers can test their mettle. How should the client borrow, protect, and invest funds? What safeguards should be set up to avoid self-dealing? What are the fiduciary duties of the board members, and how should the board relate to the staff? What political or lobbying contributions are legal or appropriate? The lawyer's experience, and the experience available from colleagues, on mixed issues of law and business judgment can spell the difference between success and failure. For young lawyers accustomed to having filters block out the light of their ideas, this can be at once frightening and energizing.

One of my law firm's pro bono clients is a nonprofit known as Ashoka: Innovators for the Public. Ashoka supports 350 or so local public policy entrepreneurs in developing countries, usually by providing three-year stipends that allow the fellows to pursue their programs in education, low-cost housing, women's economic development, and other fields. When Ashoka needs legal or strategic advice, the call is urgent: a donor wants to form a joint venture to support environmental fellows in Latin America. How should it be funded and how can Ashoka ensure program quality? Quasi-governmental matching funds are available. Can Ashoka protect its independence? A large gift is offered. How will it affect Ashoka's status as a public charity? There is a short-term cash flow problem. What can be pledged for a bank loan? These are sophisticated questions on which this pro bono client needs prompt legal analysis and wise counsel. There are no beauty contests, no fee negotiations, no limits on the role of outside counsel, and, always, an enormously grateful client. Most important is the connection to the work of the fellows worldwide and the opportunity to discuss with many of them their visions for their countries.

Lawyer morale benefits from pro bono work in other ways as well. Lawyers talk to their nonlawyer friends and family disproportionately about direct public service and pro bono work. That work is easier to explain and discuss than the trust indentures, registration statements, and multidistrict litigation that are the ordinary stuff of a corporate law practice. Pro bono work often deals overtly with public policy issues, such as homelessness, or with hands-on situations, such as eviction. The value questions are more explicit, less clouded by process and intermediaries. "Shelf registration" of corporate securities may ultimately benefit our society by reducing the cost of capital. So, too, may the prosecution or defense of product liability cases ultimately result in higher quality or lower cost goods for the consumer. Yet these conclusions are neither accessible nor interesting to most of a lawyer's friends, and the judgment of friends and family about a lawyer's work very much affects the lawyer's morale.

Public service need not be selfless or self-effacing to raise morale. Indeed, one of its attractions can be that the faceless lawyer develops some notoriety, opening new options in building a law practice or embarking on other careers. Renewed ambition can add a new dimension to a career gone flat.

Direct public service and pro bono work also have in common that they offer a lawyer another point of reference for valuing and validating his or her professional and personal worth. Compensation and promotion decisions can then be seen for what they are: the law firm's view of the lawyer's contribution to its profitability, not a judgment on the lawyer's contribution to society.

No panacea, public service can be a promising part of a firm's, and a lawyer's, strategy for infusing professional life with more immediacy, reducing the paradoxical isolation many lawyers find in large firm practice. It remains to press law firms for greater flexibility to encourage and accommodate these opportunities.

Notes

1. For an account that argues that differences in culture or house norms of firms play a dominant role in the way a lawyer practices, see Michael J. Kelly, *Lives of Lawyers: Journeys in the Organizations of Practice* (University of Michigan Press, 1994).
2. "These [large corporate] firms are elite institutions. They attract the best law school graduates, have the most powerful clients, and possess the greatest clout within the profession. They also make the most money." Anthony T. Kronman, *The Lost Lawyer: Failing Ideals of the Legal Profession* (Harvard University Press, 1993), p. 272.
3. Steven Brill, "Short-Term Pain, Long-Term Gain," *American Lawyer*, vol. 13, no. 1 (January/February 1991), p. 5. Eleven of twelve major law firms surveyed showed declines in profits per partner in 1990. In 1992 aggregate revenue of the top one hundred

firms was only up 3 percent (in comparison with 9 percent in 1990, and 17 percent in 1989). Robert Safian, "Bottoming Out," *American Lawyer*, vol. 14, no. 6 (July/August 1992), p. 9. Revenue per lawyer rose only 3 percent in 1990, dropped by 0.3 percent in 1991, and just barely started to recover in 1992, rising 3 percent. Likewise, profits per partner showed similar trends, dropping 2 percent in 1990 and 6 percent in 1991, and in 1992 rising only 1.5 percent. "Bouncing Back: Revenue Per Lawyer Rebounds" and "Profits Per Partner Pick Up—But Barely," *American Lawyer*, vol. 15, no. 6 (July/August 1993), pp. 31, 45.

4. Randall Samborn, "Rudnick and Wolfe Partners 'De-Equitized'," *National Law Journal*, November 20, 1989, p. 2. "New York firms [felt] the pinch first, and even the most prominent firms [had] layoffs. Cahill Gordon & Reindel, whose representation of Drexel Burnham at one time accounted for roughly 25% of its revenue, [had] to terminate 30 associate lawyers in the wake of Drexel's collapse and the broad decline in merger and acquisition work." Ellen Joan Pollock, "Slowdown Hits Legal Profession After '80s Boom," *The Wall Street Journal*, November 1, 1990, p. B1.

5. William C. Cobb, "The Shift to the New Competitive Model and the Impact on Management Issues," *Law Practice Management*, vol. 19, no. 4 (May/June 1993), p. 32.

6. "On January 28, when the 250-attorney Shea & Gould announced its dissolution, it became the second largest New York firm to close its doors, topped only by the 1988 bankruptcy of 700-lawyer Finley, Kumble, Wagner, Heine, Underberg, Manley, Myerson & Casey." "Shea & Gould: Hither & Yon," *New York Law Journal*, April 1, 1994, p. 2.

7. At Winston & Strawn on March 23, 1992, "Almost 20 partners had visits that day from pairs of their fellow partners who carried letters signed by [the] managing partner. . . . asking each of the partners to 'relocate to a position of alternative professional responsibility outside the firm.'" Emily Barker, "Winston & Strawn Gets Ruthless," *American Lawyer*, vol. 15, no. 5 (June 1993), p. 70. Sharon Walsh, "Key Lawyers' Departure Hits Washington, Perito: Law Firm Asks Partners to Help on Expenses," *Washington Post*, March 21, 1991, p. B1.

8. "Thirty years ago most corporate law firms had a relatively stable set of clients and represented them in matters both ordinary and exceptional. Today, their clientele tends to be more fluid and relations with individual clients less continuous—restricted, for the most part, to extraordinary events that demand a form of specialized legal knowledge that even very large companies often find it uneconomical to develop their own." Kronman, *The Lost Lawyer*, p. 277.

9. "The social questions of our time simply do not come up frequently in large-firm practice." Robert L. Nelson, "Ideology, Practice, and Professional Autonomy: Social Values and Client Relationships in the Large Law Firm," *Stanford Law Review*, vol. 37, no. 2 (January 1985), pp. 503–64.

10. 1991 survey findings showed that "lawyers are working more now than they did in 1984—50% of all lawyers in private practice now work 2,400 hours a year or more and 45% bill 1,920 hours a year or more. . . . 55% of male lawyers and 61% of female lawyers reported that they do not have enough time for themselves." *The Emerging Crisis in the Quality of Lawyers' Health and Lives—Its Impact on Law Firms and Client Services*, report prepared by the American Bar Association for national conference "At the Breaking Point" (Airlie, Virginia: Airlie House), April 5–6, 1991.

11. Powell also provided pro bono services to the Virginia Home for Incurables, the Retreat for the Sick Hospital, and the Red Cross. John C. Jeffries, Jr., *Justice Lewis F. Powell, Jr.* (New York: Charles Scribner's Sons, 1994), p. 123. Other examples abound of lawyers whose commercial practices were enhanced by their public, charitable, and pro bono activities. Victoria Slind-Flor, "Preston Gates & Ellis: Firm Has a History of Public Service," *National Law Journal*, July 25, 1994, p. A23; Sol M. Linowitz and Martin

Mayer, *The Betrayed Profession: Lawyering at the End of the Twentieth Century* (New York: Charles Scribner's Sons, 1994), pp. 59–60.

12. Lisa Brennan, "Philadelphia Lawyers Help Clinton Transition," *The Legal Intelligencer,* March 3, 1993, p. 1.

13. Warren Christopher, then chairman of Los Angeles's O'Melveny & Meyers, recruited more than forty lawyers, many of them prominent partners in the city's major firms, to investigate the city's police department. D.M. Osborne, "All Eyes on Los Angeles's Christopher Commission," *American Lawyer,* vol. 13, no. 5 (June 1991), p. 14.

14. Pedro E. Ponce, "Non-Litigators Go *Pro Bono:* Volunteer Hours Dip as Focus Shifts, Lengthy Projects End," *Legal Times,* July 18, 1994, pp. S43–S44. The president of one community bank commended "banking lawyers who . . . use their own skills and highly refined legal talent in that field in a *pro bono* way which is not often available."

5

Community Service Makes Better Lawyers

Donald W. Hoagland

The bar associations and other sincere sources of emphasis on the lawyer's ethical obligation to serve poor people are missing a crucial point. There is a powerful weapon available to them that they are not using. Not only is the weapon useful for motivating lawyers to engage in more pro bono activity, but it should serve, in doing so, to blunt the sharp and widespread criticism of lawyers as a guild that has lost its sense of professional responsibility and is focused solely on its own financial interests.

That weapon is the ability to persuade law firms that lawyers whose customary work is in the general commercial and business context will actually improve in that work as they do free legal work for poor people. If this proposition is persuasively circulated, more business lawyers and, indeed, lawyers of many specialties, may increase their pro bono legal work. The need for that kind of work is very large.[1] Meeting a significantly larger portion of it on a pro bono basis will help materially in meeting the legitimate needs of poor people for legal services.

However far you may choose to carry your analysis of the effects of the current need for legal services, there is little disagreement with the idea that it is in the public interest for the poor to have better access to

* This chapter was produced, in part, as a project of the community service subcommittee of the Colorado Bar Association. Its participating members were Jonathan Asher, A. Edgar Benton, Jane Gill, Edward Kahn, Diane King, and Joseph Meyer III.

legal services. The question I shall focus on now is whether it can be shown persuasively that it is in a law firm's own interest to encourage pro bono work by its own lawyers in order to improve their professional abilities.

As Barrington D. Parker, Jr., has put it, the challenge of trying to support this conclusion is considerable. "Why during periods of relative economic uncertainty and professional insecurity a large proportion of the bar would commit to, in effect, spending significant amounts of time and money on indigent clients is a question that affords no easy answers." [2] But I will try, in this chapter, to add to the strong reasons already advanced in other chapters. What follows is written against a background of some forty-five years in and around the legal system, supported and enriched by extensive discussions with those in a position to offer considered judgments about the question before us.

Method of Inquiry

To pursue this inquiry, I undertook qualitative research consisting of three categories of research people: 1) lawyers of all ages who had done pro bono work, 2) lawyers who had supervised or evaluated lawyers who had (and had not) done pro bono work, and 3) executives of substantial private and public entities who had occasion to hire or supervise lawyers from time to time for assignments that were not of a limited and technical character.[3]

In interviewing for this purpose, it was important to have some consistency in the use of the term "community legal service," or "pro bono" services; the two terms are used interchangeably. For our purposes, these terms refer to free legal services for low-income people or for organizations formed to provide services to these people who are unable to pay for legal services. This latter category would include formation of and operating advice for nonprofit, tax-exempt organizations such as community health clinics or legal services units, but would not include service on the boards of directors of major art museums, universities, business-based service clubs, or other organizations that tend to provide prestige and business contacts to participating lawyers.

Admittedly, there are forms of service other than providing legal services that could have at least some, if not all, of the same desired effects on a lawyer's abilities. Tutoring young children, teaching literacy, and providing meals or other services to the homebound and disabled can also have the desired effect, but for practical reasons they are beyond the scope of this particular inquiry.

Lawyers and Community Legal Service

Community legal services are now being provided in a wide range of organizational structures. Interviews with lawyers who have participated substantially in these programs have yielded a number of comments.

One interesting group is the Colorado "Lend-A-Lawyer" program. This program, which now exists in similar form in other states, was developed in Colorado by a creative bar association president named Chris Brauchli. It involved sending lawyers to small rural towns for four months each to provide free legal services to people who could not afford to hire a lawyer, while their firm continued to pay their regular salaries. Of the five participants I interviewed, all had been outstanding law students.[4] They had been doing responsible work on commercial transactions or disputes, operating at the second or third tier of responsibility and authority. In the Lend-A-Lawyer program, however, they had to make all the decisions, take the lead, and operate independently. The sheltering wing of a large, well-staffed, and protective support system was gone. They had been sitting in handsome offices on the upper floors of their city's tallest office building, looking out at sweeping views of the plains and the Rockies. Now they were in windowless offices with no law books, in the basements of cottage-level office buildings in towns of less than 10,000 inhabitants and with a regional bar of twelve lawyers.

The participants had access to mentors, but rarely had time for more than a passing word with them. This did wonders for their confidence and their maturity, as well as for their otherwise unserved clients. Beyond that, and more important, it alerted them to the critical human elements of disagreements and negotiations—a sensitivity that became a permanent ingredient in their professional skills. Their supervisors recognized the acceleration of their professional maturity when they came back.

When asked, the individuals repeatedly confirmed that the experience had added materially to their professional abilities. As younger, though not inexperienced, lawyers, they found new strengths of several kinds. Here are some samples of their comments:

> To learn what it means to be an advocate and a counselor, for lawyers often forget they are both, is to me perhaps the most invaluable lesson

to be learned from the program. The impact which the local community had on me was also tremendous and was in no small part responsible for the growth achieved in my professional development. It was primarily an understanding that circumstances and factors seemingly beyond a person's control and comprehension can conspire and result in otherwise good and decent people finding themselves in embarrassing and precarious predicaments.

—Jim Puga

[About lawyers who have not done community legal service work:] They don't see the human aspect of the major business deals their clients face.

—Jim Puga

This experience gave me much more confidence that I could handle difficult legal work. It also gave me a greater sense of worth.

—Diane King

Law schools give you the impression that there is a formula—that you apply the formulas to cases and get answers. In real life the facts have a lot more to do with the result than those formulas. I am no longer easily intimidated. In [the firm] my confidence level went down. In Rocky Ford I found out I really *was* a lawyer. You don't have time to think, you just *do it.*

—Lori Bauer Apodaca

The experience was invaluable. You develop instinctive and innate skills in understanding legal theory and how to handle a case. You find out what works in negotiated settlements. . . . Most important one: the intangibles—the level of confidence. . . . You become more understanding of people.

—Joe Rogers

As a lawyer who often represents corporations in employment disputes, the opportunity to represent individuals gave me a greater understanding of the complexities of individual decisionmaking and a greater appreciation for how individual employees respond in settlement negotiations, deposition, and trial. In turn, this has improved my preparations for each.

—Chris Leh

It put a human face on legal problems and policy issues. These experiences have had a major impact on my practice now, because in working with trickier witnesses I could relate to them before a jury and that made their testimony more valuable. . . . you begin to look at the human dimensions of the people you deal with . . . women tend to do that but it is trained out of us in large firms.

—Diane King

It is significant that of these five early stage Lend-a-Lawyer participants, only one is still with a large firm. The reasons for this are predictably different in each case and only partly discoverable. It is impossible to determine which ones left their firm out of a desire to be more active in pursuit of the legitimate interests of poor people—as at least one did— and which ones left for other reasons. Although all were strengthened by their experience, their former firm is only receiving the benefit in one instance.

Coupled with those facts, we are obligated to look at the current patterns in the Lend-a-Lawyer program. It has given up trying to recruit lawyers from the largest Colorado firms and is successfully offering $500 per month, with free office space and a collaborative arrangement, to lawyers who are willing to work in a legal services program. This is making legal services more accessible to people who might not otherwise have been able to obtain them. That is a plus, of course. But the large firms are missing the opportunity to provide their younger lawyers with this maturing and sensitizing experience that some of them need to become the kind of broad-gauged counselors that they could become—but may not if they stay in their narrow career path. Of course, many will get there anyway, but some will not, and their shortfall could be avoided by some such experience.

The individuals themselves face the difficult culture shift from the career and public service optimism of the 1960s to the blend of cynicism, commercialism, and time stress that weighs on younger lawyers today. The need to give family life a fair share of young lawyers' time is much more clearly recognized today, but the probability that both spouses are trained and employed makes the time-management pressure even more difficult. We cannot advocate that family time be reduced to allow for community service. The only acceptable resolution is to manage time more efficiently, to be more skeptical about the amount of permissible "leisure" time, and to seek a recognition by law firms that it is in their interest to accommodate community service hours at a reasonable level.

Firms that expect less than 2,000 hours of chargeable time should not have to lower those numbers. Firms that expect 2,500 to 3,000 hours of chargeable time should take a hard look at their priorities.

An experienced lawyer in both commercial and community service practice and a senior partner in the Denver office of Faegre & Benson, Bruce Sattler, puts it this way:

> Community legal service experience gives a lawyer experience in communicating with low income clients, service providers, uncooperative and cooperative bureaucrats, community groups and other diverse audiences. This experience enables the lawyer (when working in a large firm) to communicate more effectively with other audiences and enhances the lawyer's ability to select appropriate themes for jury trials, and participate in multi-party disputes, legislative efforts, consensus building and other activities. Also, with community legal service experience, lawyers know they can work their way through problems with difficult clients, thus they are more confident when they deal directly with corporate clients. They understand the client is truly who matters, not the partner." [5]

Harold R. Tyler, Jr., now a partner in the well-known New York firm of Patterson, Belknap, Webb & Tyler, is also on record on this point. This fine former federal judge and recidivist public servant, who has responded frequently to emergency calls for demanding public interest legal services, reported that people had said to him that "you don't need to do this stuff anymore." He then said, "It's not a matter of my need. I owe something. I owe something to this city and this country. And I get so much out of this. *It has made me a better lawyer.*" [6]

This is not exactly a new thought—perhaps it is more an overlooked one. U.S. Senior Circuit Judge Frank M. Coffin has quoted the revered Supreme Court Justice Louis D. Brandeis as saying, "no hermit can be a great lawyer, least of all a commercial lawyer. When from a knowledge of the law, you pass to its application, the needs of a full knowledge of men and of their affairs becomes even more apparent." [7] Justice Brandeis was way ahead of his time in this respect. He tied the problem of lawyers' narrowing their focus to the growth of urban centers: "When communities were small, every lawyer was apt to be a general practitioner, so that in addition to his legal education, his diversified practice and clientele were giving him an economic and social education." [8] If this is a correct thought, as I believe it is, then it is time to reassert it and *act* on it. Many prominent lawyers agree with this.

For example, Assistant U.S. Attorney General for Civil Rights Deval Patrick was quoted as follows:

> As I look back and think about people I have interviewed for positions at my firm, those with legal aid experience or its equivalent in clinical programs bring a different perspective and added strength. They have experience with the gritty business of solving people's problems. I think what separates great lawyers from good lawyers is not primarily academic training. Of course, you have to be fluent in the law and procedure, and you have to communicate effectively. But the most intractable legal problems are rarely solved without careful, patient listening and the innovation that comes from varied experiences. Those are the skills that you develop at the [Legal Aid] Bureau." [9]

A leading corporate lawyer in Denver, A. Edgar Benton, had these observations in response to my questions:

> One of the criticisms that clients have of corporate law practice is that it takes too much lawyering and therefore too much time and money to get things done. Clients are very interested in getting a good result for less investment. It seems to me that when a young lawyer is representing poor people there is a high premium on making judgments, presumably competent judgments, as soon as possible. There is neither the time nor the resources to exhaust the subject at hand to the nth degree. So, I think that ought to put a focus on good analytical judgment, and efficient follow through on the judgment made with a usable and competent result. Such skills developed in the diversity of legal representation of the poor ought to be directly transferable to corporate law with enhanced effectiveness for the clients being served.
>
> And beyond that is the question of extending one's relationships to the broader community. . . . The ability of the young lawyer to operate as a person connected with the community should, I think, diminish the fatigue and maybe the disillusionment which is so common in the profession among young lawyers, and not just young lawyers but lawyers generally. It should provide a much larger stage upon which lawyering and matters relating to lawyering can take place, and thus provide some additional margin for the lawyer to function, not just as a legal technician, but as a human being connected with significant numbers of other human beings. [10]

Susan Kohlmann is the partner who supervises the pro bono activities of Winthrop, Stimson, Putnam & Roberts in New York. She has been involved in that work since she started with the firm in 1981. Having observed years of participation in community service legal work by large firm lawyers, she has concluded that encouraging this kind of work is really in the firm's interest, not just so litigators will get more frontline experience more quickly, but also so any lawyer will learn how to define legal problems in a way that is understandable to clients. She has seen corporate lawyers volunteer to provide simple wills and guardianship assistance to indigent AIDS patients and come out of their experience (especially the younger ones) with a clearer sense of what client responsibilities really are at a one-to-one, personal level.[11]

One of the Colorado district's most senior federal judges, Judge Richard Matsch, has a range of experience that gives him an unusually relevant basis for developing an opinion on this issue. Before coming to the federal bench, he had served substantial periods of time as a practicing lawyer in the offices of the U.S. Attorney, the Denver City Attorney, and the strong private law firm of Holme, Roberts & Owen. He thus has had the opportunity to observe the performances of lawyers representing the poorest of the poor and the most corporate of the corporate. He has watched, supervised, or collaborated with lawyers from green to grizzled, and from poised to puzzled. When asked whether community service makes better lawyers or makes good lawyers sloppy, he said this:

Anything that humanizes lawyers improves their performance. I've seen it in my own experience. The closer you are to working with the human problems, the more realistic the problem becomes. Working with people at all levels of society increases not only your dedication, but also your skills. Nobody is born a good lawyer—it is a learned skill and a learned art. Too many people in large mills see problems legally in the abstract, not recognizing the human dimension which has a lot to do with finding the best course of action. This is not just applicable to trial practice—it also applies to transaction work. Students become really enthusiastic about cases when you open up the people side. Keep in mind also that judges are human too. Lawyers should recognize the human level at which they address decision-making.[12]

Edwin Kahn is a Rocky Mountain–area lawyer best known for sustaining a practice that blends representation of strong business organizations with prominent representation of disadvantaged individuals and groups in his community. He has found that: "Becoming familiar with the emotional content of such work as pro bono divorce cases has made me a better lawyer in dealing with employment termination, partnership break-ups, and similar situations with emotional overtones. In general, I'm sure pro bono work has improved my ability to deal with the emotional content of commercial disputes and negotiations." [13]

James R. McCotter, associate general counsel of the El Paso Natural Gas Company, adds: "My experience and observations have been that the representation of pro bono clients often brings out the best skills in a lawyer because, without any financial motivation, he or she really becomes identified with the client's position and is interested in bringing the matter to a successful conclusion as efficiently as possible. If this balance between 'results' and time, with a good dose of enthusiasm for the client's cause, can be achieved for paying clients as well, I believe that in many instances those clients will be better served." [14]

Granfield Research

An interesting and related line of research has been pursued for the past eight years by Professor Robert Granfield of the University of Denver Department of Sociology. He set about interviewing students at Harvard Law School and Northeastern Law School to investigate the effect of their law school experience on their interest in public service and public policy. The first stage of this work resulted in a book that was based on interviews with students upon entering and then upon completing law school.[15] Although it contains some interesting comparative observations about the two law schools, the author found it necessary to limit the book's analysis of student evolution to forty Harvard students.

Since writing that book, Dr. Granfield has returned to that same group of students to inquire about their careers and their interests now that they have been out of law school for an average of about five years. Although Dr. Granfield did not initially focus on the thesis of this chapter, his work offered a potentially fertile resource for testing its thesis, and Dr. Granfield agreed that it would be useful from his standpoint also. This offered a promising opportunity to find out whether they had provided pro bono services after law school, and how they, their employers, and their clients regarded this aspect of the practice.

Predictably, their answers were not uniform. But certain themes came through clearly: many were involved in community service, but few had been encouraged to do so. More than half of the young attorneys who participated in follow-up interviews reported having engaged in some pro bono activity since graduating from Harvard Law School. Most of the thirty young lawyers employed in private firms reported some pro bono activity, while none of the attorneys employed in public interest or government settings participated in pro bono. Respondents who reported having done no pro bono work claimed that either their organization did not encourage it, or that they simply had no additional time for it. Only nine respondents indicated that they received any encouragement or support for pro bono work, and only three of these nine worked in settings with in-house pro bono programs.[16]

Clinical education has been receiving much more attention from law schools in recent years. Daniel Greenberg, director of clinical programs at Harvard Law School, supplied these comments:

A major purpose of the practice of law is to solve problems working with the people who have the problems. Clinical programs teach a student to problem-solve with real clients with all the texture inherent in our lives. This is especially important because the traditional curriculum is more theoretical, more abstract, with facts laid out in unidimensional form.

In reality, clients rarely present themselves with a canned set of facts. Indeed, even if they say they have a certain kind of problem, a good lawyer will see beyond that. In the poverty-law context of clinical education, for example, an elderly client with an eviction notice can rarely focus past the housing problem. We teach students, however, to see that eligibility for Social Security, disability or other government benefits may obviate the problem.

. . . It is rare that new lawyers are systematically trained to envision the full breadth of a problem. They are increasingly segmented into narrow, arcane areas of law. . . . Lawyers who go into practice without having had this experience in law school, can obtain some of its benefits by engaging in pro bono practice during their legal careers. They should be sure to handle their first cases under the guidance of specialists in the area, in order to replicate the instruction which is inherent in clinical education.[17]

How Can Pro Bono Work Improve Lawyers' Abilities?

These interviews suggest that providing community legal services can make better lawyers for several reasons:

—By dealing with a broader cross-section of people in the community, the lawyer becomes more alert to the attitudes and values of the entire community. This improves the lawyer's ability to manage a team effort, select a jury, interrogate a witness, negotiate a transaction, or interview a prospective client or colleague.

—It improves a lawyer's understanding of other people and sensitivity to their needs.

—The resultant broadening of perspective will better prepare a lawyer to perceive and analyze the broadest potential consequences of a possible course of action; predict the probable public reaction to a proposed course of action; explain to a client the full policy and personal implications of the client's position and possible courses of action; and discharge a lawyer's professional responsibilities not only to the client but as an officer of the court.

—Younger lawyers will mature more rapidly and be able to take on more responsibility than they would in the structured setting of most law firms.

—Many aspects of the law have developed, and continue to be developed, out of generations of the judicial system's probing into the essentials of desirable behavior. There is a continuing risk in legal analysis that yesterday's conceptual restatement of the conclusion to be reached has become inappropriate because of changes in our lives that were not present when the old concept was formulated. Community service by lawyers gives them a better grasp of the currently operative policy elements in that balancing process and gives them a better basis for predicting what courts will do. This is what lawyers are really doing whenever they purport to say what the law "is."

Litigation has something of a life of its own in this connection. It is difficult for talented young lawyers to get the level of litigation experience they want and need in large law firms. Some do get it, but many do not. The classic and most prestigious avenue for gaining this kind of experience in the northeast is the office of the U.S. Attorney for the Southern District of New York. The pattern is equally effective in district attorneys' offices all over the country, and that kind of experience has proven its value repeatedly. When supplemented by community service, it can make a powerful combination. As Neil Peck, a veteran of both of these patterns of experience now practicing in Denver, puts it: "In-house lawyers like to pick such people." [18]

For transaction lawyers, however, there is no such established pattern. Only community legal services offers a comparable independence, responsibility, and exposure to the broad realities of life outside the comfortable but limiting corporate practice environment. Those responsible for the development of transaction lawyers would do well to consider it seriously. [19]

As Barrington D. Parker, Jr., also pointed out to us, "A progressively greater proportion of the time and professional attention of more and more lawyers is devoted to discrete specialties or subspecialties. The consequence is a narrowing of the range of matters to which a lawyer is expected to turn."

How Can Pro Bono Work Improve Law Firm Performance?

In the past ten years or so, law firms that deal primarily with the problems of business have put increasing pressure on their lawyers to record more billable hours. They also have become more commercially oriented in their value systems, marketing activities, compensation techniques, and entire professional culture. Among the perils of these developments are disincentives to community service and an overshadowing of humanistic concerns. These developments contribute to the disaffection of many talented young lawyers. It seems likely that, as a result, the quality of professional performance suffers. Although the responses to our interviews are anecdotal and not statistically compiled, they do suggest certain advantages pro bono work could present not only to the lawyers involved, but also to law firms, the profession, and the public interest. For example:

—Business-oriented law firms would find their experienced lawyers more widely sought after and relied on in decisionmaking involving crucial blends of business and human considerations and the evolution of public policy; for example, business decisions in sensitive areas such as plant construction and relocation, benefit plan negotiations, and environmental disputes.

—Lawyers and law firms would more effectively meet the public interest in providing greater access to legal services for deserving individuals and entities that cannot afford those services.

—Law firms would find that their younger lawyers would become more productive, more skillful negotiators, more sensitive interrogators, and more creative problem-solvers.

—Younger lawyers would see that the profession offers a broader way of life than the endless office-bound replication of bloodless complex documents.

—A stronger sense of professionalism would develop throughout the lawyer group (whatever its size), and its members would be more stable, loyal, proud, and committed to their colleagues and their profession.

—With a broader knowledge of the needs and expectations of the entire community, lawyers would be active participants in efforts to make the legal system more accessible and affordable to all. This knowledge would significantly increase the likelihood that the changes they suggest would attract broad-based support, rather than seeming to be an adversarial contest among narrow special interest groups. This in turn would give the public more reason to respect and trust the legal system and its professionals.

Business Community Recognition

At least some in the business community may be way ahead of the legal profession in recognizing the contribution that community service makes to a lawyer's abilities. This surfaced when the Clinton administration was launching a new community service program known as "AmeriCorps." Designed to enlist educated young people in a domestic peace corps, the corps provides mentors, organizers, and motivators to work with youngsters who might otherwise become dropouts, hostile gang members, or otherwise destructive and to engage them in useful community service activities. Corps members would be offered the added inducement of financial help for further education.

The first rally to launch this ambitious program was held on the Harvard campus in May 10, 1994. One of the speakers was Jeffrey Swartz, the vigorous young chief operating officer of Timberland, an equally vigorous outdoor clothing and equipment manufacturer. As part of his rapid-fire call to constructive arms, he said essentially this: When he is interviewing candidates for jobs in his company, he wants to hear their record of community service, because it gives them special skills he wants to see in his people. His response regarding lawyers and community service was: "We seek people who have the capacity and willingness to bring a fierce sense of ownership and accountability to everything they do. The best employees, business partners, the best people are the ones who have been struck by the realization that relying upon someone else to make it happen is a half truth—they know that their active contribution is always required. . . . When we find those people we usually find community service in their background." [20]

According to a recent newspaper article, United Parcel Service is encouraging its employees to tackle social issues and has an extensive training program for this purpose. Its program may play a key role in its low employee turnover rate. Their stated hope is *that this will translate into better management.* [21]

The business sector is now the fastest-growing provider of volunteers. According to a December 1993 article in *Hemispheres* magazine, "Business people say that charity and business make a natural marriage. Not only does volunteering time to a good cause make people happier, *it also makes them better at their jobs.*" [22]

Samuel Gary, one of the Rocky Mountain region's most energetic and successful oil finders in the high-activity period of the 1970s and early 1980s, has said: "Many people don't realize how important it is—that sensitivity to the human element sharpens a person's professional capacity. . . . There is an insulation that comes from dealing almost exclusively with other lawyers or with successful business people, and . . . lawyers insulated in that way can really miss the key elements in a problem." [23]

This attitude has, in fact, leaked over to the selection of lawyers by major businesses facing tough legal challenges; for example, major industrial companies that face potentially multibillion-dollar liability charges for environmental damage and risk caused by various forms of pollution. One Rocky Mountain area megacompany faced with this kind of liability looked widely for the best legal representation. It knew there were available lawyers worldwide with overwhelming prestige, authority, and presence. It knew there were available lawyers with dramatic styles that were sure to capture the attention of the public and the jury. It also knew there were available lawyers with graduate degrees in chemistry and geology that would intimidate any opposing expert witnesses and insulate his own from contrary examination.

But whom did this company select? It chose a prestigious all-purpose local business lawyer who had immersed himself in delicate and tricky community issues. He had not only counseled boards of directors of private-sector clients, but also, as a nonpaid elected official, had faced crowds of angry citizens at public meetings who were passionate about both sides of a sensitive, critical social policy issue: segregation in the public schools. The company knew that it needed a competent lawyer, but it also knew that it needed someone who had been out on the street, out of the office, who had dealt with an aroused public, and who was able to make constructive progress toward mutually acceptable solutions in that kind of an unstable atmosphere. That is a skill an office-bound lawyer will not develop.

A different and equally dramatic example is found in connection with the negotiation of investment proposals in underdeveloped countries. As the economy of the United States slowly gropes toward the international awareness of all other industrialized nations, its lawyers are finding themselves more and more involved in transactions in strange legal environments. We are seeing the potentially desirable expansion of U.S. foreign business interests, including, but also going beyond, natural resource development in third world countries.

American lawyers who deal with these opportunities find themselves in a new form of dialogue. They are no longer working with opposing counsel who were trained in the same general conceptual and linguistic culture. They may be dealing more with government officials than with lawyers. Suddenly all conceptual fundamentals are open for reconsideration, and policy—not precedent and habit—is all that counts. It is the "haves" against the "have-nots," and any proposals that do not accommodate this underlying framework will fail. How will counsel develop an adequate sensitivity to the needs and reactions of an impoverished nation if they have never worked outside their sheltered, glossy environments? How will they be able to anticipate the impact of indemnity and compensation provisions that they assume to be common practice boilerplate, when they do not accurately anticipate the way they will sound to the leaders of people who do not know where their next meal will come from?

It is worth reflecting on this question in the context of a startling article by Robert Kaplan in the February 1994 issue of *Atlantic Monthly*. In it he wrote: "Think of a stretch limo in the potholed streets of New York City, where homeless beggars live. Inside the limo are the air-conditioned post-industrial regions of North America, Europe, the emerging Pacific Rim, and a few other isolated places, with their trade summitry and computer information highways. Outside is the rest of mankind, going in a completely different direction." [24]

How should American lawyers prepare themselves to cope with that kind of a world? Should they not become involved in these underserved portions of our own communities that contain most of the frustrating forces of poverty, environmental degradation, family violence, undereducation, and individual desperation that exist in the third world? These are the things that must be dealt with if any kind of common purposes can be identified and constructively pursued by the legal profession, either in a third world country or right here in our own backyards.

Are Codes of Ethics a Barrier to Community Legal Service?

Some lawyers and law firms refuse to take many pro bono assignments because they say they are ethically obliged to decline matters they are not competent to handle. Is this a weak excuse from lawyers who do not want to do the work anyway, or is it a realistic appraisal of their qualifications and of the codes of ethics?

The state of Colorado adopted its current code to be effective January 1, 1993, under the title "Rules of Professional Conduct." The first rule (identical to the ABA Model Rule) deals with this issue:

Rule 1.1 Competence
A lawyer shall provide competent representation to a client. Competent representation requires the legal knowledge, skill, thoroughness and preparation reasonably necessary for the representation.

The explanatory comment under this rule warns lawyers not to "accept employment in any area of the law in which the lawyer is not qualified." Many lawyers may, defensively, stop right there. But it goes on to say, however, that "a lawyer may accept such employment if in good faith the lawyer expects to become qualified through study and investigation, as long as such preparation would not result in unreasonable delay or expense to clients." It also states that a "lawyer may accept representation where the requisite level of competence can be achieved by reasonable preparation. This applies as well to a lawyer who is appointed counsel for an unrepresented person."

There seems to be considerable room in these comments to allow—if not encourage—a lawyer to take on a pro bono case even if he or she has never handled such a matter before, so long as the subject is one the lawyer can come to grips with in a reasonable length of time. Corporate lawyers contemplating divorce and adoption cases are good and common examples. When you consider that in these civil matters little or no income tax or financial complexity will be involved, lawyers should be expected to make the extra effort to become moderately competent to represent people who might otherwise have no lawyer at all.

Jonathan Asher, the highly respected executive director of the Legal Aid Society of metropolitan Denver, reminds us that although unfamiliarity with the law involved is a frequent excuse from lawyers who refuse a pro bono referral, we should consider whether lawyers in moderate to large law firms would stretch themselves to handle new subject matter for existing clients—or for new clients who seem capable of paying for the work.[25]

For example: twenty or thirty years ago, bankruptcy law and international law were unknown to most Denver law firms, but Asher points out that when their clients became involved in those fields in the rocky times of the 1980s, or as international business grew, they found it possible to do the necessary homework and serve their clients in those fields. Consider also the practice of law in small towns, and in any city decades ago when ten or twelve was a large law firm. Did those lawyers hesitate to move into new subject matter? Of course not. They relied on their fundamental capacity to brief themselves quickly and to find the crucial issues in a complex situation without necessarily becoming fluent with all of the details at the outset. Crossing the line between civil and criminal matters raises more demanding obstacles, but moving into strange areas of civil matters should not—in most of the matters that come up in representing the poor—stop a careful lawyer from offering useful and responsible pro bono services.

Clearly a law firm under financial pressure will worry about malpractice claims and the diversion of hours from billable to nonbillable time. These concerns will discourage lawyers from undertaking the time-consuming processes of counseling that so often are necessary for low-income clients. This could also become a habit in dealing with business clients, especially those who insist on fixed fee retainer arrangements or hard-content proof of the value of each billed hour. This may well be the place to consider what has been clearly established in medicine: that the frequency and severity of malpractice claims varies inversely with the amount of time the physician spends with the patient.[26]

It would be instructive at this point to look at the case load of a lawyer who takes pro bono whatever comes in the door. Here is an estimate from a few such lawyers in the Lend-A-Lawyer program:

Family law (including divorce, dependency, and neglect; child 40%
support collections or controversies)
Juvenile delinquency 20%
Mental health commitments 5%
Landlord and tenant issues 10%
Wills and advance directives 10%
Other (including guardian *ad litem* appointments, civil forfeiture, 15%
debtor-creditor controversies)

If the same estimate were made for the cases placed with pro bono volunteers in the Denver bar by the Legal Services Agency (through the Denver Bar Association's volunteer program), the numbers would be about the same, except that public benefits claims would be in the 15-percent range and court appointments in juvenile and mental health cases would be smaller.

Except for debtor-creditor and landlord-tenant disputes or transactions, almost none of this is run-of-the mill business law. Yet these subjects can be crucial in the lives of people affected by them. As with all legal subjects, each has its own universe of potential detail and complication, but the underlying issues and principles are not beyond the grasp of any serious lawyer willing to do some intense studying. Most important, the people involved will probably not get legal help any other way.

Physicians and hospitals are ethically and legally obliged to give some level of care to patients in an emergency condition, whether they can pay or not. Yet it is disturbing for a lawyer to compare the relative approaches of the legal and medical professions to the needs of the poor. Medical education routinely confronts its students with the stressful demands of poor patients in public hospitals. Clinical programs in law schools exist, but not uniformly and not with the intensity of medical internships and residencies. Access to health care, the goal of universal coverage of health insurance, and quality of care have become dominant public policy issues in the last four years. The quality of care offered by providers has been subjected to data-based statistical analysis and attempts to give the public useable comparisons of the relative quality of the care offered by different providers. Does the legal system offer comparable assurances to the illegally evicted tenant, the single mother unable to provide food and shelter without the defaulted support payments, or the abused child needing a restraining order to be protected from a violent family member? If we are going to apply all of the demanding tests of access, cost, and quality to the health care system, and the extent to which it serves the community's needs, why not make the same demands of the legal system?

Conclusion

The legal system is not providing affordable services of a predictable quality to a significant portion of our population—not just its poor people, but also small businesses and families of low to moderate income. Observers have estimated that as much as 85 percent of the legitimate legal needs of the poor go unmet. The professionals trained to provide all legal services have tended in recent decades to regard success as being included in a firm of high-earning lawyers that either exceeds or hopes to exceed fifty in number, and in many instances comprises several hundred lawyers branched into several cities.

Yet within the last ten years, these firms have been jolted in several ways. Their clients have become more critical and selective; their talented young recruits are increasingly unsure that the life they offer is satisfactory; their incomes have declined; talented females have left in large numbers; and they have become the butt of widespread public disrespect, dislike, and outright bashing. The perceived rapaciousness of many lawyers has made the term "legal tender" an oxymoron to many people. The legal system itself is losing the public's respect and confidence.

Judge Frank Coffin has suggested another way of testing the thesis that community service makes better lawyers: "Another test is to contemplate lawyers and firms acting on the assumption that pro bono service adds nothing to a lawyer's equipment. Such an assumption proceeds from a narrow view of linkage between a lawyer's capacity and the kind of law he practices. In other words, only information, learning, and experience dealing with a specialty are relevant." [27]

Such tunnel vision would not seem to either foster a sense of personal fulfillment or supply a basis for thinking of personal development. Such a professional viewpoint would seem to constrict the choices available to a young lawyer as he or she attains seniority. One cogent illustration is the basis for selection as a judicial appointment, used not only by bar association voting groups but also by senators' and governors' (and presidents') selection of officials and committees: purely technical proficiency, without broad exposure to and service on behalf of groups and individuals in need of pro bono efforts, or equivalent broadening experience, is likely to be a losing card.

In short, there seems to be no advantage and probably some disadvantage in conducting personal and firm business on a negative pro bono assumption. Perhaps, when we consider the question of making room for significant pro bono activity, we should ask not "Why?" but "Why not?" [28]

Fuller recognition that the involvement of business lawyers in community legal services will actually improve their general lawyering abilities is a realistic way to attacking these problems. This concept is not in fact limited to the legal profession, but it may currently be least understood and applied there. It is not excessively dramatic to say that a full appreciation of it in all elements of our society may well be necessary to achieve the kind of stability and fairness that we all want. Professionalism among lawyers can properly be asked to lead us in that direction, and to be active about it.

Notes

1. The American Bar Association has reported on this extensively. See "Major Findings of the Comprehensive Legal Needs Study," in American Bar Association Consortium on Legal Services and the Public, *Legal Needs and Civil Justice*, (Chicago: American Bar Association, 1994), p. 23.
2. Statement provided by Judge Parker at a meeting of the Governance Institute Steering Committee on the legal profession, Washington, D.C., June 11, 1994.
3. Initially I had thought that a data-based research design could be constructed to pursue this inquiry. Although a literature search confirmed that the thesis had not been professionally researched, we concluded that the subject matter was too subjective and imprecise to lend itself to a structure of double-blind, data-based, large-sample sociological research.
4. Jim Puga, Diane King, Laurie Bauer-Apodaca, Joe Rogers, and Chris Leh were interviewed between April 20 and August 30, 1994. See also King, Bauer-Apodaca, and Puga, "Lend-A-Lawyer: A Firsthand View," *Colorado Lawyer*, vol. 20, no. 6 (June 1991), pp. 1151–53.
5. Correspondence dated June 24, 1994.
6. See profile on Harold R. Tyler, Jr., in "Private Lawyer, Public Citizen: Columbia's Pro Bono Requirement," *Columbia Law School Report* (Spring 1993), p. 9.
7. Keynote address, Judge Frank M. Coffin, Program on Professional Ethics and Responsibility, Boston University School of Law, January 8, 1990.
8. Louis D. Brandeis, *The Curse of Bigness*, miscellaneous papers, edited by Osmond K. Fraenkel (Viking Press, 1934), p. 324.
9. Deval Patrick, assistant attorney general of the United States, quoted in "Clinical Education at Harvard Law School—Real Clients, Real Cases," *Harvard Law Bulletin*, vol. 45, no. 2 (Winter 1994), p. 36.
10. A. Edgar Benton, interview on April 20, 1994, and correspondence concluded August 3, 1994.
11. Telephone interview with Susan Kohlmann on July 26, 1994.
12. Judge Richard Matsch, interview on July 17, 1994.
13. Edwin Kahn, interview on July 17, 1994.

14. Correspondence with James R. McCotter dated August 3, 1994.
15. Robert Granfield, *Making Elite Lawyers: Visions of Law at Harvard and Beyond*, (New York: Routledge, Chapman & Hill, Inc., 1992).
16. "Does Ethical Training Matter? Between Ethics in the Books and Ethics in Practice," paper presented by Robert Granfield at the Law and Society Association meetings, Phoenix, Arizona, June 1994.
17. Comments received from Daniel Greenberg on July 22, 1994.
18. Interview on March 21, 1994.
19. Information provided at Governance Institute Steering Committee meeting, Washington, D.C., June 11, 1994.
20. Confirmed in correspondence dated June 9, 1994.
21. Kathleen Murray, "At Work: Listening to the Other America," *New York Times*, April 25, 1993, section 3, p. 25.
22. Andrea Atkins, "Mixing Business with Volunteer Work," *Hemispheres*, December 1993, p. 37.
23. Correspondence with Samuel Gary dated July 14, 1994, and September 9, 1994.
24. Robert Kaplan, "The Coming Anarchy," *Atlantic Monthly* (February 1994), p. 60.
25. Interview and correspondence with Jonathan Asher concluding July 29, 1994.
26. Patricia Danzon, "The Frequency and Severity of Medical Malpractice Claims," *Journal of Law and Economics*, vol. 27, no. 1 (April 1984), pp. 115–48.
27. Frank M. Coffin, information provided at Governance Institute Steering Committee meeting, Washington, D.C., June 11, 1994.
28. Suggested in Governance Institute Steering Committee meeting, Washington, D.C., June 11, 1994.

6

Private Enforcement
of Public Rights:

The Role of Fee-Shifting Statutes
in Pro Bono Lawyering

William A. Bradford, Jr.

A law firm's decision as to what its pro bono effort is to be, by its nature, will be a product of conflicting views held by members of the firm as to what is "in the public interest." Lawyers practicing in large firms have as many ideological stripes as the public at large, and what is one lawyer's public interest is another lawyer's anathematic interference with individual rights, assault on the free enterprise system, or support of bureaucrats run wild.

The institutional decision by a law firm to undertake a particular pro bono matter thus reflects a consensus, often uneasy, as to what is in the public interest. Compromises are made, controversies are avoided, and "easy cases" sometimes fill a firm's pro bono docket. It is noncontroversial to assist indigent elderly persons with wills; to staff a neighborhood poverty law office; and to assist neighborhood residents with debt, consumer, and tenant problems. These are all worthwhile projects and can properly be a part of any firm's pro bono docket. These projects provide meaningful and rewarding client contact and access to the legal system for those who would otherwise be denied it.

However, those matters do not take full advantage of what law firms, particularly large law firms, can offer: for example, exhaustive legal research on difficult issues; the ability to conduct extensive discovery; the ability to staff matters with a range of legal talent from the very experienced supervising lawyer to first-year associates, legal assistants, and file clerks; and the ability to retain and effectively use experts and consultants. While most American lawyers do not practice in law firms of over fifty lawyers, it is those larger firms that often have the flexibility, personnel, and economic resources to provide effective pro bono lawyering on an institutional basis, and in many instances to take on pro bono matters that could not be handled by smaller firms or solo practitioners.[1]

To assist large law firms in defining the public interest in a manner that takes full advantage of their resources—both personal and financial—this chapter suggests as a source for pro bono representation the recent proliferation of legislation containing fee-shifting statutes. The rights articulated in those statutes have already been defined, as a matter of law, as being in the public interest. In addition, the legislatures, in passing those statutes, have determined that the services of the private bar are needed to secure fully the rights set forth in the statutes. The democratic process has spoken, and it is difficult to argue that helping to secure a right, or to curb an activity deemed unlawful, by a statute giving incentive to the bar to do just that, is not in the public interest. This chapter further recommends that if such cases are undertaken as a part of a law firm's institutionalized pro bono activity, some or all of any fee award (after the firm's expenses) be donated to the charitable public interest organization that referred the case, to an analogous public interest nonprofit law firm, or to a fund for pro bono litigation expenses.

The American Rule and the Public Interest Exception

For almost the entire history of our country's jurisprudence the "American Rule" has governed the question of which side pays attorney's fees once litigation is concluded. Alone among legal systems in industrialized nations, the American Rule provides that each side in a lawsuit bear its own attorney's fees.[2] "[The] general 'American Rule' [is] that the prevailing party may not recover attorneys' fees as costs or otherwise." [3] The rule was recognized in an early Supreme Court case and was later codified for federal courts in the 1853 Fee Bill, now found at 28 U.S.C. §1920 and §1923.[4, 5]

The American Rule does, however, permit attorney's fees to be assessed in favor of the prevailing party when its opponent has litigated in bad faith.[6] This equitable exception to the rule that each side bears its own attorney's fees was joined briefly in the early 1970s by a court-constructed "private attorney general" exception.

Congress, in the Civil Rights Act of 1964, provided that a prevailing party in Title II litigation to enjoin racial discrimination in public accommodations could be awarded attorney's fees at the court's discretion.[7] In 1968 the Supreme Court held that the discretion to *withhold* an award of attorney's fees was to be exercised only in "special circumstances," and that the prevailing party in Title II litigation "should ordinarily recover an attorney's fee[.]"[8] In thus reinforcing the fee-shifting provision of the 1964 Civil Rights Act, the Supreme Court used language that has set the tone for the myriad public interest fee-shifting statutes that have followed:

> When the Civil Rights Act of 1964 was passed, it was evident that enforcement would prove difficult and that the Nation would have to rely in part upon private litigation as a means of securing broad compliance with the law. A Title II suit is thus private in form only. When a plaintiff brings an action under that Title, he cannot recover damages. If he obtains an injunction, he does so not for himself alone but also as a "private attorney general," vindicating a policy that Congress considered of the highest priority. If successful plaintiffs were routinely forced to bear their own attorneys' fees, few aggrieved parties would be in a position to advance the public interest by invoking the injunctive powers of the federal courts. Congress therefore enacted the provision for counsel fees—not simply to penalize litigants who deliberately advance arguments they know to be untenable but, more broadly, to encourage individuals injured by racial discrimination to seek judicial relief under Title II.[9]

Although the Supreme Court in *Newman* v. *Piggie Park Enterprises, Inc.,* was construing a fee-shifting *statute,* the Court's private attorney general language encouraged the U.S. Court of Appeals for the District of Columbia Circuit in a 1974 case to shift fees in furtherance of the public interest in the absence of specific statutory authority.[10] The D.C. Circuit was reversed in 1975 in *Alyeska Pipeline Service Co.* v. *Wilderness Society,* and the Supreme Court stated forcefully that the use of fee shifting to encourage public interest litigation was a matter for Congress, not for the courts:

> [C]ongressional utilization of the private attorney general concept can in no sense be construed as a grant of authority to the Judiciary to

jettison the traditional rule against nonstatutory allowances to the prevailing party and to award attorneys' fees whenever the courts deem
the public policy furthered by a particular statute important enough
to warrant the award. Congress itself presumably has the power and
judgment to pick and to choose among its statutes and to allow attorneys' fees under some, but not others.[11]

This invitation to Congress in *Alyeska* helped spawn the scores of public
interest fee-shifting statutes that came afterward, and that still emerge
with great regularity from Congress.

Public Interest Fee-Shifting Statutes

Congress's immediate reaction to *Alyeska*'s holding that fee shifting in
the public interest has to be directed by Congress, not constructed by
the courts, was the passage of the Civil Rights Attorney's Fees Awards
Act of 1976. This act, codified at 42 U.S.C. § 1988, provides that a prevailing party (other than the United States) in lawsuits under the civil rights
statutes may be awarded reasonable attorney's fees.[12] Congress stated,
when passing the Fees Awards Act, that the enforcement of the important
rights embodied in civil rights legislation "depends largely on the efforts
of private citizens" and that fee awards were a necessary incentive to
accomplish private enforcement.[13]

Clearly, public interest fee-shifting statutes had their modern birth in
the Civil Rights Act of 1964 and the augmenting Civil Rights Attorney's
Fees Awards Act of 1976. As the country's concerns moved in the 1970s
and 1980s to issues such as consumer rights, the environment, and rights
of the disabled, fee-shifting provisions accompanied virtually every piece
of legislation dealing with those issues.[14]

To be sure, some fee-shifting statutes predate the civil rights revolution
and may have little to do with the public interest as that term is understood
in the private attorney general formulation. If fee-shifting statutes are to
serve as a source of a law firm's pro bono efforts, then, there should
be a mechanism for identifying public interest fee-shifting statutes. No
mechanism can be totally free from debate about its uses as a tool to
determine whether a particular statute furthers the public interest. And
none can give a definitive answer as to whether the public interest is
furthered until the statute is applied to the facts of a particular case. A
helpful start, however, in isolating appropriate public interest fee-shifting

statutes from the more than two hundred fee statutes in the United States Code alone is to ask these questions: [15]

— Is the award of fees primarily to permit access to the courts for a meritorious claim, rather than to punish the defendant?
— Are the substantive rights to be protected in the underlying statute clearly defined?
— Are the rights to be vindicated in the statute widely applicable to the public at large?
— Is the underlying lawsuit permitted by the statute not one for pain and suffering or punitive or other damages that would attract a contingent fee attorney?
— Is the party represented in the action giving rise to fees an individual, or a class of individuals, not a for-profit corporation?

Affirmative answers to these questions, keeping in mind the rationale of the private attorney general theory, make it easier to separate the public interest fee-shifting statutes from the others. Derfner and Wolf, in their comprehensive *Court Awarded Attorney Fees,* have divided federal fee-shifting statutes into thirteen substantive areas: economic regulations; securities litigation; consumer protection; consumer safety; environmental protection; civil rights; employment; labor organizations; sunshine and privacy; abuse of process; federal liability statutes; intellectual property; and debtors' estates.[16]

Many of these categories can be eliminated entirely as not involving public interest statutes. Economic regulations statutes are primarily relied on by corporations to fight unfair competition, and the treble damages allowed in many of the statutes (notably including the antitrust statutes) make the cases attractive to lawyers. Similarly, securities litigation statutes are meant to enforce the rights of shareholders, not rights enjoyed by the public at large, and the damages awarded often make the cases attractive to the bar. Consumer safety statutes primarily allow for an award of damages for injuries caused by products or for other injunctive relief having to do with the safety of consumer products. While they may benefit particular individuals, typically such cases attract the plaintiffs' bar because of the availability of contingent fees. The labor organizations category enforces the rights of union members vis-à-vis their unions and their employers; these are not rights enjoyed by the public at large. The abuse of process category protects the rights of litigants in lawsuits in general; no substantive rights are defined in those statutes. Federal liability statutes, such as the Equal Access to Justice Act, likewise do not encourage enforcement of substantive provisions of law, but allow parties who litigate against the United States to get attorney's fees if they prevail under certain circumstances, and, in the case of EAJA, if the litigation position of the government agency was not "substantially justified." [17, 18] Both the intellectual property and debtors' estates categories of fee-shifting statutes apply to private disputes under the patent, trademark, and hallmark laws and between debtors and creditors in the bankruptcy courts.

This process of elimination leaves the following categories of fee-shifting statutes as likely to contain provisions that further the public interest:

—Consumer protection,[19]
—Environmental protection,[20]
—Civil rights,[21]
—Employment,[22] and
—Sunshine and privacy.[23]

Of course, a particular case brought under any of the statutes within these categories may not meet the public interest test as defined above, but that can usually be determined by asking the questions and applying the private attorney general rationale.

Fee-Shifting Statutes and a Firm's Pro Bono Docket

How well will public interest fee-shifting statutes accomplish their role as a source for a law firm's pro bono docket? Their use could raise questions from those accustomed to a more traditional pro bono docket. Since by definition a lawyer is compensated for his or her successful work in a fee-shifting case, such cases could be criticized as not pro bono lawyering at all but rather another form of contingent fee practice. But because in a fee-shifting case the wrongdoer pays the fee rather than the contingent fee plaintiff paying it from his or her award, society is imposing an additional cost on the wrongdoer as a deterrent. This difference is crucial to show that there is thus nothing antithetical to pro bono lawyering in such a reward for the pro bono lawyer. Moreover, unlike traditional contingent fee cases, the right vindicated in a successful public interest fee-shifting case has been defined by the legislature as one in furtherance of the public interest.

An even better response, however, to the criticism that fee-shifting cases reward the lawyer would be for the pro bono lawyer to donate all or part of the fee award to the public interest group that referred the case or, if there was no such referral, to a public interest organization linked to the issue that was litigated. An alternative use of the award could be the funding within the law firm or elsewhere of a pool of monies to be used to pay the disbursements associated with pro bono cases. Often the firm management, while tolerant and even encouraging of the pro bono hours logged by firm lawyers (which in most cases do not replace fee-generating work, but are an addition thereto), look askance at the "hard money" spent on depositions, computer research, messengers, postage, copying, word processing, and expert witnesses. It often attempts to make the payment of such disbursements the responsibility of the pro bono client or the referring public interest organization. The payment of these disbursements can be the source of friction between the law firm and the pro bono client. And the retainer agreements making the pro bono client responsible for those disbursements can sometimes be a bar at the outset to representation. For all these reasons, a fund for pro bono disbursements created out of fee-shifting awards could greatly facilitate a law firm's pro bono representation.

The donation of the fees to a public interest group or to a disbursement fund will also go far toward allaying the dismay or even anger of the client who recovers no monetary award at the end of a successful case but rather receives an injunction or declaratory judgment vindicating his or her rights. Such a client often cannot understand why the lawyer receives tens of thousands of dollars, or more, as a fee award when the client receives no monetary compensation. This anomaly will be better accepted if the client understands that the fee is being donated to assist other similarly situated plaintiffs or other needy clients.

Another possible criticism of fee-shifting cases forming a part of a larger law firm's pro bono docket is that such a practice takes the cases away from the specialized bar, which may have a high percentage of minority lawyers. Many fee-shifting statutes generate lawyers who specialize in such cases (that is, the Title VII bar, the Americans With Disabilities Act bar, and so forth), and some argue that siphoning off these cases to large law firms weakens the specialized bars and therefore runs counter to the public interest. After all, the argument continues, a large law firm's pro bono docket is subject to the vicissitudes of that firm's pro bono administration, and even the economic health of the law firm. Thus, while certain fee-shifting cases might be popular with large law firms one year, they may be out of favor the next year. On the contrary, the *raison d'être* of the specialized bars is to handle fee-shifting cases; the specialized bars intend always to provide that service, but if they are weakened by case-siphoning, they may not be able to fulfill that goal.

This argument, however, is unduly speculative. No hard evidence has entered the debate showing that the specialized bars have been damaged by case-siphoning from large law firms or that such would be the case if large law firms increase their fee-shifting docket. There would seem to be enough cases for all interested lawyers; after all, Congress believed that the need was so great as to justify the fee-shifting mechanism in the applicable statutes. Moreover, the case selection methods of large law firms are likely to produce difficult cases "on the edge" of the law that, if successful, will expand the definition of rights covered by the statutes—thus actually producing more work for the specialized bars.

The same response goes far to answer the criticism that large firms should spend their pro bono resources on more innovative cases designed to reform the law rather than on the more mundane issues that are dealt with in fee-shifting statutes. The premise of this criticism is faulty. There is just as much room for innovation and creative lawyering in the context of a fee-shifting statute as in other contexts. Indeed, one could argue that large law firms with their concomitant resources are best suited to fortify and expand the rights set forth in fee-shifting statutes.

Another criticism that might be raised about using fee-shifting cases in a pro bono docket is the impropriety of exposing a pro bono client to the possibility of being liable for the *defendant's* legal fees if the client does not prevail. Some fee-shifting statutes permit the prevailing party, whether plaintiff or defendant, to be awarded fees.[24] This criticism can be answered by full disclosure of, and counseling with respect to, the possible liability for fees when discussing the initial retention in the case. A firm should not be deterred from taking fee-shifting cases, with the advantages that have been described, because of the possibility of reverse liability. That possibility is simply the price of admission of taking certain cases, and the risks associated with that possibility can be minimized by selecting strong cases to begin with, and by a sharp-penciled attack on the defendant's fee petition if that becomes necessary.

Stemming Criticism of Pro Bono Programs

The more substantial a law firm's pro bono docket, the more likely it is to be criticized. Criticism comes from within—from lawyers at the firm who disagree with the docket's reflection of the public interest—and from without. The external criticism comes largely from groups that do not see themselves as benefiting from the largesse of the firm's donation of legal time.

Whatever the motivation of pro bono critics, the criticism often manifests itself in a disagreement over ideology. In an effort that was well publicized at the time, a conservative think tank, the Washington Legal Foundation, issued in 1988 a one-hundred-page treatise highly critical of the pro bono dockets of Washington law firms.[25] Its major tenet was that, rather than providing direct legal assistance to people who could not afford lawyers, the pro bono dockets of Washington firms were furthering liberal social engineering:

> When most people think of pro bono, they think of lawyers accepting cases at no charge involving indigents who are suddenly confronted by everyday legal problems. Examples of typical pro bono cases have consisted of providing legal assistance to criminal defendants, tenants with housing problems, and consumers with credit disputes. Instead of labeling the law firms' activit[ies] . . . [currently reflected on their pro bono dockets] as pro bono service, it is more accurately described as "legal engineering" of society from the firms' ideological blueprints.[26]

While critical of the firms' representation of such groups as the American Civil Liberties Union, Amnesty International, the Maine Audubon Society, People for the American Way, the National Association for the Advancement of Colored People, the Wilderness Society, and the Washington Lawyers Committee for Civil Rights Under Law as not fulfilling the firms' professional obligation to help the poor, the Washington Legal Foundation's report ironically laments the failure of the firms to represent conservative public interest groups, nonprofit businesses, established religious groups, and family-owned small businesses.[27] Yet it is difficult to imagine that conservatives would object, for instance, to pro bono projects on victims' rights, *amicus* briefs in favor of private landowners in Takings Clause suits, or drafting commercial or securities litigation for a nation in the former Soviet Union. It seems that the objection is based on ideological orientation rather than on the principle of pro bono work not directly performed on behalf of low-income clients.

A slightly different tact of criticism has been taken more recently in an article in the *Journal of the Legal Profession*.[28] Like the Washington

Legal Foundation, the author posits that pro bono lawyering should be to help the "poor and disadvantaged," citing the eclipsed American Bar Association Code of Professional Responsibility rather than the current model rules.[29] The author suggests that ancillary benefits of pro bono programs to law firms—such as recruiting, associate training and legal education, publicity, business contacts, and "one-upmanship"—might create violations of the ethical requirements of lawyers to conduct themselves in a dignified manner, to respect the client's goals and integrity, and to avoid the appearance of impropriety.[30] The author concludes: "The bar should give up its efforts to encourage law firms to provide pro bono services. Instead, the bar should compel the large law firms to help the indigent in the most meaningful way possible—by donating money." [31] Indeed, the author has this to say about fee-shifting cases on a firm's pro bono docket:

[I]ndigents are not really helped when law firms take on cases under reimbursable fee statutes, retain the money collected, and subsequently characterize these cases as pro bono since the services were rendered at a reduced rate. Nevertheless, these cases occupy time that firms might otherwise devote to indigent causes. Unless the law firms return the money received under reimbursable fee statutes to charitable organizations, indigent causes will be effectively displaced by high-profile suits brought under reimbursable fee statutes.[32]

The Washington Legal Foundation's report is likewise critical of the use of fee-shifting statutes, although the criticism has more of an ideological tone: "Despite the best intentions of the drafters, fee-shifting statutes have largely become a tool of liberal public interest lawyers to fleece businessmen and taxpayers." [33] After asserting that most fee awards come from government entities, the final criticism of the Washington Legal Foundation is a philippic against lawyers getting rich at taxpayers' expense: "Fee shifting statutes must not be used as a guise for increasing firm revenues. Taxpayers should not be forced to pay for unnecessary legal work, or work which doesn't clearly deserve reward. In general, the goal of pro bono must not be abandoned in the pursuit of financial gains." [34]

While the criticisms reflected in the two publications discussed do not find wide currency, they tend to embody the arguments made by those opposed to the current formulation of law firms' pro bono efforts. The use of public interest fee-shifting statutes to fill a part of a firm's pro bono docket may help to mute those criticisms, particularly when the fee awards are donated, as suggested earlier.

The most persuasive arguments brought by public interest fee-shifting statutes to the debate about whether a pro bono docket is serving the public interest, or serving the poor and disadvantaged, are that the statutes reflect Congress's judgment that 1) the rights advanced by the statute are in the public interest, and 2) the bar needs the inducement of fee shifting to take the cases. The second argument means that the clients in a fee-shifting case are in a class found by Congress to be "disadvantaged" in the ability to attract lawyers absent fee-shifting provisions. One might disagree with Congress's choice of rights or class of litigants for which to assign fee shifting, but that choice is the political choice of our democracy, circumscribed only by the Constitution. Law firms can take comfort in following Congress's definition of merit and need. Taking cases sanctioned by our political process can blunt both the ideological criticism and the "ulterior motive" criticism. The contribution of the fees to a public interest group or to a pro bono disbursement fund (after paying the expenses of the litigation) would deflect the charge that the lawyer time had not been provided gratis, or that the motivation of the firm in taking the case had been influenced by the possible generation of fee revenue.

In sum, adding public interest fee-shifting cases to a firm's pro bono docket would meet a public need defined by our political process, would provide lawyers to classes of persons who would otherwise have difficulty attracting and paying lawyers, and would generate money for the use of nonprofit public interest groups or otherwise to further pro bono lawyering.

Notes

1. In 1993 there were approximately 777,000 lawyers in the United States. See U.S. Bureau of the Census, *Statistical Abstract of the United States 1994*, 114th ed. (1994), p. 407. In 1993 more than 102,000 lawyers worked at the 714 American firms with fifty or more lawyers. See *Of Counsel*, vol. 13, no. 9 (May 2–16, 1994), p. 5.
2. Mary Francis Derfner and Arthur D. Wolf, *Court Awarded Attorney Fees*, vol. 1 (New York: Matthew Bender Co., 1994), pp. 1–2, 3.
3. *Alyeska Pipeline Service Co.* v. *Wilderness Society*, 421 U.S. 240, 245 (1975).
4. *Arcambel* v. *Wiseman*, 3 U.S. (3 Dall.) 306 (1796).
5. Some state law has deviated from the American Rule. Derfner and Wolf, *Court Awarded Attorney Fees*, pp. 1–17, 18.
6. *Alyeska Pipeline Service Co.* v. *Wilderness Society*, 421 U.S. 240, 245 (1975).
7. 42 U.S.C. §2000a-3(b).
8. *Newman* v. *Piggie Park Enterprises, Inc.*, 390 U.S. 400, 402 (1968).

9. Ibid., pp. 401–02.
10. *Wilderness Society* v. *Morton*, 495 F 2d 1026 (1974); reversed *Alyeska Pipeline Service Co.* v. *Wilderness Society*, 421 U.S. 240 (1975).
11. *Alyeska Pipeline Service Co.* v. *Wilderness Society*, 421 U.S. 240, 263 (1975).
12. 42 U.S.C. 1981, 1982, 1983, 1985, 1986; Title IX of Public Law 92-318, 20 U.S.C. §1681 et seq.; Title VI of the Civil Rights Act of 1964, 42 U.S.C. §2000d et seq.
13. H. Rept. 1558, 94 Cong. 2 sess. (GPO, 1976), p. 1; and S. Rept. 1011, 94 Cong. 2 sess. (GPO, 1976), pp. 2–6.
14. See, for example, Consumer Credit Protection Act, P.L. 90-321, 82 Stat. 156 (1968), codified at 15 U.S.C. §1640(a) (consumer rights); Endangered Species Act, P.L. 93-205, 87 Stat. 897 (1973), codified at 16 U.S.C. §1540g(4) (environmental protection); Rehabilitation, Comprehensive Services, and Developmental Disabilities Amendments of 1978, P.L. 95-602, sec. 120, 92 Stat. 2982 (1978), codified at 29 U.S.C. §794(a) (rights of the disabled).
15. Derfner and Wolf, *Court Awarded Attorney Fees*, p. 5-3.
16. Ibid., pp. 5-21–5.66.
17. P.L. 96-481, Title II, 94 Stat. 2325 (1980), codified at 5 U.S.C. §504 and 28 U.S.C §2412.
18. 5 U.S.C. 504.
19. See, for example, Equal Credit Opportunity Act, P.L. 90-321, Title VII, 88 Stat. 1524 (15 U.S.C. §1691e(d)).
20. See, for example, Clean Air Act, P.L. 91-604, 84 Stat. 1706 (42 U.S.C. §7604(d)).
21. See, for example, Fair Housing Amendments Act of 1988, P.L. 100-430, 102 Stat. 1633 (42 U.S.C. §3613(c)(2)).
22. See, for example, Age Discrimination in Employment Act of 1967, P.L. 90-202, 81 Stat. 604 (29 U.S.C. §626(b)).
23. See, for example, Privacy Protection Act of 1980, P.L. 96-440, 94 Stat. 1880 (42 U.S.C. §§2000aa–6(g)).
24. Derfner and Wolf, *Court Awarded Attorney Fees*, pp. 5-5, 5-6.
25. Washington Legal Foundation, *Washington Law Firms' Pro Bono Work: Shortchanging the Poor?* (Washington, D.C., 1988).
26. Ibid., pp. 4, 6.
27. Ibid., pp. 20, 29.
28. Carolyn Elefant, "Can Law Firms Do Pro Bono Work? A Skeptical View of Law Firms' Pro Bono Programs," *The Journal of the Legal Profession*, vol. 16 (1991), pp. 95–124.
29. Ibid., p. 96 and passim. Center for Professional Responsibility, American Bar Association, Model Rules of Professional Conduct, 1992 ed. Model Rule 6.1, Voluntary Pro Bono Publico Service, substantially modified in February 1993, is as follows: "A lawyer should aspire to render at least (50) hours of pro bono publico legal services per year. In fulfilling this responsibility, the lawyer should: (a) provide a substantial majority of the (50) hours of legal services without fee or expectation of fee to: (1) persons of limited means or (2) charitable, religious, civic, community, governmental and educational organizations in matters which are designed primarily to address the needs of persons of limited means; and (b) provide any additional services through: (1) delivery of legal services at no fee or substantially reduced fee to individuals, groups or organizations seeking to secure or protect civil rights, civil liberties or public rights, or charitable, religious, civic, community, governmental and educational organizations in matters in furtherance of their organizational purposes, where the payment of standard legal fees would significantly deplete the organization's economic resources or would be otherwise inappropriate; (2) delivery of legal services at a substantially reduced fee to persons of limited means; or (3) participation in activities for improving the law, the legal system or the legal profession. In addition, a lawyer should voluntarily contribute financial support to organizations that provide legal services to persons of limited means."

30. American Bar Association/Bureau of National Affairs, Inc., *Lawyers Manual of Professional Conduct* (1994), DR 2-101, Canon 5 and Canon 6 of the Model Code; Elefant, "Can Law Firms Do Pro Bono Work?" p. 104.
31. Elefant, "Can Law Firms Do Pro Bono Work?" p. 120.
32. Ibid., p. 119.
33. Washington Legal Foundation, *Washington Law Firms' Pro Bono Work,* p. 50.
34. Ibid., pp. 54–55.

7

Community Service as Pro Bono Work

Edwin L. Noel, Anthony F. Earley, Jr., and Lewis F. Powell, III

P ro bono lawyering has many levels and dimensions. For a firm, devising appropriate standards and criteria is delicate. The task is not easily susceptible to hard-and-fast definitions but rather requires a sensitive recognition of a diversity of factors, all of which must be weighed as the balance is struck. In this chapter we analyze various dimensions to be considered in weighing pro bono, including a discussion of the important efforts of the American Bar Association, possible standards for crediting pro bono activity, practice management issues, and some illustrations of how factors might be evaluated in crediting pro bono work.

Bar Association Guidelines

The American Bar Association has long advocated that lawyers do pro bono work. As far back as 1908, the ABA Canons of Ethics recognized the inherent duty of a lawyer to provide legal representation to indigents in criminal cases. In 1969 the ABA adopted Ethical Consideration 2-25

* The authors wish to thank Countess W. Price, an associate with Armstrong, Teasdale, Schlafly & Davis in St. Louis, Missouri, and Michelle M. Ketchum, a third-year law student at the University of Missouri-Kansas City Law School, for their most able assistance in the preparation of this chapter.

to their Model Rules of Professional Conduct. This implored "every lawyer, regardless of professional prominence or professional work load, [to] find time to participate in serving the disadvantaged."

In 1983, in what is commonly referred to as the Montreal Resolution, the ABA moved from this broad definition of public service to a requirement that pro bono service be in the form of "legal service provided without a fee or at a substantially reduced fee." In 1988 the ABA narrowed the definition of pro bono service further by adopting the so-called Toronto Resolution, which urged all lawyers "to devote a reasonable amount of time, but in no event less than fifty hours per year, to pro bono or other public service activities that serve those in need or improve the law, the legal system or the legal profession."[1]

Model Rule 6.1

In 1993 the ABA House of Delegates adopted, by a vote of 228 to 215, proposed Model Rule 6.1 on Voluntary Pro Bono Public Service, which provides as follows:

> A lawyer should aspire to render at least (50) hours of pro bono publico legal services per year. In fulfilling this responsibility, the lawyer should:
> (a) provide a substantial majority of the (50) hours of legal services without fee or expectation of fee to:
> (1) persons of limited means or
> (2) charitable, religious, civic, community, governmental and educational organizations in matters which are designed primarily to address the needs of persons of limited means; and
> (b) provide any additional services through:
> (1) delivery of legal services at no fee or substantially reduced fee to individuals, groups or organizations seeking to secure or protect civil rights, civil liberties or public rights, or charitable, religious, civic, community, governmental and educational organizations in matters in furtherance of their organizational purposes, where the payment of standard legal fees would significantly deplete the organization's economic resources or would be otherwise inappropriate;
> (2) delivery of legal services at a substantially reduced fee to persons of limited means; or

(3) participation in activities for improving the law, the legal system or the legal profession.

In addition, a lawyer should voluntarily contribute financial support to organizations that provide legal services to persons of limited means.[2]

ABA Law Firm Pro Bono Project

Also in 1993, the ABA's Law Firm Pro Bono Project promulgated guidelines for large law firms, asking that each firm make an institutional commitment to contribute, by no later than the close of calendar year 1995, from 3 to 5 percent of the firm's total billable hours to pro bono work. In defining these goals, the project requests each firm to agree that at least 50 percent of the pro bono time will consist of the delivery of "legal services on a pro bono basis to persons of limited means or to charitable, religious, civic, community, governmental and educational organizations in matters which are designed primarily to address the needs of persons of limited means." The firm's pro bono activities not designed primarily to address the needs of persons of limited means are to involve the provision of "legal assistance" either to "groups seeking to secure or protect civil rights, civil liberties or public rights," or to charitable and other groups "in matters in furtherance of their organizational purposes where payment of standard legal fees would be otherwise inappropriate." The project also requests that each firm ensure that a majority of both partners and associates in the firm participate annually in pro bono activities.

Other Guidelines

At this point the ABA pronouncements are merely aspirational goals. The state of Florida, however, has gone further. Effective October 1, 1993, most of the state's 50,000 lawyers will be expected to provide twenty hours of free legal services to the poor each year or donate $350 to a legal aid program.[3] Although the pro bono standard is not mandatory, lawyers who fail to report their pro bono service on their annual dues statement will be subject to possible disciplinary action by the Florida bar. Interestingly, the rule also applies to Florida's 10,000 nonresident lawyers, who will be expected to perform their pro bono work where they live or practice. Other states have proposed mandatory pro bono programs,[4] and numerous scholars[5] seriously advocate mandatory pro bono programs, notwithstanding obvious constitutional challenges.

Whether pro bono service remains an aspirational goal or becomes mandatory, we believe that the ABA should, over time, consider a broader, more flexible definition of pro bono for at least a portion of the lawyer's time devoted toward pro bono activities. This is consistent with the recognition of the many roles that lawyers play outside of the adversarial legal system in today's complex society. An inclusive definition of pro bono service also recognizes the legitimate practice management and quality control concerns of today's highly specialized law practice and allows greater opportunities for lawyers—especially those who do not practice in the courtroom—to participate in pro bono programs in a meaningful way. While we recognize the initial advantage of, and need for, hard-and-fast categories as the ABA launched the Law Firm Pro Bono Challenge—a singularly important and highly desirable development—the definitions should gradually be made more flexible once firms have satisfied the Challenge minima.

Crediting Pro Bono Activity

While a broad definition of public service for lawyers is more consistent with the wide array of public service performed by lawyers and needed by community groups, obviously not every project a lawyer undertakes without pay is pro bono in nature. For the reasons we outline below, at least three restrictions ought to apply in determining which activities meet even the broad definition of pro bono service: 1) the services should be for a public service organization that has a financial need for free or significantly reduced fee services; 2) the activity should call upon the lawyer's skills and training, even if legal services in the strict sense are not being performed; and 3) the services should be provided for little or no compensation.

Services Should Be for a Public Service Organization

With respect to the first test, the very nature of pro bono activity means that, whatever the service, it is performed for individuals or organizations who could not otherwise afford the service. While most nonprofit civic, charitable, educational, and bar institutions clearly have a financial need, the question may arise whether a specific organization could obtain these services if not obtained free of charge. Indeed, there are some organizations that clearly can afford such advice. Major charities (the American Cancer Society, American Heart Association, for instance) and educational institutions (well-endowed universities, for instance) have the resources to obtain whatever legal and/or business advice they need. Equally obvious, however, is the fact that these organizations are better able to serve their public charitable missions if they do not have to pay for such services.

Rather than delve into the financial strength or weakness of a public service organization, the matter can be decided by relying on the commercial instincts of lawyers. Many lawyers specialize in representing and advising nonprofit organizations. If there is direct compensation for the activity, it should not be considered pro bono work. If, however, the lawyer freely volunteers his or her services for an organization providing a public service, then it should be considered pro bono, even if the organization otherwise could afford paid counsel.

Activity Should Call Upon Lawyer's Skills and Training

The second test is more difficult to analyze. The easiest cases are those that involve the direct rendering of legal services to a charitable, civic, or public service organization. But the fact that a lawyer sitting on a board is not asked to provide direct legal services should not disqualify the activity altogether. By giving counsel and providing informed, reasoned judgments, a lawyer brings to any board the analytical skills of the profession. Moreover, it is almost impossible to find any activity of a public or private entity, large or small, that does not have legal complications or consequences. The presence of a lawyer helps ensure that the implications of these issues are not overlooked. Thus, where the pro bono activity reasonably calls on a lawyer's professional skills to benefit an organization, the activity should be considered within the scope of the pro bono obligation.

Nonetheless, there may be circumstances where a particular activity is so far removed from the provision of legal services that it could not be fairly considered as a pro bono activity. Thus, a lawyer who volunteers in a soup kitchen or works at a church bazaar, while certainly providing a public service, does not by this activity fulfill his or her professional obligation to the public. Also, if the activity—while superficially public—directly serves the lawyer's personal interests (for example, bringing an environmental challenge to a major development near a lawyer's property), it should not be treated as pro bono. This is true even if the work is done for free and is done for an organization that legitimately qualifies based on financial need.

Similarly, doing free legal work for one's secretary, staff, or another lawyer in the firm should not qualify, because these activities are usually done on a personal favor basis or are considered a fringe benefit of employment in a law firm. Also, volunteer activities for one's church have a strong personal element and, depending on the nature of the service, may be too far removed from the notion of public service to be considered a pro bono activity.

In short, although pro bono activities need not directly require the rendering of legal advice, they should, at a minimum, require some of the skills and knowledge associated with the profession for which commercial clients typically pay, but not be so limited in focus, or personal in nature, as not to be truly considered for the public interest.

Services Should Be Provided for Little or No Compensation

Last, to qualify for this broad interpretation of pro bono activity, the services provided should not result in any substantial direct remuneration. And while indirect financial benefit, such as meeting potential referral sources for future paying work or developing legal and management skills, should not automatically exclude an activity, the nature and relationship of the benefit to the activity should be examined. Thus, where a lawyer serves on the board of a charitable organization (for no fee), but the lawyer's firm receives substantial fees for legal services to the charitable organization, it should not be considered a pro bono activity, but more of a business development activity. On the other hand, if the fees received from the charitable organization are *de minimis* compared to the amount of time volunteered by the lawyer, it may well be appropriate to consider the time as pro bono work. Nor should indirect financial benefits flowing from contacts made or visibility achieved by board membership disqualify the activity.

This financial benefit test clearly eliminates full-time paid government service from the pro bono category.[6] Although this type of activity is often called public service, it should not fall within the category of activities discussed here. However, part-time governmental service, even if it involves some remuneration, should not be automatically disqualified if the amount of the remuneration is small in comparison to the fair value of the time involved.

Although guidelines such as these may be helpful for each lawyer and for each firm in determining compliance with professional responsibility guidelines, no rigid tests should be defined or legislated. Rather, a broadly defined scope for pro bono activities is consistent with the underlying reasons for the obligation to provide such services. As long as these services are provided at little or no compensation for a public service organization that may not otherwise have access to the services, and the services are reasonably related either to providing legal advice or employing skills associated with the legal profession and legal training, then they should fulfill, at least in part, a lawyer's pro bono obligation.

Practice Management Issues

Practice management issues also favor a flexible definition of pro bono work. The poor have every expectation and right to competent legal services, even if provided without charge. Accordingly, law firm practitioners should take the same precautions that they do for paying clients to make sure that the quality of their services is consistently high.

Law firms, especially larger ones, do not routinely practice in the areas of law in which the poor typically have problems. It is rare, for example, for a law firm practitioner to represent tenants in housing foreclosure cases, individual debtors in debtor's rights cases, welfare or social security recipients in entitlement cases, or other areas where the poor may need legal help the most. In fact, to the extent that law firms have had experiences in these areas, it is more likely that they have represented clients whose positions were adverse to those of the poor.

These factors complicate what types of cases law firm practitioners typically can agree to take. Law firms that represent landlords and developers, for example, most likely will not handle plaintiff housing cases for fear that they would either have a direct conflict of interest with one of their existing or prospective clients, or that the representation could create a positional conflict of interest if they advocate a result that might set a precedent adverse to clients in future cases.

Another law practice management issue prevalent in law firms, especially the larger firms, is rooted in the way these firms typically staff their client matters. In order to staff cases efficiently and cost-effectively for their clients, law firms typically assign less-experienced, less-expensive lawyers to do much of a client's work under the supervision of more experienced lawyers. It is this practice of supervision that gives a large firm confidence that its work product is consistently of high quality. With numerous lawyers working on many different matters, the only way to guarantee consistency in the quality of the work product is to have it supervised by more experienced practitioners. This does not mean that every legal issue has to be approached in exactly the same way throughout a firm, but it does ensure that the quality standards and judgment of senior lawyers are imparted on each client matter.

Careful review of client matters before they are accepted to ensure that the firm has expertise in the area and has adequate staffing to handle the cases is a common practice in law firms. The same careful screening and supervision need to be present in any law firm's pro bono program. For these reasons, many law firms develop areas of special expertise for their pro bono programs. A law firm may decide, for example, to accept pro bono cases only in specific areas, such as domestic relations, social security, and other entitlement program appeals, or other areas that are unlikely to require the advocacy of positions that would pose ethical conflicts with commercial clients or otherwise impede the commercial practice of the firm.

Successful pro bono programs in many firms have one or more designated pro bono lawyers familiar with a specific area of the law supervising the work of others. The others need not always be junior lawyers. In fact, it should not be uncommon for a senior lawyer to accept a pro bono assignment in an unfamiliar area and to be supervised by a younger lawyer who is experienced in that particular area.

Some firms seek out very large and complex pro bono cases that might involve, for example, class actions or other mechanisms to enforce the rights of a group of people who are financially unable to maintain protracted litigation. Large law firms are well versed in many of the procedural issues and staffing of complex cases, making this an appropriate use of their talents on behalf of public interest groups. It is important that pro bono cases, whether they be for individual clients or for larger public interest groups, be staffed and supervised in the same manner as are cases for regular paying clients.

A common and long-outdated myth is that if a lawyer is a member of the bar, he or she can be a skillful practitioner in all areas of the law. Thus, in jurisdictions where court appointments still prevail, lawyers are appointed to cases irrespective of their areas of specialty. The realities of today's law practice, however, do not comport with the image of the lawyer as a jack-of-all-trades. Many lawyers, especially in larger firms, practice in very restricted areas and may never see the inside of a courtroom during their entire professional life. They should not be expected to handle adversarial matters of any nature. To require them to do so will not serve the poor effectively and may invite a malpractice suit.

For these lawyers, an alternative method of meeting the obligation to do pro bono work for the poor may be necessary. Their areas of expertise, such as tax law, pension and benefit law, or even general corporate law, are specialized areas in which poor people typically do not need assistance. Lawyers in these fields should still be asked to meet a pro bono standard, but it may be that their menu of activities should not be limited only to an annual amount of defined services for people of limited means.

The realities of law firm practice, including the need for conflict clearance, supervision to maintain high and consistent quality control, and increasing specialization, all point to a more flexible, less rigid definition of *pro bono publico* in determining what services a law firm practitioner reasonably should be asked to provide.[7]

Service to the Legal Profession

There are many ways a lawyer can contribute to society through service to the legal profession itself. Indeed, much of what lawyers traditionally considered as pro bono work fell within the rubric of service to the legal community. This includes bar-related activities and court appointments. For this reason, these categories deserve special mention.

Service on Bar Committees

Many lawyers who are active in the organized bar provide a tremendous amount of volunteer service for the betterment of the legal profession. Often this is done through organized bar activities to promote the self-interests of the legal profession. For example, lawyers who lobby for the passage of limited liability corporation acts for lawyers in their state legislature or for revisions in the law solely as they pertain to the profession would not qualify for pro bono recognition because their work would not be perceived as benefiting the public in general. Similarly, lawyers who sponsor bar social activities, even though providing a service to the profession, also do not meet the pro bono test of providing a service to the public in general. In these respects, a bar association is not radically different from any other trade association.

Certain bar activities, however, differ in many important respects from trade association work. There are numerous issues in which lawyers do not share a common interest. For every lawyer who is interested in advancing more aggressive enforcement of environmental laws, for example, there is another lawyer who believes that we have already become too regulated in this area and is urging a more cautious approach.[8] Bar committees that sponsor debates on such legal issues serve a larger public interest by providing an open societal forum for discussion and change.

Lawyers also serve on a variety of bar-sponsored committees that analyze access to the justice system not only for those who cannot afford it, but also for those who can, thereby providing a more efficient and fair administration of justice.[9] Certainly, this work benefits the public, is done without compensation, and is done through associations that could hardly afford to pay for the legal talent brought together. Thus, unless the lawyer has a personal stake in serving on these committees—such as a client that has asked the lawyer to advocate tort reform—this work should also fall within the broad definition of pro bono work.

Court Appointments

Perhaps the most common form of service to the low-income public comes in the form of court appointments for criminal and civil cases. While many jurisdictions have a public defender's office that provides legal services to indigents in criminal cases, court appointments are still a common occurrence in jurisdictions that do not have public defender's offices and also in cases where that office would have a conflict in representing more than one defendant. While there is compensation available for some of this work,[10] by most law firm standards it is certainly uneconomical to accept these cases.

Similarly, in civil cases courts often appoint lawyers to represent a variety of indigents who have filed *pro se* complaints. These run the range from employment-related and housing disputes to prisoners' petitions. Even less money is available to compensate lawyers for representing appointed clients in civil cases than there is for criminal cases.[11]

As a practical matter, few lawyers have any realistic alternative but to accept these court appointments, because lawyers who practice in firms that appear regularly before the judges who appoint them do not have the audacity to challenge the appointments.[12] As a result, some argue that taking these types of cases is not true pro bono service. Also, some lawyers seek out these appointments because they are an important source of experience for them. Again, the motive for accepting court appointments does not undermine their essential pro bono nature or the importance to the administration of justice that the appointments represent.

These appointments have all of the attributes of other, more traditional pro bono work. The clients are typically indigent and need the services of a lawyer. Moreover, by providing these services, the lawyer is ensuring fairness in our adversarial system and an equal administration of justice. Thus there is no basis for according court appointments anything less than the same level of importance as other broadly defined public service undertakings.[13]

In summary, most of what lawyers do in connection with bar association work or service to the legal profession would appear to qualify under a broad-based definition of pro bono service. Only in those instances where the lawyer can be said to be acting in his or her own personal interest, in the interest of the legal profession as a trade association, or in the interest of a client, would service on bar-related committees fail to count as pro bono service.

Reconciling the Benefits of a Broad Approach with the Acute Need to Serve the Poor

How, then, can the desirability of a more flexible definition of pro bono work be reconciled with the important needs of the poor in obtaining legal representation in adversarial proceedings and other traditional legal service matters? The criteria for crediting pro bono work certainly should not become so diffuse that we forget the important gatekeeper role that lawyers—especially those who practice regularly in adversarial proceedings—play in the legal system. Thus it is fair that a large percentage of a law firm's pro bono commitment be directed toward serving the needs of the poor.

Both the ABA's Model Rule and the Law Firm Pro Bono Project deal with this issue by allowing at least a portion (but not all) of a lawyer's pro bono commitment to be met by work done for a broader array of community groups. Model Rule 6.1 sets forth an aspirational goal of fifty hours per year and requests that a "substantial majority," or the core requirement, of this commitment be spent on behalf of people of limited means or for organizations that are designed primarily to address the needs of persons of limited means. The ABA's Law Firm Pro Bono Project requests that between fifty and eighty-five hours per lawyer—assuming an average of 1,700 billable hours per year per lawyer—be set aside for pro bono work and that a majority of this commitment be met by the delivery of legal services to persons of limited means or organizations that are designed to address the needs of such people. In both instances, for the remainder of a lawyer's or law firm's commitment, greater flexibility is contemplated.

Model Rule 6.1 gives pro bono credit for the delivery of "legal services" at no fee to organizations seeking to protect "civil rights, civil liberties or public rights" or to a broad variety of community organizations in furtherance of their organizational purposes. It also recognizes "participation in activities for improving the law, the legal system or the legal profession." Thus a broad range of bar activities is given recognition as completing a part of one's pro bono goal. Indeed, Model Rule 6.1 is so broad in this respect that it may encompass a lawyer's bar work that advances only the interests of the profession and not the public:

> Serving on bar association committees; serving on boards of pro bono or legal services programs; taking part in Law Day activities; acting as a continuing legal education instructor, a mediator, or an arbitrator; and engaging in legislative lobbying to improve the law, the legal system, or the profession are a few examples of activities that fall within this paragraph.

While the ABA is understandably very supportive of bar activities, interestingly, the Law Firm Pro Bono Project does not appear to recognize these types of activities. Under the project's definition of pro bono, only three categories of service would qualify for recognition:

—Delivery of legal services to persons of limited means or to charitable, religious, civic, community, governmental, and educational organizations in matters that are designed primarily to address the needs of persons of limited means;

—Provision of legal assistance to individuals, groups, or organizations seeking to secure or protect civil rights, civil liberties, or public rights; and

—Provision of legal assistance to charitable, religious, civic, community, governmental, or educational organizations in matters in furtherance of their organizational purposes, where the payment of standard legal fees would significantly deplete the organization's economic resources or would be otherwise inappropriate.

The project's deletion of bar activities from its definition of pro bono seems to us to be unduly restrictive because it appears not to recognize the tremendous amount of important time lawyers give to the improvement of the law through bar work.

Both Model Rule 6.1 and the Statement of Principles of the Law Firm Pro Bono Project contain restrictions that pro bono work be in the form of providing either "legal services" or "legal assistance." The comments do not define either term. If a broad definition of "legal services" or "legal assistance"—as we have advocated—includes giving advice and rendering judgments in leadership capacities on community service groups, then the definition appears to be appropriate for all the reasons stated above. If, however, it is contemplated that legal services are restricted only to those issues where lawyers are actually engaging in the practice of law as narrowly conceived—adversarial proceedings, drafting bylaws, giving legal advice on employment situations, and so on—then the definition is too restrictive.

Both Model Rule 6.1 and the Law Firm Pro Bono Project recognize that not every lawyer will be able to meet a pro bono commitment every year. The model rule does not state this explicitly, but its comments contain the following provision:

> Because the provision of pro bono services is a professional responsibility, it is the individual ethical commitment of each lawyer. Nevertheless, there may be times when it is not feasible for a lawyer to engage in pro bono services. At such times a lawyer may discharge the pro bono responsibility by providing financial support to organizations providing free legal services to persons of limited means. Such financial support should be reasonably equivalent to the value of the hours of service that would have otherwise been provided. In addition, at times it may be more feasible to satisfy the pro bono responsibility collectively, as by a firm's aggregate pro bono activities.

The Law Firm Pro Bono Project recognizes this fact in its statement of principles:

> Recognizing that broad-based participation in pro bono activities is desirable, our firm agrees that, in meeting the minimum goals discussed above, we will use our best efforts to ensure that a majority of both partners and associates in the firm participate annually in pro bono activities.

To the extent that both Model Rule 6.1 and the Law Firm Pro Bono Project's Statement of Principles recognize that the need for flexibility exists in assigning lawyers to pro bono projects within a law firm, they reflect realistic solutions. The Law Firm Pro Bono Project encourages law firms to require a majority of both partners and associates to participate annually in pro bono activities, in addition to ensuring that the firm as a whole meets designated pro bono goals. As long as certain lawyers in a firm are not routinely exempted from pro bono service, this seems to be a reasonable compromise.

The model rule and the project treat appointed cases slightly differently. The model rule includes court appointments, where substantially reduced fees are obtained, in the broader definition of pro bono, but does not count these cases toward meeting the "substantial majority" of services without fee or expectation of fee to the poor. The project simply defines pro bono as "activities of the firm undertaken normally without expectation of fee and not in the course of ordinary commercial practice." It would seem that if a law firm wished to consider appointed cases as part of its core pro bono service (the 50 percent to "persons of limited means"), then it should commit to set aside those fees to be given to appropriate charitable organizations designed to meet the needs of the poor prior to accepting the appointment. In such instances, appointed cases could be said to be undertaken by the firm without expectation of fee and would meet the test of providing legal services for persons of limited means. If the fees were retained by the firm, then only a portion of the work could be said to be truly pro bono in nature.

In summary, both Model Rule 6.1 and the ABA's Law Firm Pro Bono Project strive to obtain a fair balance between the desire and necessity for flexibility in defining pro bono service and the very important goal of our society to ensure that persons of limited means are given fair access to legal services. A 50-percent rule appears to be a fair compromise, requiring that at least a majority of any lawyer's pro bono time be focused on providing legal services to persons of limited means or organizations supporting such groups.

However, both the Model Rule and the ABA's Law Firm Pro Bono Project appear to be somewhat restrictive in their treatment of the remaining 50 percent of a lawyer's pro bono undertaking. These services should not be restricted solely to "legal services" or "legal assistance" in the traditional sense, but rather should allow for greater flexibility in public service, recognizing that many of the talents lawyers bring to community organizations are other than their ability to practice law.

For instance, Model Rule 6.1's inclusion of bar activities for this type of pro bono service is very sensible, although it may be too broad to the extent that it would include lawyer social activities or other more typical trade association work. Additionally, both the model rule and the project allow lawyers the flexibility to satisfy the pro bono responsibility collectively through a law firm's aggregate pro bono activities. This also is a sound result, although in no case should any single lawyer or group of lawyers be automatically exempt from pro bono service.

Some have suggested that the best way for a lawyer or a law firm to meet the pro bono obligation is simply to pay for it.[14] Indeed, the Florida rule allows lawyers to escape pro bono altogether for a $350 fee.[15] While simple in its approach, allowing lawyers or entire law firms to buy out of their pro bono commitments is not in the best interest of the profession or the individual lawyers. The advantages to society and the lawyers involved in providing pro bono services are many, beyond just the service provided. Pro bono service expands a lawyer's understanding of the law and the legal system and sensitizes a lawyer to the problems of those less fortunate. Also, it enhances the role of the lawyer as a member of a noble profession and gives lawyers a way to serve more than just the commercial interests of the profession. Furthermore, diversity of legal services is satisfying professionally and may mitigate lawyer "burnout." Thus lawyers should not routinely and consistently avoid pro bono services simply by paying money to the state bar association.

Some Illustrations

While eschewing any rigid formulas regarding counting pro bono, the following illustrations may help demonstrate what we advocate:

—A does legal work without fee for B, a small company with considerable prospects that cannot afford A's standard billing rate. This work should not qualify for any pro bono credit since B is not a public service organization.

—A drafts a set of bylaws without charge for B, a nonprofit school that A's child attends and that could not otherwise easily afford A's services. This work should qualify for broad pro bono credit, but would not qualify for the core "substantial majority" requirement since B is not an organization designed primarily to address the needs of persons of limited means. The fact that A's child attends school at B should not be a disqualifying factor.

—Same as the previous illustration except A's work is calling other parents for fundraising. This work should not qualify for any pro bono credit because the work does not call upon A's skills as a lawyer, even in a broad sense.

—A serves without compensation as a member of the board of directors of B, a nonprofit organization designed to serve the needs of the poor. A does not serve as B's counsel but does render legal judgments and give informal advice as a board member. A's work should count for both the broad pro bono credit and the core requirement even though the services rendered may not be "legal service" as traditionally defined.

—Same as the previous illustration except B is a well-endowed institution that pays A's firm substantial fees at prevailing rates for legal services. A's work should not count for any pro bono credit because A serves as a director as a service to a paying firm client who happens to be a nonprofit organization.

—A serves as a part-time alderman for city B at little or no compensation. A does not serve as B's counsel but does render legal judgments. A's work should count toward the broad pro bono credit, but not the core requirement, because B is not an organization designed specifically to address the needs of the poor.

—A serves on an organized bar committee designed to revise and streamline A's state tax laws. A's service should qualify for broad public service credit, but not for core credit, as the work is not aimed at assisting the poor.

—Same as the previous illustration except A is asked to serve by B, a client of A's, to attempt to revise state tax laws for the benefit of B. This work should not qualify for any pro bono credit, even if A performs the work without compensation, because A's motivation is not to provide a public service.

—A serves on two bar committees, one designed to revise state laws to aid the access of the poor to the legal system, and the other to create laws to limit malpractice liability of lawyers by shortening applicable statutes of limitations. A's work on the legal system access project should qualify toward both the broad pro bono credit and the core requirement, even though A's services are not "legal services" in the strictest sense. A's work on the limitation of liability project should not count for any pro bono credit because it does not provide a service to the public beyond the legal profession's self-interest.

—A is appointed by a court to represent an indigent in a criminal case. A serves without fee or at a substantially reduced fee. A's work should qualify for the core pro bono requirement even if undertaken by court order and even if A did not have a meaningful choice whether to accept the appointment, because a member of the indigent public is served by the lawyer's representation.

—A is a member of a large law firm that has an active and sizable pro bono practice; however, A does no pro bono work. A is not required to do pro bono work in any given year, but the law firm should develop opportunities for and encourage A to do substantial pro bono work over a period of years.

—A represents a class of indigent plaintiffs in a voting rights case on a contingent fee basis. This work should only be treated as pro bono if A agrees at the time of undertaking the representation to pay all fees earned to a nonprofit organization designed primarily to serve the poor. If so, this work should count for both the broad and the core pro bono requirement.

—A is asked by B, an organization formed to protect the First Amendment, to write an amicus brief in a First Amendment case dealing with free speech in schools. A does so without charge. A's work should count toward the broader pro bono credit but not the core requirement, because B is not an organization designed primarily to serve the needs of the poor.

These illustrations are not exhaustive, as there are countless tasks to which lawyers can and should apply their skills to assist those who need legal guidance. It is to be hoped, however, they will serve to illustrate the concepts developed in this chapter as to how our profession should carry out its public service obligations.

Conclusion

Lawyers are trained to see every side of an issue. Out of this training springs a desire to debate every side of an issue. The debate on why lawyers should and do perform pro bono service has gone on too long. It is now time to stop talking about pro bono work and start doing it. As Thomas Jefferson described the practice of law:

> The study of the law is useful in a variety of points of view. It qualifies a man to be useful to himself, to his neighbors, and to the public.[16]

Currently, the public perception is that lawyers use their law degree to profit only themselves. We need to revise this image by providing greater service to our neighbors and to the public. In so doing, we need to encourage lawyers to become involved in a broad array of the community's social and political structures. Allowing lawyers flexibility in defining their own pro bono commitments and permitting them to do pro bono work in areas of interest should encourage them to undertake more pro bono work.

Notes

1. For further discussion of the history of the American Bar Association's studies on pro bono service, see the American Bar Association Standing Committee on Lawyers' Public Service Responsibility Report to the House of Delegates (February 1993).
2. Center for Professional Responsibility, American Bar Association, *Model Rules of Professional Conduct* (Chicago: American Bar Association, 1992), pp. 98–99.
3. Florida Statutes Annotated Bar Rule 4–6.1 (St. Paul, Minnesota: West, 1994), p. 811, provides that:

> (a) Professional Responsibility. Each member of The Florida Bar in good standing, as part of that member's professional responsibility, should (1) render pro bono legal services to the poor and (2) participate, to the extent possible, in other pro bono service activities that directly relate to the legal needs of the poor. This professional responsibility does not apply to members of the judiciary or their staffs or to government lawyers who are prohibited from performing legal services by constitutional, statutory, rule, or regulatory prohibitions. Neither does this professional responsibility apply to those members of the bar who are retired, inactive, or suspended, or who have been placed on the inactive list for incapacity not related to discipline.
> (b) Discharge of the Professional Responsibility to Provide pro bono Legal Service to the Poor. The professional responsibility to provide pro bono legal services as established under this rule is aspirational rather than mandatory in nature. The failure to fulfill one's professional responsibility under this rule will not subject a lawyer to discipline. The professional responsibility to provide pro bono legal service to the poor may be discharged by (1) annually providing at least 20 hours of pro bono legal service to the poor; or (2) making an annual contribution of at least $350 to a legal aid organization.
> (c) Collective Discharge of the Professional Responsibility to Provide pro bono Legal Service to the Poor. Each member of the bar should strive to individually satisfy the member's professional responsibility to provide pro bono legal service to the poor. Collective satisfaction of this professional responsibility is permitted by law firms only under a collective satisfaction plan that has been filed previously with the circuit pro bono committee and only when providing pro bono legal service to the poor (1) in a major case or matter involving a substantial expenditure of time and resources; or (2) through a full-time community or public service staff; or (3) in any other manner that has been approved by the circuit pro bono committee in the circuit in which the firm practices.
> (d) Reporting Requirement. Each member of the bar shall annually report whether the member has satisfied the member's professional responsibility to provide pro bono legal services to the poor. Each member shall report this information through a simplified reporting form that is made a part of the member's annual dues statement.

See "Reporting Pro Bono: Fla.'s Requirement Could Lead to Blacklisting, Some Say," *American Bar Association Journal,* vol. 79 (October 1993), p. 16.

4. The Nevada Bar Association filed a petition in late 1994 with the Nevada Supreme Court asking the court to adopt a mandatory pro bono plan quite similar to that of Florida. See Hope Viner Samborn, "Court Weighs Required Pro Bono," *American Bar Association Journal*, vol. 101 (February 1995), p. 24. Also in 1990 the Marrero Committee, appointed by then Chief Judge Wachtler of the New York Court of Appeals, recommended in its final report the establishment of a system of mandatory pro bono for all New York lawyers. New York lawyers were to provide a minimum of forty hours of qualifying pro bono service every two years. Unlike the ABA's Model Rule 6.1, the pro bono work would be limited strictly to services provided on behalf of the poor. Committee to Improve the Availability of Legal Services, "Final Report to the Chief Judge of the State of New York," *Hofstra Law Review*, vol. 19 (Summer 1991), p. 755. Additionally, in Texas Section 31 of the 1991 amendatory act mandates:

> The State Bar of Texas shall study provision of pro bono or free legal services by the attorneys in this state and shall report to the legislature and the Supreme Court of Texas not later than January 1, 1993, on the advisability of a mandatory pro bono program to provide legal services for those unable to afford legal assistance and on the procedures necessary to implement the program if it is advisable. V.T.C.A. § 81.012 (1994).

Some federal district court bars have adopted mandatory pro bono programs, including the districts of Arkansas, Iowa, and Connecticut. Some local bars have also imposed such requirements, including Orange, Leon, and Palm Beach Counties in Florida, although these are not mandatory bars requiring admission in order to practice in that locale. For further discussion, see chapter 3.

5. See, for example, Chesterfield H. Smith, "A Mandatory Pro Bono Service Standard— Its Time Has Come," *University of Miami Law Review*, vol. 35, no. 4 (July 1981), note 1, p. 727. But see Jonathan R. Macey, "Mandatory Pro Bono: Comfort for the Poor or Welfare for the Rich?" *Cornell Law Review*, vol. 77 (July 1992), note 1, p. 1115, for a contrary view.

6. For an excellent discussion of the pro bono obligations of government lawyers, see Lisa G. Lerman, "Public Service by Public Servants," *Hofstra Law Review*, vol. 19, no. 4 (Summer 1991), p. 1141.

7. Large law firms as a group appear to be making increasing efforts to increase their pro bono obligations. Between 1990 and 1992, total hours of pro bono work increased by 37 percent at the seventy-two large firms sampled (see chapter 2). For a general discussion of some of the programs of large law firms, see Ronald J. Tabak, "How Law Firms Can Act to Increase the Pro Bono Representation of the Poor," *Annual Survey of American Law*, Book I (1989), p. 87. See also Eric Schnapper, "Advocates Deterred by Fee Issues," *National Law Journal*, March 28, 1994, pp. C-1–C-16.

8. Nearly all of the ABA's substantive law committees have members with opposing viewpoints who debate issues. In many respects, this may be one of the few effective ways that many nonlitigators can engage in public service, because the opportunities for public service in the corporate law arena are much more limited.

9. These are among the most important issues confronting our legal system, because even those who can afford access are often faced with frustrating delays due to docket backlogs. Identifying methods for improving our dispute resolution system benefits not only lawyers—in fact, it is often cynically noted that lawyers who try to improve the administration of the justice system are only hurting themselves since lawyers benefit financially from long delays and crowded dockets—but, more important, serves to improve the lives of those that the profession serves. These and many other legal service projects are important commitments that lawyers give to the public and should be encouraged.

10. See, for example, Criminal Justice Act, 18 U.S.C.A. § 3006(A)(d)(2), (West, 1992), p. 313:

> For representation of a defendant before the United States magistrate or the district court, or both, the compensation to be paid to an attorney or to a bar association or legal aid agency or community defender organization shall not exceed $3,500 for each attorney in a case in which one or more felonies are charged, and $1,000 for each attorney in a case in which only misdemeanors are charged. For representation of a defendant in an appellate court, the compensation to be paid to an attorney or to a bar association or legal aid agency or community defender organization shall not exceed $2,500 for each attorney in each court. . . .

11. For example, the U.S. Court of Appeals for the Eighth Circuit will reimburse a lawyer only for reasonable expenses, but not for his or her time.
12. One lawyer who had the temerity to challenge a federal court's appointment was John E. Mallard. In *Mallard* v. *United States Dist. Court,* 490 U.S. 296 (1989), the court declared that an attorney may not be compelled pursuant to 28 U.S.C. § 1915(d) to represent an indigent client in a civil case.
13. Many civil court appointments are in areas where there are fee-shifting statutes allowing the successful plaintiff to recover his or her attorneys' fees. However, these cases typically are not viewed as potentially profitable sources of business and, therefore, are more fairly characterized as public service undertakings by lawyers who are appointed to these types of cases. If, however, the cases result in fees that are not donated to community groups, they certainly should not be treated as pro bono in nature. For an excellent discussion of fee-shifting statutes in these areas, see chapter 6.
14. See Bill Winter, "'Buy Out': Is it a Pro-Bono Cop-Out?" *American Bar Association Journal,* vol. 66 (November 1980), p. 1351.
15. Florida Statutes Annotated Bar Rule 4–6.1. The proposed Nevada rule would contain a similar exemption upon payment of $500.
16. Letter from Thomas Jefferson to Thomas Mann Randolph, May 30, 1790. Julian P. Boyd, ed., *The Papers of Thomas Jefferson,* vol. 16 (November 30, 1789 to July 4, 1790) (Princeton University Press, 1961), p. 449.

8

Monitoring Compliance with the ABA Law Firm Pro Bono Challenge

Barrington D. Parker, Jr.

Т he existence of the American Bar Association Pro Bono Challenge
is, I believe, a message from the legal community, the significance of
which should not be overlooked. Firms large and small, and even those
whose primary goals seem to be commercial, now commonly wrestle
with questions such as: Who are we? What continues to separate us as
professionals from purely commercial organizations? What would return
a sense of importance and vitality to what we do?

A significant part of the answer to these and related questions lies, I
believe, in a purposeful expansion and redefinition of our concept of what
work lawyers are regularly able to chose and to do. Pro bono work, in
a major way, facilitates this process of choice and, in doing this, can
greatly help revitalize the practice of law. But how this can occur is not
clearly understood since pro bono work is so typically seen, even by its
proponents, as charity or as activity peripheral to a firm's "real work."

The Challenge presents a seminal opportunity to reeducate the bar on
these issues. How is this opportunity to be exploited? As important as
the promulgation of the Challenge was, the steps taken to ensure adherence
to it and to expand and institutionalize pro bono work are equally as

---

* I am indebted to Esther Lardent for a long and helpful conversation while I was preparing
this chapter.

important. It is still too early to judge which firms have taken the Challenge seriously. It is likely that some have used the Challenge as an opportunity to expand their pro bono work, some have used it as a wedge to introduce pro bono activities where intrafirm politics previously made this unfeasible, and some signed on to the Challenge but did not take it seriously. What happens to the Challenge must await the further receipt and analysis of additional information. Reports, audits, and critiques of the pro bono programs of Challenge members are basic compliance mechanisms, the essential features of which are outlined later in this chapter.

But I suggest that a somewhat different and perhaps more important opportunity is presented by pro bono work and by the Challenge. I believe that a major impediment to more extensive involvement by law firms, at least the major law firms, in pro bono activity is a pervasive misunderstanding of its value. In this chapter I urge that a successful monitoring program can, and should, serve not merely as a mechanism to facilitate compliance, but also as a device that provides important information about the intrinsic benefits of pro bono to lawyers and their firms. In that sense the monitoring mechanisms reinforce the value of pro bono. I also suggest that the economic costs of pro bono work to law firms have similarly been widely overstated. Making a reeducation effort around issues such as these a central component of compliance monitoring activities could well, in the long run, be the Challenge's most important contribution to the public and to the bar.

Teaching the Value of Pro Bono

The information collected in a monitoring effort can buttress support for pro bono in a variety of ways. First, such a program can reinvigorate a profession plagued by increasingly serious morale problems by requiring lawyers more fully to appreciate that, as law is a service profession, the greatest rewards flow from service to the human community. Second, such a program can assist lawyers who view pro bono work primarily as a distraction or an economic drain to understand how a strong pro bono program generates, at all levels of professional lives, better, more imaginative, and more mature lawyers. Third, as lawyers are forced to give more and more attention to economic concerns, a sound monitoring program can demonstrate that pro bono work results in a competitive advantage in paying work that has generally been either missed or seriously underestimated.

One of the important steps to encourage compliance with the Challenge is to present the case, as Denver-based lawyer Donald Hoagland does, that pro bono work can play a critical role in facilitating the professional and personal growth and maturation of lawyers—associates as well as specialists—and that law firms will be the beneficiaries in terms of broadened skills, widened experience, and increased enthusiasm for—and commitment to—the practice of law in its broadest sense. This effort would help displace the stereotype among the more commercially oriented members of large firms that pro bono work is extrinsic to the overall success and profitability of a firm, that it is a "favor" and, in times of economic pressure, a luxury.

An initial problem lies with the Challenge's own concept of pro bono. In its statement of principles, pro bono is cast as a "contribution to others" and as a way of meeting the "special needs of the poor for legal services." Pro bono work is seen as a donation to "persons of limited means" or to "charitable, religious or civic organizations who are concerned primarily with persons of limited means."

While pro bono in its classic sense involves work for others and for the public, an exclusive reliance on this component misses the importance of pro bono activities to the development of lawyers and law firms. In a fuller sense, pro bono work is not simply work done for the poor, but valuable, legal professional work that differs from other legal work because it is done without the expectation of direct remuneration. The work in question is selected not only for its usefulness to others, but because of its intrinsic value and interest to the lawyer performing the work. Pro bono work provides a partial, but nonetheless potent, antidote to the serious problems posed by the intellectual, self-limiting nature of legal specialization.

Whether these considerations are sufficiently more compelling to prevail in a climate in which economic concerns increasingly predominate remains to be seen. But to encourage firms as part of their commitment to the Challenge to take a look at the broad benefits of pro bono work could be one of the most valuable roles the project plays.

The Challenge could facilitate this process of professional growth and self-examination. It could solicit somewhat personal written information from lawyers working on pro bono projects about what benefits were derived. Relevant questions would extend beyond a description of the project and might include information on:

— Why and how a project was chosen;
— What skills were engaged;

— What was learned;
— How the project differed from regular client work; and
— What mistakes were made in the selection process.

The project would also seek evaluations from those with managerial and supervisory authority as to their perceptions about the value of pro bono work in the development of legal skills, along the lines that Hoagland suggests, and from clients as well. Hopefully, the results would track over time the maturation and development of particular lawyers. The best examples of this process would be included in case studies showing how consistent attention to pro bono work led to the evolution of leaders in practice areas, the firm, and the bar.

Many well-known leading lawyers have had extensive and interesting pro bono projects throughout their careers, but the exact nature and extent of the work is little known, even within their firms. Here again, case studies could be prepared with prominent lawyers—such as Robert MacCrate, Jay Topkis, Cyrus Vance, or David Kendall—discussing historically on a year-by-year basis such topics as:

— What pro bono projects they took on;
— How they obtained the work;
— Exactly what they did; and
— What they learned.

Examination of these case studies would teach lawyers at all levels, but particularly younger ones, at least two valuable lessons: 1) pro bono work can be among the most interesting work available, and 2) those who do pro bono work consistently and with commitment grow in professional, intellectual, and personal capacity.

Measuring Costs

The conventional wisdom is that pro bono work involves a financial sacrifice to the firm since it is work given away. This conclusion is sufficiently widely held so that it generally goes unchallenged, even among strong proponents of pro bono work. A closer look at law firm economics causes this conclusion to unravel. Since the real financial costs of pro bono work are typically greatly exaggerated, once the intangible benefits of pro bono work are returned to the equation, the work may not be especially costly to a firm at all.

Thus a second area in which efforts to monitor compliance with the Challenge can possibly significantly expand pro bono work is to assist firms to conduct far more careful analyses than most have done in the past of the real cost of such work. The traditional analysis of the economics of pro bono work starts from the assumption that it is a drag on the firm's revenue because the time spent would otherwise have been devoted to revenue-producing work. The amount of the drag is calculated by taking the number of hours spent on a particular pro bono project multiplied by the hourly billing rate of the attorney involved. Thus if an attorney bills at $175 per hour and during the course of the year spends one hundred hours on pro bono projects, it is commonly believed that the firm has "donated" $17,500 to the recipient of the pro bono services. This drain on firm revenues is thought to be increased by out-of-pocket expenses such as court reporting fees and secretarial overtime expenses that must be borne by the firm. Thus pro bono costs are thought to be measured in two ways: revenue foregone and cash out-of-pocket. Ironically, the Challenge reinforces this stereotypical approach by encouraging firms participating in the Challenge, whether at the 3 or the 5 percent level, to measure the cost of participating by simply multiplying the selected level of participation by the law firm's gross revenues.

But this type of analysis generates a highly misleading picture of the real cost of pro bono activities. Obtaining a more accurate picture may be difficult since it is likely to vary from firm to firm depending on a variety of factors relating to client base, billing practices, and internal operating efficiencies. Out-of-pocket expenditures can be a real and easily measured cost, but they generally are small amounts compared with foregone revenue. Notwithstanding those considerations, as Jack Londen, one of the profession's leading advocates of pro bono work points out, the analysis based on hours spent and billing rates, widely used and encouraged by the Challenge, substantially overstates the true cost of pro bono work.[1]

Consider a hypothetical large firm of 350 lawyers, Atchison & Baker ("AB"), with little institutional background in pro bono work, that is contemplating accepting the Pro Bono Challenge. The average billing rate of AB's 350 lawyers is $175. AB's gross-to-net expense ratio is 40 percent. The average lawyer at AB bills 1,800 hours a year, but management wants to increase this number to 2,000. AB's management committee wants to accept the Challenge but also wants to increase its partner income, which has been static over the past few years. A small group of highly productive, commercially oriented lawyers at AB is opposed to participation in the Challenge because of financial considerations.

The management committee is favorably disposed but is worried that if it accepts the Challenge, time that would otherwise be devoted to revenue-producing activity would go to pro bono work, and revenues would continue to stagnate. A major role in monitoring compliance would be to assist firms such as AB in alleviating this anxiety. Assuming AB's lawyers are diligent and efficient, the reason the lawyers are billing 1,800 rather than 2,000 hours is, most probably, that the extra work is just not there. Thus it is the lack of new business, not the Challenge, that is the impediment to the extra 200 hours per lawyer.

It is in this "real world" context that the cost to AB of accepting the Challenge must be measured. It is highly likely that the infrastructure that would permit each lawyer at AB to bill the additional two hundred hours already exists, since the increase translates to less than one additional hour per day per lawyer. As Londen points out, if the extra two hundred hours per year in paying work does not exist, then the cost of filling that time with pro bono work would be the true "cost" to the firm of joining the Challenge. While these costs are hard to quantify precisely, they are not large and, in any event, are far less than pro bono hours times billing rules.

In the real world, this gap between the hours the managers desire and plan for and the hours that lawyers actually generate almost always exists. Law firms rarely operate at full capacity, and when they do it is only for brief periods of time. In reality, in any given year a certain proportion of lawyers meet and a certain proportion of lawyers typically do not meet the hours expectations set by managers, and the identities of those who do and do not changes from year to year. Consequently, there is almost always time available for some lawyers in practically every firm to use excess capacity for pro bono work. In most cases, the cost to the firm of pro bono work is simply the cost of using existing firm resources (that is, lawyer time, office equipment, and support staff) that would lie fallow if not devoted to pro bono activities.

Paradoxically, the farther the average lawyer at the AB firm falls below the expected 1,800 hours because paying work is unavailable, the more compelling the case for pro bono work becomes. Challenging professional work can make lawyers more experienced and efficient and, hence, more valuable to the firm and its clients. Conversely, underutilizing lawyers is wasteful and detrimental to morale, particularly when others in the firm are substantially more busy.

If professionally challenging pro bono work could be found, then the lawyers at AB who fall below hours expectations should be put to work during slack time developing the same kinds of skills—writing briefs, arguing motions, drafting legal documents—they would be developing if there were enough paying work in the firm. Again, the costs of doing this would not be income that could otherwise be generated but would be the out-of-pocket expenses plus the costs of using an existing but underutilized infrastructure. It is simply against a firm's self-interest to restrict pro bono work during slow periods on the grounds that its lawyers are not sufficiently busy on income-generating activities, and the Challenge should assist firms to recognize and verify these conclusions.

Assuming AB's marketing and business-generating programs begin to succeed and the average billable hours for AB's lawyers increased from 1,800 to 2,000 hours per year (a ten-hour work day every business day of the year), AB's lawyers would, arguably, have little, if any, time for pro bono work. But in the real world of law firms this situation is unlikely to occur. Cases settle and deals close. Consequently, firms rarely operate at peak capacity for extended periods of time, and excess capacity reappears. If AB wished to remain successful, it would not risk an extended period near peak capacity since it would never wish to turn down new work for satisfied, valuable, regular clients on the grounds that it was too busy to service them.

What AB would do, in all probability, is to add more lawyers at lower salaries to increase capacity and partner income. This expansion would quickly lower the average hours lawyers worked and recreate the capacity for pro bono work. In the busiest firms, as with others, the cost of pro bono time is not hours times rates but typically the cost of using excess capacity. In the busiest firms, however, unlike the firms that cannot raise hours, there is a possibility that pro bono work would displace paying work. But the cost is likely to be far less than AB's managers think, because AB's lawyers will not work at peak capacity for any extended period of time. At 2,000 hours, AB's managers are less likely to complain than they might have been when their lawyers were at 1,800 hours, because partner incomes will be significantly larger than those of their competitors. As a result, the sacrifice to each individual partner of complying with the Challenge will be substantially reduced. Moreover, in most firms, human realities impose practical limitations on the amount of time lawyers are willing to devote to their work. Since, as Londen suggests, lawyers who do pro bono work tend to do so out of personal choice or conviction, such lawyers are more likely to spend more time doing pro bono plus billable work than they would be willing to spend on billable work alone.

Moreover, many firms now have extensive training programs that are often run at real cost to the firms. Those monitoring compliance with the Challenge could help firms realize that supervised work on substantial pro bono work is, in many respects, a superior training vehicle to in-house training programs or, at the very least, an extremely useful supplement.

This analysis ignores the nonmonetary benefits of pro bono work such as increased morale, enthusiasm, and professional stature, because they tend to be difficult to quantify. When such intangible benefits are recognized and when hidden benefits such as training are quantified and added to the realistically calculated costs of pro bono work, they come much closer to balancing one another than is previously understood. Sharing this information as part of the monitoring process might greatly expand participation in, and enthusiasm for, the Challenge.

Compliance Mechanisms

Once the substantial nonmonetary benefits of pro bono work are demonstrated, and once the confusion about its real costs are alleviated, the question remains: What additional compliance mechanisms will best ensure that firms that have agreed to participate in the Challenge fulfill their obligations?

In order to be effective, the mechanisms must anticipate a rather lengthy list of complications. Firms have disparate cultures. Many have virtually no history of pro bono work. In others, pro bono work might be done by younger partners or associates but seldom by powerful managing or other key partners. Pro bono work might be done by only a small number of lawyers in a specific practice group, typically litigation. In some firms, pro bono work may not be seen as a vehicle for advancement, and the work is given little real credit toward billing or hours expectations or achieving partnership. At an extreme, the firm's culture might tolerate partners who actively discourage pro bono work.

Firm structures can also inadvertently discourage pro bono work. Firms theoretically committed to increasing pro bono work find themselves handicapped by the absence of written pro bono policies. Many firms interested in training lawyers to do pro bono work may have no formal training policies or procedures. Experienced lawyers who are willing to devote substantial time to pro bono work may not have the necessary connections in the community to identify and secure challenging and interesting pro bono projects. Firms may lack policies or procedures for accepting and staffing pro bono work, or for generating records and statistics about pro bono work.

Other changes in the legal environment complicate the development of a uniform compliance mechanism. Many firms are experiencing dramatic changes in size. These changes may be fueled by internal growth, but are increasingly brought about by lateral hiring, mergers, and downsizing compelled by economic factors. Many firms are drifting away from the notion of a common partnership and evolving into groups of semiautonomous boutiques. These changes may mean there is no consistent firm culture, or that the culture changes as dominant lawyers or dominant business developers with differing views on the importance of pro bono work come or go. Economic uncertainty and major changes in a firm's makeup affect associates, making associates skittish about major commitments to pro bono projects thought to offer little to career advancement because of their lack of immediate economic value.

Effective compliance also raises geographic concerns. Cities such as San Francisco and Washington, D.C., with the most venerable histories of pro bono work, are not particularly dynamic legal markets. On the other hand, many large cities—such as Dallas, Phoenix, and Los Angeles— that are experiencing comparatively rapid growth have little history of pro bono activities and lack strong, citywide pro bono leadership.

What approaches to monitoring compliance to pro bono work are likely to succeed in light of these various considerations, and what tendencies should a compliance program reinforce? As a threshold matter, the Challenge should be—and is—requiring written reports from all participants. The reporting format, as presently envisioned, contains specific requests for information concerning the percentage of firm billable hours spent on pro bono work, the percentage of such work spent on those of limited means, and the numbers of partners and associates involved.

Optional categories of information include whether the participating firm has a written pro bono policy, whether it has developed any innovative pro bono activities, whether it has a pro bono committee, or whether it publishes an annual report of pro bono activities. In addition, a firm may report on whether the Challenge has caused the firm to alter its policies on advancement and promotion, or whether the firm has made a monetary contribution to organizations that provide free legal services to the poor.

In exchange for this information, the Challenge made a significant concession. It agreed not to disclose the information contained in the reports in a disaggregated form that identifies individual law firms. This concession was a controversial one but resulted from the conclusion that, in its absence, the number of firms willing to join the Challenge would be significantly reduced. While it is obviously important that the Challenge's managers keep track of those who meet their goals, the absence of the peer pressure created by identifiable, published statistics is a significant but perhaps unavoidable weakness in the reporting format.

A second compliance activity would involve the submission to, and critique by, the Challenge's sponsors of pro bono policies. This process would ensure that firms participating in the Challenge are more likely to incorporate in their pro bono policies those features the Challenge has identified as essential. These include a clear definition of what constitutes pro bono work, an institutional commitment by the firm's leaders to an unambiguous encouragement of pro bono work, a commitment to treat pro bono matters like other work for the firm's paying clients, assistance in identifying a wide range of pro bono activities, and a clear-cut assignment of supervisory and administrative responsibility for pro bono work. This process should also include comments and suggestions for changes in the submitted policies, as well as technical assistance such as identifying new, or changes to, computer software that facilitate tracking pro bono activities.

Activities such as the requirement for written reports and the evaluations of in-place pro bono policies have inherent limitations. The Challenge's initial success was achieved, at least in part, because firms were convinced that it would not be an intrusive process and would not constitute an invitation to "outsiders" to meddle in private firm matters. Since these assurances were critical to the understanding under which most firms joined the Challenge, it is unlikely that they could be changed without endangering the goals of the Challenge.

As a result, increasing the degree of compliance with the Challenge's goals and the enthusiasm with which pro bono activities are pursued are likely to be more effectively achieved by softer approaches. The more important approaches, as previously discussed, involve convincing firms during the monitoring process that pro bono work provides major professional benefits and does not cost what firms think it costs.

A number of additional steps can reinforce this message. A surprisingly large number of firms are committed to the goals of the Challenge but, having comparatively little experience with a full-blown pro bono program, are unsure about how to meet the goals or expand their programs. Assistance in these areas thus becomes as important as reporting activities. The Challenge's sponsors can, and intend to, for example, serve as a clearinghouse for information on what types of pro bono projects participating firms are working on. (For example, certain firms have developed highly innovative projects such as using combinations of corporate and real estate attorneys to develop low-cost housing and using financial services attorneys to assist in the formation of credit unions or community development corporations.) This information is an important source of new leads and ideas. While this information will continue to be of importance to litigation attorneys, it is likely to be even more useful for other practice areas that have tended to lag in pro bono activities.

Key to the success of pro bono work is the functioning of pro bono coordinators and supervisors. As part of its follow-up activities, the Challenge should attempt to ensure that all coordinators and supervisors meet minimum standards of proficiency. The Challenge should develop and disseminate standard training materials to all coordinators and supervisors at all participating firms.

Law schools have, for a number of years, keyed into the level of pro bono activity as a selection factor in the recruiting process. To the extent the guidelines permit, the Challenge's sponsor should supply law schools with information concerning compliance by Challenge members. The sponsors can also encourage law schools and law students to be more specific and more aggressive in requiring law schools which recruit on campuses to provide detailed and specific information about pro bono activities.

The ABA's Minority Demonstration Program was highly successful in increasing the number of minority lawyers at majority firms and in increasing the use of minority firms by major corporations. The key to this success was client pressure. Since many large corporations have somewhat diverse customer bases and work forces, the case that suppliers of services should mirror client diversity is an easier and more compelling one to make than the one for pro bono work. But the analogy still holds. Corporate counsel should be pressured to include inquiries about pro bono activities as part of the firm retention process. Corporate counsel should be encouraged to stress that his or her company believes in the importance of being a good citizen, takes its social obligations seriously, and looks for a similar commitment from those who provide services to the corporation. While the approach may have weaknesses, its message, considering its source, will not be lost on law firm managers.

Probably the most important factor in achieving an overall increase in pro bono activity is publicity. Most major law firms are hypersensitive to criticism in the media, especially the popular professional media. While the ABA cannot, because of assurances it issued when recruiting members for the Challenge, publish levels of activity, other publications like the *American Lawyer* and the *National Law Journal* can and are beginning to do so. In the past, their rating or evaluation process has been handicapped, to some extent, by the lack of a uniform definition of what constitutes pro bono work. Should leading publications be induced to adopt the definition promulgated by the Challenge, meaningful comparisons would be possible. Publicity of this sort would be an enormous incentive for firms to take the Challenge seriously and to meet or exceed its goals. Just as this type of publicity played a major factor in encouraging pervasive competition among law firms over income levels, perhaps it will result in a similar competition in pro bono activity.

These steps taken by the ABA to assist participants in the Challenge to increase the level of pro bono activity seem appropriate during the Challenge's relatively early stages. The need to carefully foster a continuing commitment to, and enthusiasm for, the Challenge is great. For firms that are genuinely addressing problems associated with increasing their pro bono commitment, the current approach of those administering the Challenge—assistance and gentle reinforcement—is wise.

But undoubtedly a certain proportion of firms that have signed on to the Challenge will not meet their commitment. Similarly, other firms will continue to decline to join the Challenge or to otherwise make any meaningful commitment to pro bono activities. As we have seen, the response of the Challenge's administrators to these latter two categories has generally been to support and praise firms that fulfill their commitments, but to avoid criticizing or publicly commenting on firms that do not.

This approach might be a salutary one during the initial phases of the Challenge, but as its stature and effectiveness increases, the case, I believe, for continuing this passive approach weakens. A lawyer's obligation to do pro bono work has consistently been recognized by the courts.[2]

Thus for firms that refuse to comply with, or join in, the Challenge, those administering the Challenge could impose, or at least should consider, a variety of additional, more aggressive compliance mechanisms:

— Publicly and specifically recognize the most successful participants in the Challenge.

— Require different reporting formats for noncomplying participants, such as more frequent and more detailed reports that include self-generated analyses of the reasons for noncompliance and commit the participants to specific remedial steps.

— Supply more detailed critiques of the policies and procedures of noncomplying firms and more detailed discussions of, or responses to, the reasons for noncompliance.

— Actively encourage the legal media to publicize the identity of, and to report on, firms that have not joined the Challenge or that do little pro bono work.

— Encourage law schools to solicit and disseminate in connection with on-campus interviews the names of firms that have declined to join the Challenge or that do little pro bono work.

Since the existence of a professional obligation to do pro bono on the part of all lawyers is undisputed, those administering the Challenge should be emboldened. As the bar grows more comfortable with the existence and operation of the Challenge, more pressure should be applied to firms that do not comply or do not join.

The Challenge's point of departure should be that the obligation to render pro bono services must be regarded no differently from other professional obligations, such as to avoid conflicts of interest or prevent the unauthorized practice of law. The higher the obligation to render pro bono service is viewed in the calculus of professional obligations, the stronger the conclusion becomes that pro bono work is a duty and not a favor, and that fulfilling that obligation not only strengthens the profession but also serves the public good by greatly enhancing respect for the rule of law.

Notes

1. Jack Londen, "The Economics of Pro Bono Work," *Center for Pro Bono Exchange*, vol. 2, no. 2 (August 1993), p. 1.
2. See *Mallard* v. *U.S. District Court for the Southern District of Iowa*, 490 U.S. 296, 310 (1989): "In a time when the need for legal services among the poor is growing and public funding for such services has not kept pace, lawyers' ethical obligation to volunteer their time and skill *pro bono publico* is manifest. . . . A court's power to require a lawyer to

render assistance to the indigent is firmly rooted in the authority to define the terms and conditions upon which members are admitted to the bar"; *Barnard* v. *Thornstenn,* 489 U.S. 546, 549 (1989); and *United States* v. *Dillon,* 346 F.2d 633 (9th Cir. 1965), emphasizing that one who is allowed the privilege to practice law accepts a professional obligation to defend the poor.

9

Afterword

Frank M. Coffin

I venture this afterword as an empathetic outsider, privileged, as a director of the Governance Institute, to sit in on the unique deliberations that have produced this balanced testament to "pro bono." Although as an appellate judge I have been on the receiving end of lawyers' advocacy for nearly thirty years, this has been a rare opportunity to observe, over a period of four years, a group of responsible partners of large law firms come to terms with the question: How, if at all, should a large law firm respond to the call to contribute its time and talent to the public good?

What was unique about this project was that insiders, mostly key partners of large firms living through the trauma of the slide from the high-flying 1980s to the slower and lower 1990s, were devoting an impressive amount of otherwise billable hours to reexamining conventional rubrics, going back to basics, engaging in fresh thinking about their profession, and combining in all their explorations both idealism and realism.

They began with a perspective informed by realism. Academia, through Professors Galanter and Palay, depicted the seismic changes in law firm size and structure during this century, changes that cannot be fairly capsuled as a commercialization of a once noble profession. Truth is, the legal profession has always been an alloy of lucre and magnanimity. But the contemporary phenomena of size, specialization, cost-pushed pricing, and competitive pressures both disable the large firm from carrying on a traditional kind of pro bono practice and enable it to pursue cutting-edge kinds of pro bono work, as well as, of course, to give financial help to those directly performing more conventional services. In short, for today's law firm of any size, as is true of all complex institutions, coping constructively with a pro bono commitment is no longer a matter of doing what comes naturally. Hard analysis of strengths and weaknesses, a rigorous search for opportunities, creative thinking and planning, and painstaking follow-through are indispensable.

A second realist perspective has been contributed by Esther Lardent, who bears the title and the burden of director of the American Bar Association Pro Bono Challenge project. Today's pro bono scene occupies an extremely wide spectrum of law firm activities across the nation. They range from subsidies to public interest law groups and lending firm lawyers to clinics to a full-fledged community service department led by a prominent partner. Even an impressionistic catalogue of contemporary pro bono work done by large law firms constitutes an impressive rebuttal to those who are quick to label such firms as apostles of greed.

Yet to accept this panorama as sufficient proof of an adequate response by the profession would be a misuse of evidence. The lawyers involved in this study were all too aware of the extent of the unmet legal needs of the indigent throughout the United States. They also were not loath to say that paper claims often gilded a frail lily, and that in many firms what passed for a pro bono program were the unsupported, unguided, uncredited, and often maladroit efforts of junior associates.

So the group continued its inquiry. Although each member probably had an instinctive feeling that community service was a legitimate concern for a law firm, it was agreed that this must not be assumed without examination. What, they asked, is the legal profession's ethical obligation, if any? What distinguishes lawyers from, say, plumbers or taxi drivers? At rock bottom, the group found, three factors coalesced to form the intellectual foundation of the pro bono obligation: 1) the claim of the profession to maximum autonomy if it were to fulfill the role of independent advocate (even against the state); 2) the grant by the state to the profession not only of a monopoly in providing access to courts but of an unregulated monopoly; and 3) the resulting commitment by the profession to render public service to the goals of the adversary system, not merely by faithfully and competently representing paying clients, even unpopular ones, but by helping to realize the premise of the system, equality before the law, in serving those unable to meet the monetary price for that equality.

But a sense of obligation alone in this flawed human world is seldom enough to move large institutions and keep them on course. Perhaps this group's most persuasive contribution to the pro bono debate is its illumining the nature and extent of enlightened individual and firm self-interest served by appropriate pro bono activity.

This fascinating story divests the emperor of at least a few clothes, making the point that the costs of pro bono work to a law firm are usually substantially overstated. The conventional approach is to multiply hours spent on pro bono work by the hourly rate regularly billed to paying clients. But realism compels the concession that in most firms, most of the time, there exists some excess capacity, and that the true cost of much pro bono is the cost of using resources of time, staff, and equipment that would otherwise lie fallow. The group does not argue that pro bono is done on the cheap, with no costs; its stance is rather one of skepticism at claims of awesome sacrifice.

If sacrifice is overstated, benefits to a firm are understated in two respects—both of them as vital to the individual as to the collective firm. The first is related to the recent changes in the structure, operations, and expectations of law firms. Associates and junior partners, even some seniors, experience lower expectations of tenure and advancement, income, collegiality, and client relationships, together with an anticipation of greater isolation, specialization, expenditure of bureaucratic time, and investment in billable hours. Intellectual challenge is limited. Specialization may even reduce the lawyer's value to a client as a source of general judgment. Little time for refreshment and regeneration can be squeezed out of an already overburdened day. The syndrome can be summarized in one phrase: a diminished quality of life.

Against this somber background, the potential contribution to individuals of pro bono service emerges as a beacon of opportunity: opportunity to work one-on-one with human clients, to gather new experiences of interest to others, to reduce one's sense of isolation, to generate new pride in legal work. As all the pressures continue to increase, so, in all likelihood, will the saving attractiveness of a healthy component of pro bono involvement.

The second area of understated benefit is the contribution of pro bono work to the making of a lawyer. Although hard empirical data on this point are lacking, perhaps necessarily so, the group had the benefit of interviews with both those who had done direct pro bono work in the field and those who had supervised such work. The values served that seemed relevant to a lawyer's development were identified: a general increase of sensitivity to individuals and the human factor in legal cases; exposure to community attitudes and values—relevant to everything from selecting a jury to negotiating, problemsolving, weighing potential consequences and public reaction to a course of conduct; the early assumption of greater responsibilities, thus stimulating confidence, the ability to organize time, and maturity. In an era of centrifugal and fractionating specialization, pro bono promises to supply an organizing, centripetal, maturing opportunity.

With pro bono credentials solidly established, the project faced the problems of definition, implementation, and future direction. In 1993, several years after the group began its work, definition was largely preempted by the ABA's Model Rule 6.1 and its Law Firm Pro Bono Challenge project, with emphasis on contributed direct work for persons of limited means or organizations serving them by at least a majority of partners and associates.

Also, as one of the chapters has pointed out, of some two hundred fee-shifting statutes, those dealing with protection of the consumer, the environment, civil rights, employment fairness, and privacy go far to identify what Congress has deemed areas of public interest where large firms may possess a unique capacity. Success in litigation under these statutes may result in substantial recoveries of monies that may most appropriately be deposited in funds devoted to meeting disbursements in pro bono cases.

Another chapter, while recognizing the need of the ABA to establish concrete goals, would allow some flexibility. For example, some bar association activities benefiting only the profession or a class of clients would not seem to fit within the spirit of pro bono, whereas projects seeking more general improvements in the administration of justice would. Similarly, while membership on a prestigious art museum board would fall outside any pro bono claim, rendering a lawyer's general kind of advice to a board concerned with enhancing the lot of the poor could be recognized as pro bono, even though the advice was not given in connection with any litigation. In short, carving out what is legitimate pro bono work and what is obviously self-serving, or indirect firm protection or aggrandizement, or, at most, neutral is more a matter of carrying out the spirit of a genuine commitment than finding the applicable niche in a detailed code. At least when the ABA Challenge minima are met, a principle-guided flexibility would seem called for by a law firm.

Already ABA Challenge guides for translating a firm's pro bono commitment into a working, practical, effective program are in circulation:

the participation and leadership of key partners; a pro bono committee; a written policy; procedures for accepting pro bono work, training, staffing, supervising, and keeping records; and the full crediting of pro bono work for working time and advancement. The first reports from the 164 law firms that have accepted the Challenge have yet to be filed. But even in advance of these reports, our group called for continuing and escalating efforts to obtain more detailed reports, to submit firms' programs to informed peer review, to recognize leaders in pro bono, and to encourage legal media and law schools to identify firms that have rejected any meaningful pro bono program.

* * *

An epilogue in a literary work often deals with the future of the leading characters. What I can say along those lines is that a beginning has been made in the task of persuading that unique American institution, the large law firm, to lead the profession in rendering effective service for the public good. Our lawyers in this project, like the storied and sculpted Burghers of Calais, have come forth seeking to ransom their beloved profession. They have acted in the highest traditions of that profession. They have responsibly and imaginatively provided the intellectual underpinning for sophisticated, serious, and sustained pro bono programming on a substantial scale. They have done so by pointing out the fit between pro bono commitment and public service, on the one hand, and the individual's interest in the quality of firm life, the firm's interest in lawyerly development, and the profession's inherent ethical obligation, on the other.

If efforts like this catch on, first with large firms, then with others, one can hope that the legal profession as a whole will make a seminal contribution to realizing the goal of equal access to the law. In the course of so doing, it will have ensured its own revitalization, refreshment, and reputation.

Contributors and Steering Committee Members

William A. Bradford, Jr., is a partner in the Washington, D.C., firm of Hogan & Hartson. Mr. Bradford's practice is primarily commercial and administrative litigation, including breach of contract and government procurement cases. He has practiced actively in local District of Columbia courts; in the federal courts of the District of Columbia, Maryland, and Virginia; and in the U.S. Court of Federal Claims. His practice also includes work before specialized procurement tribunals such as the Armed Services Board of Contract Appeals and the GSA Board of Contract Appeals. He has extensive experience in cases involving the Foreign Sovereign Immunities Act in which foreign states or their instrumentalities are parties. Mr. Bradford formerly served as the partner in charge of Hogan & Hartson's community services department; in that capacity he gained wide experience in constitutional and civil rights litigation and in the delivery of pro bono legal services. He received his undergraduate degree from Swarthmore College, with honors, in 1966 and graduated from the Yale Law School in 1969.

Frank M. Coffin has been a U.S. Court of Appeals judge for nearly thirty years, part of which he served as chief judge of the First Circuit and as chair of the U.S. Judicial Conference Committee on the Judicial Branch. In his earlier public service career, he served all three branches of government—as a trial lawyer, member of the U.S. House of Representatives from Maine, and deputy administrator of the Agency for International Development. He is a founding director of the Governance Institute and a trustee emeritus of Bates College. His books are *Witness for AID, The Ways of a Judge: Reflections from the Appellate Bench, A Lexicon of Oral Advocacy,* and *On Appeal: Courts, Lawyering, Judging.* Judge Coffin is a graduate of Bates College (*summa cum laude*) and of the Harvard Law School.

Anthony F. Earley, Jr., is president and chief operating officer of Detroit Edison. Mr. Earley's utilities career began in 1985, when he was named general counsel for the Long Island Lighting Co. (LILCO) in Hicksville, N.Y. He became executive vice president for LILCO in 1988 and president and chief operating officer in 1989. Mr. Earley was instrumental in negotiating a complex agreement transferring the Shoreham Nuclear Power Station to the state of New York and in developing a new strategic plan for LILCO that focused on customer service. Before joining LILCO, Earley specialized in energy and the environment as a partner in the Richmond, Virginia, law firm of Hunton & Williams. He has been active in community affairs and is a director of Mutual of America Capital Management Corporation. An attorney and an engineer, Mr. Earley holds a bachelor of science degree in physics, a master of science degree in engineering, and a *summa cum laude* juris doctor degree, all from the University of Notre Dame.

Marc Galanter is Evjue-Bascom Professor of Law and South Asian Studies and director of the Institute for Legal Studies at the University of Wisconsin-Madison. During the early years of his academic career, Professor Galanter was most visible as a comparativist and is still recognized as an expert on Indian law. He is the author of *Competing Equalities: Law and the Backward Classes in India* (1984, 1991) and *Law and Society in Modern India* (1989). In recent years he has published a number of studies of litigation and disputing in the United States, including studies on the impact of disputant capability in courts, the relation of public legal institutions to unofficial and informal regulation, and patterns of litigation in the United States. *Tournament of Lawyers: The Transformation of the Big Law Firm* (1991) is his most recent book (with Thomas Palay). Professor Galanter was editor of the *Law & Society Review* and president of the Law & Society Association from 1983 to 1985. He received degrees in philosophy and law from the University of Chicago.

Donald W. Hoagland is counsel to the Denver firm of Davis, Graham & Stubbs. He has been with that firm since 1951, except for a leave of absence as assistant administrator for development finance and private enterprise in the Agency for International Development. Mr. Hoagland's practice has evolved from general practice to concentration in corporate securities and international work. He has spent many years on the management committee of Davis, Graham & Stubbs and was its chairman for four years. He has also served on the board of directors, including several years as chairman, of the Legal Aid Society of Colorado and of the Colorado Legal Aid Foundation, a support group. He has handled several pro bono cases personally and is currently chairman of the Subcommittee on Community Service of the Colorado Bar Association's Committee on Professionalism, as well as a member of the Colorado Supreme Court's Grievance Committee. In recognition of his commitment to community service, the Colorado Bar Association created the Donald W. Hoagland Pro Bono Award. Mr. Hoagland is a graduate of Yale College and of the Columbia University School of Law.

Robert A. Katzmann is president of the Governance Institute; Walsh Professor of Government and professor of law at Georgetown University; and a visiting fellow in the Brookings Institution Governmental Studies program. He has been a director of the American Judicature Society; a public member of the Administrative Conference of the United States; a vice chair of the Committee on Government Organization and Separation of Powers of the ABA Section on Administrative Law and Regulatory Practice; cochair of the FTC Transition Report; and special counsel to Senator Daniel P. Moynihan on the confirmation of Justice Ruth Bader Ginsburg. In the fall of 1992 he occupied the Wayne Morse Chair in Law and Politics at the University of Oregon. Professor Katzmann is the author of *Regulatory Bureaucracy: The Federal Trade Commission and Antitrust Policy* and *Institutional Disability: The Saga of Transportation Policy for the Disabled;* editor and contributing author of *Judges and Legislators: Toward Institutional Comity;* coeditor of *Managing Appeals in Federal Court;* and is completing *Courts and Congress: Reflections From the Field.* He has also written on regulation, the administrative process, antitrust policy, institutional reform litigation, and court reform for a variety of journals. Professor Katzmann received his A.B. from Columbia College (*summa cum laude*), A.M. and Ph.D. from Harvard University (Department of Government), and J.D. from Yale Law School, where he was an article and book review editor of the *Yale Law Journal.* He has directed the Project on the Law Firm and the Public Good.

William C. Kelly, Jr., chairs the finance and real estate department of the Washington, D.C., office of Latham & Watkins, an international law firm. He practices principally in the areas of infrastructure project finance and low-income housing finance. Mr. Kelly joined the firm after serving as executive assistant to the secretary of the U.S. Department of Housing and Urban Development from 1975 to 1977. He is a member of the bar of the District of Columbia and has been admitted before the U.S. Supreme Court. In the civic realm, he serves on the boards of the National Low Income Housing Coalition, the Governance Institute, and the Sheridan School. Mr. Kelly served as a law clerk to Judge Frank M. Coffin of the U.S. Court of Appeals for the First Circuit (1971–72) and to Justice Lewis F. Powell, Jr., of the U.S. Supreme Court (1972–73). He received an A.B. *magna cum laude* in 1968 from Harvard University and a J.D. in 1971 from Yale University, where he was a note and comment editor of the *Yale Law Journal.*

Esther F. Lardent, an independent legal and public policy consultant, is director of the American Bar Association's Law Firm Pro Bono Project, which is funded through a grant from the Ford Foundation. She has written and lectured widely on the subject of *pro bono publico.* Since 1987 Ms. Lardent has also been chief consultant to the ABA Postconviction Death Penalty Representation Project. She serves as chair of the American Bar Association's Consortium on Legal Services and the Public and as a vice president of the National Legal Aid and Defenders Association. Ms. Lardent received her J.D. degree from the University of Chicago Law School and is a graduate of Pembroke College of Brown University.

Peter P. Mullen has since 1962 been a partner in the international law firm of Skadden, Arps, Slate, Meagher & Flom, engaged in the practice of corporate, securities, and business law. From 1981 to 1994 he served as executive partner of the firm. In this role as chief executive officer, in addition to managing the firm, Mr. Mullen presided over and guided the growth of the firm in the 1980s from 250 to over 1,000 lawyers. In 1994 he stepped down as executive partner but continues to act as chief of Skadden's international operations. Among his many other activities, Mr. Mullen is a director of Georgetown University (having served as chairman of the board of directors from 1985 to 1992); president and trustee of the Skadden Fellowship Foundation, which funds the work of twenty-five graduates each year in public service organizations serving the disadvantaged; chairman of the board of directors of the Gregorian University Foundation; and a member of the board of directors and executive committee and secretary of Project Orbis, Inc. He received an A.B. degree *cum laude* from Georgetown University and his LL.B. from the Columbia University Law School.

Edwin L. Noel is the managing partner of Armstrong, Teasdale, Schlafly and Davis, with offices in St. Louis and Kansas City, Missouri; Belleville, Illinois; and Olathe, Kansas. The firm's pro bono programs have won special awards from the Missouri Bar, the Bar Association of Metropolitan St. Louis, and the Legal Services of Eastern Missouri, Inc. Mr. Noel's principal practice areas include commercial litigation and environmental law. He serves on numerous civic and charitable organizations, including the Missouri Clean Water Commission; the Metropolitan Sewer District of St. Louis County, Missouri; the St. Louis Regional Commerce and Growth Association; the Edgewood Children's Center; the St. Louis Association for Retarded Citizens; the Churchill School; and the Whitfield School. Mr. Noel is a graduate of Brown University and St. Louis University School of Law (*cum laude*).

Thomas Palay is professor of law at the University of Wisconsin-Madison. Prior to joining the University of Wisconsin Law School in 1980, he was a research fellow at the Brookings Institution. Professor Palay's research interests center on the economics of contracting and the organization of businesses. His most recent work has focused on the growth and change of large law firms. He is the author, with Marc Galanter, of *Tournament of Lawyers: The Transformation of the Big Law Firm* and numerous articles on the subject. He is currently at work on studies of large English legal practices, law firm networks, and the provision of pro bono legal services. He received his B.A. from Tufts University and his J.D. and Ph.D. from the University of Pennsylvania.

Barrington D. Parker, Jr., is a U.S. district court judge in the Southern District of New York. He was for many years a practicing lawyer, most recently as a partner in the law firm of Morrison & Foerster. Among his other activities, he has served as vice president of the NAACP Legal Defense and Education Fund and as a director of the Governance Institute, the Harlem School of the Arts, the New School for Social Research, and the Federal Bar Council. As a lawyer, Judge Parker was involved in a wide range of pro bono matters, including death penalty litigation, and service by special appointment of the U.S. Supreme Court. He is a graduate of Yale College and Yale Law School.

Lewis F. Powell, III is a partner in the Richmond, Virginia-based international law firm of Hunton & Williams. He joined the firm after clerking for U.S. District Judge Robert R. Merhige, Jr. Mr. Powell's practice has ranged from nuclear regulatory litigation, to complex environmental and toxic tort cases, to personal injury and commercial disputes. He has worked on trial and appellate matters, variously, in state and federal courts in Virginia, North Carolina, Florida, Washington, D.C., New York, Georgia, Missouri, and California, including the Fourth, Eleventh, Second, and Eighth Circuits. He has led or participated in several confidential internal investigations for public and private companies. He is a member of the American Law Institute and the Fourth Circuit Judicial Conference. During the time he chaired Hunton & Williams' pro bono committee, the firm opened a storefront law office in an impoverished area of Richmond (called Church Hill) to serve those who could not qualify for Legal Aid. Mr. Powell is a graduate of Washington and Lee University and the University of Virginia Law School, where he was an executive editor of the *Virginia Law Review*.

Index